Gender, Ethics and Information Technology

Gender, Ethics and Information Technology

Alison Adam

First published in 2005 by
PALGRAVE MACMILLAN
Houndmills, Basingstoke, Hampshire RG21 6XS and
175 Fifth Avenue, New York, N.Y. 10010
Companies and representatives throughout the world.

PALGRAVE MACMILLAN is the global academic imprint of the Palgrave Macmillan division of St. Martin's Press, LLC and of Palgrave Macmillan Ltd. Macmillan® is a registered trademark in the United States, United Kingdom and other countries. Palgrave is a registered trademark in the European Union and other countries.

ISBN-13: 978–1–4039–1506–1
ISBN-10: 1–4039–1506–7

This book is printed on paper suitable for recycling and made from fully managed and sustained forest sources.

Logging, pulping and manufacturing processes are expected to conform to the environmental regulations of the country of origin.

A catalogue record for this book is available from the British Library.

Library of Congress Cataloging-in-Publication Data

Adam, Alison.
    Gender, ethics and information technology / Alison Adam.
        p. cm.
    Includes bibliographical references and index.
    ISBN 1–4039–1506–7
        1. Women—Effect of technological innovations on. 2. Information technology—Moral and ethical aspects. 3. Computer crimes. 4. Feminist theory. I. Title.
HQ1233.G452 2005
174'.9004'082—dc22   2004059128

Transferred to digital print on demand, 2007

Printed and bound in Great Britain by
CPI Antony Rowe, Chippenham and Eastbourne

Contents

Acknowledgements

I would like to thank the many colleagues and friends who have supported me throughout the writing of this book, particularly colleagues from the ISOS research group at the University of Salford, and especially Ben Light, Elaine Ferneley, Frances Bell, Helen Richardson, Debra Howcroft and Nathalie Audren for keeping me cheerful. I am indebted to the 'invisible college' of international gender and technology researchers and the computer ethics community, especially those involved in CEPE conferences where I have presented some of the ideas from this book. Particular thanks are due to Paul Spedding, Marja Vehviläinen and the two anonymous reviewers for reading and commenting on drafts of this book. Naturally, any errors and omissions are entirely down to me. Without the love and support of my family these projects are just not possible. Thank you to Craig, Nicol and Sibyl for once more tolerating the mad woman in the attic.

Earlier versions of some of the ideas in Chapters 4, 5 and 6 appeared in Adam (2001a, 2001b, 2002) and in Adam and Ofori-Amanfo (2000). An earlier version of Chapter 7 was presented at the CEPE 2003 conference.

1
Gender and Information and Communications Technologies – It's not for Girls!

Introduction: setting the scene

This book is about the intersection of two areas; first, gender and information and communications technologies (ICTs) and second, computer ethics. It is born from my long-standing interest in gender and computer technologies, a more recent research and teaching interest in the discipline which is often known as 'computer ethics' and my concern that research on computer ethics problems should be brought to a wider audience beyond the academy and information technology (IT) profession, as so many of the issues involved have a substantial bearing on aspects of our everyday lives, lived with ICTs.

The rationale for this book derives from my claim that many ethics topics relating to information technologies, such as hacking, software and electronic funds crime, online harassment and cyberstalking, Internet pornography, computer-mediated communications, privacy and online community and democracy, have a gender dimension which, to date, has rarely been explored, and, where it has been tackled, has generally not been subject to thorough theoretical analysis. Indeed a web search of any news website (such as the BBC) for legal and ethical violations on the Internet throws up items such as sales of Internet twins, hackers, Internet sales of vital organs, Internet paedophiles, and so on. I argue that these are all concerns that cry out for extended gender analyses against the backcloth of appropriate feminist theory.

I believe that there are (at least) four major reasons why such analyses are not yet forthcoming. First, computer ethics, the academic discipline that has formed round legal and ethical concerns over behaviour on the Internet, tends to be relatively traditional in theoretical terms. This is described in Chapter 4. Second, on the other hand, writers from within the rapidly growing domain of feminist ethics, and related areas, rarely explore computer ethics issues. Third, academic science and technology studies have spent the last three decades working hard to achieve epistemological neutrality. Effectively their project involves treating 'true' and 'false' knowledge in the same way in terms of explaining how that knowledge came about. Epistemological neutrality has tended to extend to ethical neutrality, so research in science and technology studies of the last two or more decades often appears to be avoiding political comment. Only recently have we seen a 'turn to the ethical' with renewed interest not only in biomedical issues, as in cloning and genetically modified (GM) foods, but also computer and engineering related concerns such as systems failures and Internet security. Finally, although research on gender and technology thrives, mainstream feminism tends to shy away from dealing with technology and science. The latter point offers a further reason as to why the well-established literatures of feminist ethics, legal studies and politics do not permeate into studies of science and technology as much as they should do.

Taken together, all these elements suggest that there are a number of feminist, and other, disciplines dealing with potentially related subject matter, but which currently tend to pull in different directions. These would benefit from a more integrated approach in terms of their treatments of ethical issues in cyberspace. Nevertheless, the situation I characterize should not necessarily be seen as a 'problem' consisting of entirely negative aspects. Instead, such tensions offer all sorts of exciting possibilities for creating interesting synergies and novel directions. Indeed a gendered analysis of ethical issues involved in ICTs might be one way of bringing together the various disciplines which I describe above and which have hitherto developed largely separately. Ideally, we may hope to foster a two-way transfer of ideas from feminist ethics to computer ethics and vice versa. Importantly we need a transfer of ideas out from both areas to reach the forum of wider public debate.

I suspect that many people working in the field of computing doubt that gender issues and feminist analyses have much to do with their subject, however, once one's consciousness is raised, questions of gender can be seen everywhere in computing. When I was a student in the 1970s I had not developed much of a political consciousness, but this soon changed when I entered the world of work in the data processing department of a large chemical company. It was 1977 and a far cry from the world of today's ICTs. Large mainframe computers, batch processing and decks of cards were the norm. Indeed, I once dropped a deck of cards and, like all the king's horses and all the king's men, I just could not get the deck back together again, at least not in its original order.

Perhaps I should have taken more notice of the burgeoning women's movement developing in the mid-1970s but I did not. However, it was commonplace remarks like the following, which turned me into a feminist almost, overnight. One day, whilst I was working at a computer screen, two male colleagues stood a short distance away, but well within my earshot, discussing who would be a suitable candidate for a new, and fairly senior post, which was being created in the data processing department. They identified a male colleague, in his forties, who was not generally noted for being particularly able or effective. However, he had a certain gravitas, which often attaches to middle-aged men in the workplace. Let us call him Fred Smith. 'For this new post we need someone like Fred Smith. It's not for little girls.' 'No', agreed his colleague, pointedly, 'it's not for little girls'.

This exchange demonstrates a number of interesting things. First, there is the whole way that language is used to keep women junior and the pejorative way that the term 'girl' is used. Think of 'big girl's blouses' and 'throwing like a girl'. My teenage son tells me that the term 'girl' can be used as an insult to both females and males. In the UK a chocolate bar, apparently aimed at the truck-driving market has as its advertising slogan 'It's not for girls.' This is accompanied by a logo of a figure of a woman in a skirt (the kind of symbol one often sees on the doors of public toilets) holding a handbag. This figure is enclosed in a roundel with a diagonal red stripe on top thus making it akin to a 'no entry' traffic sign and underlining the chocolate bar's relationship with the haulage industry.

My erstwhile colleagues might as well have attached this logo to the office door of this new post. This serves to reinforce the way that women often feel marginalized, excluded and belittled in working life. It could be argued that my 'little girls' experience was part of the cut and thrust of corporate industry of a bygone era. I hope that remarks such as the one I report are no longer made. I also believe that I could just as well have overheard the same remark in the marketing or finance department as the data processing department so it is not peculiar to the IT industry. Nevertheless, my experiences of working in the computing industry and teaching and researching computing in universities has convinced me of a strong and complex link between gender and computing technologies.

A few definitions might be useful at this stage. I use the terms IT, ICT and computing more or less interchangeably in this work. Definitions seem fairly fluid. Information technology is an older expression than ICT – the latter term includes networked technologies such as the Internet – but many people now seem to use IT to include networked technologies too. Similarly the term 'computing' is often used more or less synonymously with IT and ICT. Information technology and ICT are broader terms under which we might include fax machines, telephones, and so on. Information Technology is often, although not always, taught alongside business subjects. Information systems (IS) is the wider domain which considers the use of ICTs in social and organizational settings. Again IS as an academic subject often resides in business and management schools. Computer science is the academic discipline which includes more theoretical consideration of hardware and software and we usually find it within science, engineering or technology faculties. Software engineering, a close relation of computer science, deals more particularly with the 'engineering' of software systems. Computer ethics is probably the most common name for the discipline which has formed around ethical issues relating of ICTs, however we also find a number of terms used more or less synonymously, including Internet ethics, information ethics and cyberethics.

Over the last ten or so years, university courses on computing, software engineering and information systems have generally begun to include a module on ethical and professional issues. As Chapter 4 describes, much of the rationale for this new curriculum development derives from the pressure from professional bodies (e.g. the Association for Computing Machinery in the USA, the British Computer Society in the UK) to include the subject of 'professionalism', which often falls within the purview of computer ethics, for accreditation purposes, in university computing curricula.

When I began to teach computer ethics courses a number of years ago, I was not particularly surprised to find how little contemporary computer ethics scholarship intersected with the growing body of research on women in computing and how little gender questions found expression in computer ethics. After all, I had lived for a long time within a computing discipline where gender was a very marginal issue at best. At the time I was constructing my first computer ethics course, I was also completing a book on gender and artificial intelligence (AI) (Adam 1998). I had found the, by then, fairly substantial corpus of work on feminist philosophy, and feminist epistemology in particular, a rich hunting ground for theoretical constructs for that particular work. I had already come across feminist approaches to law in some of the AI projects with which I was involved. I began to read around the subjects of feminist ethics and feminist politics. Although I had not really expected to find significant overlap between feminist ethics and computer ethics, it was striking just how little feminist ethics had permeated computer ethics, particularly so even in studies of differences in men's and women's decision making in relation to computer ethics, where there is minimal reference to feminist ethics research. It was also notable that computer ethics tended to be fairly conservative theoretically. My gender and AI study involved bringing feminist theory to bear on a critique of AI. I have approached the current project in an analogous study where my aim is to bring feminism to a study of computer ethics, to make a richer analysis of a number of computer ethics problems.

Although I have always found computer ethics conferences and journals to be hospitable places in which to air ideas about gender and computer ethics, I am sure that many colleagues working in computer ethics will not regard gender as something which has a central place in their research repertoire. I certainly do not wish to claim that the approach, which I advocate here, is the only way to tackle computer ethics. Instead, I hope that it can be complementary to other, more mainstream approaches. However, if my claims are convincing, namely that a further dimension may be added to our explanations of a number of computer ethics problems through a gender analysis, and also that some computer ethics problems defy explanation unless understood in gendered terms, then I am hopeful that more mainstream approaches towards computer ethics will begin to take heed of feminist approaches. Apart from anything else, I believe that feminist ethics currently provides the most fertile soil for new, and potentially radical, critical ethical ideas.

It also seems to me vitally important that we find ways of bringing feminist scholarship to a mainstream audience otherwise feminist writers will remain, forever, talking to themselves. Imagine another logo. This time we will have a 'toilet door' man and he is holding an appropriately recognizable symbol of masculinity, let's say an electric drill. He is enclosed in a red roundel with a diagonal red strip across. The accompanying logo reads: 'Feminism. It's not for boys!' This is not a logo I would like. In this study, at least, I hope to show that feminism is for boys as much as it is for girls.

What do I mean by gender?

To talk of gender is to talk about masculinity and femininity and the ways in which some things in our social worlds are taken to be masculine and some things feminine. Gender is not the same thing as sex although I do recognize that different languages define things in different ways and that the definitions of sex and gender from other languages, quite literally, will not necessarily translate into English. Haraway (1991) notes that, while English distinguishes between sex and gender, German does not. The German word, *Geschlecht*, is not the same as the English 'sex' or 'gender'. Nevertheless, in English, 'sex' is usually taken to refer to biological attributes while 'gender' refers to cultural attributes which are related to biological attributes, though by no means unequivocally. These definitions are, themselves, not universally agreed. First, biological sex is by no means uncontroversial. There are individuals whose genes and sexual organs may classify them as one sex while they may know that they are the other. An individual who changes sex may know very strongly, for instance that she is a woman trapped in a man's body, or, that he is a man trapped in a woman's body.

Hence, although gender is clearly related to sex, it cannot be mapped neatly onto a biological concept of sex. Once we start to attribute feminine and masculine characteristics and suppose that they are biologically uncontroversial we sail into dangerous waters. For instance, take the notion that men are aggressive and women are passive. How much is that a biological feature or a cultural feature? Why is it that some behaviour is seen as assertive in men, but the same behaviour in women is seen as aggressive? There are all sorts of stereotypes of masculinity and femininity which must be unpacked and examined; indeed some of these stereotypes are present, unchallenged in the statistical studies of gender and computer ethics I discuss in Chapter 5. It seems impossible, and somewhat pointless, to draw the line between what is cultural and what is biological. Where to draw the line is historically and culturally contingent. Even within one culture we would never agree where it should be drawn. If a line is drawn, we have the spectre of *essentialism*, or the belief that there are essential, fixed, biological male and female characteristics. Essentialism is conceptually dangerous as it allows all sorts of stereotypes of gendered behaviour and attributes to remain unchallenged.

For the purposes of the present study, I argue that it is fruitful to treat gender as a fundamental way of classifying and ordering our social worlds. To talk of gender, then, does not (just) mean purported differences between men and women; it extends to considerations of the gendering of skills, work, crime, democracy, knowledge, ethics and, indeed, all of social life.

There are some interesting features of the concept of gender. One could be forgiven for thinking that gender is something that women have but men do not. A visit to the 'Gender' section of one's local academic bookstore will reveal many more books about women than men. As Faulkner (2000) argues, gender seems to stick more to women than to men. We talk of football and women's football, not men's football and women's football. We talk of golf and ladies' golf, not men's golf and women's golf. We talk of working mothers, rarely of working fathers. We hear the term, 'career woman' but never the term, 'career man'. We live in a society where men and masculine are the norm and where that norm is not often challenged. This is why 'gender' is usually taken to mean women.

In studies of gender and technology, and particularly gender and computing or IT, initially, much work focused on the proportion of men and women in the subject; indeed there is still a strong interest in women's poor representation in the industry especially at senior levels. I do not deny that women's under-representation continues to be important but it is clearly not all there is to the story of gender and ICTs. Indeed, focusing too sharply on numbers often tends to carry along with it an assumption that getting equal numbers of men and women into a discipline is all that is needed for equality to prevail. This is the classic liberal position of which I am so critical all the way through this book. If we have strong theoretical analyses of gender then we can move beyond considerations of presence and absence of women (as discussed in Chapter 4), towards better analyses and explanations of central computer ethics topics such as hacking, online harassment and cyberstalking, pornography and privacy. Such analyses are generally not available within our current computer ethics theoretical repertoire.

What do I mean by feminism?

The problem, then, is where to look for developed theoretical positions against which such gender analyses may be made. Feminism is not the only place but I argue that it is much the best place to look. Studies that purport to find gender differences but betray no curiosity as to why there might be differences are unsatisfactory. I am continually surprised that studies can be undertaken on gender without the authors betraying curiosity as to why things might be different for men and women. Even if differences were all that there was to say about gender one would still look for reasons for difference. I have already suggested that trying to explain in terms of gender stereotypes begs too many questions. There are biologically based theories such as sociobiology (Wilson 1975; Dawkins 1976) which tries to explain social behaviour in terms of evolutionary biology, including gendered behaviour, purporting to find many behaviours 'natural' in evolutionary terms. A notable critic, Rose (1994) points to the way that sociobiology and the new political right is something of a 'love match'. Especially in the USA, sociobiology was used by IQ advocates in arguments about race and class to justify cutting welfare benefits to poor, often black, women and their children. Sociobiological arguments are forms of 'biology as destiny' approaches and have often been used to justify white male domination over female and black subordination. Sociobiology has been used to justify some stereotypical forms of male behaviour such as promiscuity and rape and so, not surprisingly, it has been criticized by feminists (Rose 1994). Even if one were to try to dissociate sociobiology from its alliance with the extreme political right, it is still problematic in throwing explanations of behaviour into 'nature' and 'natural'. Once more we have the issue of essentialism, nothing is therefore up for explanation or alteration, it is just 'natural' and cannot be changed. So there is no hope of a political force for change from sociobiology, indeed quite the opposite as it keeps us firmly in our existing places.

Feminism seems to offer the only body of theory that challenges the existing canon, theorizes the inequalities between men and women that exist in so many walks of life, and offers political possibilities for change. Indeed, it is its political dimension, offering the potential for change, which makes it so appealing. Understandably, many feminist authors see their project in terms of improving women's estate. I believe that feminist ideas have the power to transform men's and women's lives for the better and that it is a tragedy for all of us that there is a groundswell of belief that the battles are won, that apparently we live in a post-feminist world, and that we no longer require the transformative power of feminism. In challenging this belief I follow the extraordinary work of Oakley although I cannot put the case nearly as eloquently as she does. Oakley argues that every aspect of our lives is dominated by male/female power structures and gender inequality has seriously thrown our society out of balance. She argues that the following ideas are closely and dangerously linked: 'women's continuing marginality as a minority group; feminism's "failure" to transform society; masculinist power structures; violence towards people and the material and social environment; and various ideological systems, including psychoanalysis, the worship of economic growth and sociobiology, which provide an intellectual rationale for the current state of affairs' (Oakley 2002, p. 2). Oakley is quite clear that there is no central control room where men conspire their domination over women. Indeed she argues that women and men, ' ... are jointly locked in a culture which distorts the possibilities of humanness as an ethical project. Women are outsiders in a system which often appears to them to come from another planet. And so, indeed, it has been brought to them by men, whose alienation from the experiences of others is often so complete that they can't even see their own will to power. These dual positions of aliens and outsiders are the creation of a gendered division of labour inherited from the past. But that past, where men's domination was far more concretely manifested than it is now, lives in the present through men's understandable reluctance to give up their ownership and commodification of the world' (Oakley 2002, p. 3).

Taking into account the problems with other disciplines which purport to understand gender differences, most notably sociobiology, feminism still seems to me to be much the best body of writing to turn to for projects such as mine, partly because of its explanatory power, partly because of its explicitly political commitments. I agree with Oakley in seeing men as caught up in oppressive and alienating structures where both men and women can benefit from a better understanding of these, and where hope for change only comes from such an understanding.

The contribution of feminist ethics

I argue that feminist ethics (and related areas of feminist political and legal theory) may be useful additions to current theory in computer ethics in four ways. This is because feminist ethics is a much more consciously political philosophy than many traditional ethical positions, as it is predicated on a recognition of inequalities between the genders and how to understand and lessen such inequalities. The first offers hope in countering the technological determinism and liberalism which threaten to engulf much writing on morality and computers. In other words the critical edge which is part of feminist ethics may be imported into computer ethics in order to question the supposed inevitability of technological progress and the social structures which are built on an acceptance of such progress. The second exposes continuing inequalities in power and describes how these may be understood as 'gendered'. This involves a claim that the experiences of men and women are often substantially different and are different, in some measure, because of their respective genders and because of the ways that gendered attributes are understood and valued. For instance, privacy, and how it may differ for men and women, is a key concept, as I note below. Significantly, privacy links feminist ethics with feminist jurisprudence and politics. The third aspect of this process involves offering an alternative, more collective and caring approach to the individualism of the traditional ethical theories encapsulated in the styles of writing on computer ethics which are under scrutiny here. Finally, I hope that the more collective, sharing approach signalled by feminist ethics may be brought to computer ethics in order to make thinking about computer ethics problems more relevant to a wider audience. As I argue in Chapter 4 this is vital to sustain the link between moral thinking, policy making and the application of law.

Feminist technoscience

Although I am particularly keen to make the connection between feminist ethics, law and politics and computer ethics, it is important to note the backcloth, which feminist science and technology studies or 'technoscience' forms, for studies such as mine. In other places, I review the development of this discipline, noting the obdurate nature of the association of masculinity with technology (Adam 1998). The mutual construction of masculinity and technological skill has been a constant theme of this domain, noted by many leading feminist technoscience writers (Faulkner 2000; Wajcman 2004). The strong association of technical domains with men and masculinity offers much of the rationale for women's relative absence from these domains. I take this as the starting point for the present study. However, precisely because I wish to bring in other feminist domains to make a thorough analysis of computer ethics against them, I have neither the physical nor intellectual space to bring feminist technoscience into the discussion in any great detail (although I do consider the gender and computing literature in Chapter 4). A discussion of the relationship between feminist ethics, law and politics and the breadth of feminist scholarship in science and technology studies would be a different book, although possibly one that needs to be written, as my final chapter hints.

Key themes

Technological determinism

Several intertwined key themes emerge in this study. The first is technological determinism (MacKenzie and Wajcman 1999), or the view that technological progress is inevitable and that technology drives society, rather than, perhaps, the other way round or something more mediated in between. In science and technology studies, technological determinism has been rejected in theoretical moves that have seen substantial development in the sociology of scientific knowledge (Bloor 1976), the social construction of technology (MacKenzie and Wajcman 1999) and actor–network theory (Law and Hassard 1999). Yet, as MacKenzie and Wajcman (1999) note, there *is* a common sense way in which we see technology influencing us and it appears to be this common sense, unanalysed technological determinism which is to be found in much writing on technology and morality and also, in computer ethics.

Liberalism

Why do I make such an issue of technological determinism? Part of the reason is that it has much more to do with gender issues than might be supposed at first reading. Technological determinism goes hand in hand with a liberal political position which is highly problematic in relation to gender. In the process of writing this book, I had not expected to construct such a substantial critique of liberalism. However, the feminist theories from which I draw, feminist ethics and legal theory, and particularly, feminist politics, are highly critical of liberalism. A view which takes the trajectory of technology for granted also takes the structures of society for granted and leads to the assumption that equality will be achieved without looking to the deeper reasons why the structures of inequality are as they are, in the first place. Liberalism leaves real inequalities unchallenged. Too many campaigns to persuade women to enter technical subjects have failed because of their basis in an uncontested liberalism, which fails to scratch the surface of the reasons for inequality (Henwood 1993).

Many of the cultures and communities which are springing up in relation to the Internet and other ICTs have a liberal basis. They look to freedom of entry into their communities often, supposedly on the basis of talent alone. They look to extreme forms of freedom of speech and action. As Chapters 4 and 7 note, in relation to Internet communities and hacking respectively, this leads to expressions of equality which are far from equal as they deny real differences amongst people. In addition, freedom of speech can be extremely problematic if it becomes a freedom for others to be harassed or oppressed. The freedoms espoused by some Internet communities can lead to forms of libertarianism (Winner 1997). These communities can be vociferous in allowing their members freedom at all cost, but at the expense of the chance of others to speak.

Power

Holding to a problematic liberalism disguises unequal power structures and this implies a third key theme, that of power. This is expressed in several ways. According to Foucault (1979), power is suffused through the use of technologies and heralds a disciplinary society. The power of the gaze is useful in understanding topics such as Internet pornography and cyberstalking. This also underscores women's relationship to the body which is often forgotten in traditional philosophy, including law and ethics. Power in relation to gender often means exposing inequalities in men's and women's estates, especially the ways in which women are so often cast in subordinate roles. The question of power is not new but here we must consider the disciplinary aspects of power, through new attempts at data surveillance, and how these map along gender dimensions.

Privacy

This leads on to my final key theme, that of privacy, and how privacy relates to technology and gender. I always believed that privacy would be important in a study of gender and computer ethics. However, a consideration of privacy has proved to be the single most important feature linking my case studies from data protection law, cyberstalking, Internet pornography, hacking and surveillance. There is a strong historical relationship between technology and privacy, in earlier manufacturing technologies as well as contemporary ICTs. But there is also a historical relationship between gender, technology and privacy. Nowhere is that relationship clearer than in relation to the development of domestic technologies, but it also extends into contemporary use of ICTs.

Structure of the book

This book draws on a number of important feminist arguments and I felt that it was important to lay these out in some detail in the first two chapters. Chapter 2 turns to feminist politics and feminist legal theory. The split between public and private spheres, the association of men with the former and women with the latter is a major plank of feminist political theory. This chapter raises the problems of liberalism and the ways in which it renders the power relations of the separate spheres invisible. Feminist legal theory questions the disciplinary power of law and legal knowledge, and, in particular power over women's bodies. Within feminist legal theory there has been a vociferous debate on pornography and whether there is a causal link between pornography and violence against women – this theme re-emerges in Chapter 6's consideration of Internet pornography.

Chapter 3 discusses the related topic of feminist ethics and its development from long running debates on the special nature of women's morality. It is important to distinguish between feminine and feminist ethics. Feminine ethics emphasizes women's values centring round care as opposed to men's values centring on justice. On the other hand, feminist ethics emphasizes political opposition to women's oppression. I have not made a special distinction between feminine and feminist ethics in subsequent chapters, nevertheless I feel that the political dimension of feminist ethics is an integral element in a feminist analysis; the 'feminine' approach does not contain an adequate political dimension which could offer hope for change. An important element of all branches of feminist philosophy is a critique of the traditional canon, therefore I outline a feminist critique of moral relativism, utilitarianism, Kantian or deontological theory and virtue ethics as these represent major currents in traditional ethical thinking which are also to be found in writing on computer ethics. The chapter closes by considering Gilligan's (1982) approach to ethics of care and major critiques of it, particularly in the shape of Koehn's (1998) dialalogical ethics.

Chapter 4 offers an overview of computer ethics and its roots in science and technology studies, technology ethics, business ethics and professionalism, suggesting that its critical potential is largely yet to be realized. It is here that the problematic nature of technological determinism, resting on a liberalism which cannot adequately deal with inequalities, is explored. This chapter also discusses the topic of professionalism and how much of the impetus towards developing computer ethics rests on the IT/Computing industry's attempts to form into a profession. In this chapter I also discuss the failures which can occur in our translation of moral intuitions relating to the use of ICTs into enforceable laws, by reference to some examples relating to data protection law, where vulnerable members of society were not protected as they should have been. Through a discussion of these examples, I hope to demonstrate that computer ethics is a topic whose reach extends well beyond the confines of the academic discipline where it originated. Rather, I claim that an understanding of the moral issues involved in computer-related problems is a concern of a much wider society. These discussions are notable for their lack of gender awareness and for the absence of a feminist voice. This prompts an analysis of gender in computer ethics writing in the following chapter.

Chapter 5 sets out a detailed critique of existing gender and computer ethics research, particularly those studies which undertake statistical analyses seeking potential differences between men's and women's decision making in relation to computer ethics problems. I argue that the concept of gender is undertheorized in such studies and, therefore, they struggle to explain any gender differences that they may find in a convincing way. An empirical study that I undertook with a former student cannot avoid all the problems I identify in statistical studies. Nevertheless, I offer an analysis in terms of care ethics and a consideration of power relations thus, I hope, showing that analyses which are different in inspiration from the statistical studies I find so problematic are, at least, possible.

Chapter 6 takes up the arguments of the preceding chapters to form a feminist analysis of Internet dating, cyberstalking and Internet (mainly child) pornography in terms of violations of the privacy of the body and the concept of the gaze in its ambiguity in reinforcing or resisting submission. I am particularly interested in 'third-party' or proxy cyberstalking, or the way that a stalker can cause others to harass or stalk a victim of cyberstalking. Both the fairly limited amount of academic literature on cyberstalking, and 'official' responses to the phenomenon, fail to problematize gender, treating it as an accidental rather than as a fundamental part of the problem. In addition, 'official' responses to cyberstalking follow the deterministic and liberal path which I contend is problematic in ignoring the potential causes of inequality. Cyberstalking is only understandable through a feminist ethical analysis which puts gender centre stage as an explanatory device rather than leaving it in the wings.

Chapter 7 outlines a feminist analysis of hacking. There has been much interest in the idea of women hackers and their perceived scarcity. It is interesting to compare this with discussion on the lack of women in computing in general. I have found the concept of the frontier and 'frontier masculinity' to be useful in understanding the phenomenon of the hacker. The 'hacker ethic' espouses freedom of speech and ignoring 'bogus' criteria yet it can be seen as deeply problematic in gender terms when read against an equal opportunities ethic, freedom of information ethic and work ethic.

Chapter 8 focuses on the topic of privacy which emerges as a major theme in considerations of gender and computer ethics. The historical relationship between technology and privacy is outlined through a discussion of the Panopticon and the way that it removes the exercise of power from the individual into the technology and induces those observed to discipline their own behaviour. As well as a more general relationship between technology and privacy, there is also a strong historical relationship between gender, technology and privacy stretching from technologies of production, through domestic technologies through to present day ICTs. Increased levels of data surveillance, in the wake of heightened concerns about terrorism, imply a further disciplining and regulation of society.

My final chapter represents something of a compromise and also demonstrates some of the ambiguities which are raised by a study such as this. When I originally embarked on this project I had hoped to offer some novel theoretical insights which could be incorporated into contemporary feminist ethics, derived from my case studies on gender and computer ethics. I do not wish to claim that there has been no overlap between feminist ethics and technological subjects as there has clearly been considerable interest in the politics of reproductive technologies. However, given that feminist ethics has apparently had so little intersection with other technologies, and particularly not with ICTs, I saw possible insights from technological areas as potentially very important. At the same time, I hoped to make a thoroughgoing application of care ethics in a technological subject. These were to form the basis of a 'feminist cyberethics'. My original aim now looks rather too ambitious. I hope there are insights that my study on gender, ICTs and ethics can offer feminist ethics as I still feel that there has been so little discussion of technology from feminist ethics. A study such as the present one can look overly negative, all critique, so offering positive suggestions for a way forward is extremely important. There seems little reason for others to take up the feminist challenge unless there is an optimistic future is convincingly portrayed.

Additionally, I found it was not feasible to apply care ethics to the case studies I present, in a convincing way. Much of the reason is due to my discovering the substantial set of critiques of care ethics whilst marshalling the material for this book. Care ethics now appears to me to demand too much of women's traditionally self-sacrificing natures and sets up too unequal a power differential between carer and cared for.

Where does this leave the 'feminist cyberethics' project? Not where I expected to leave it! What, I hope, is offered by the present study is a demonstration that it is not only feasible, but it is also desirable to take problems which currently concern us in computer ethics and subject them to a thoroughgoing feminist analysis. This often adds another dimension to our understanding of such problems and, as in the case of topics such as cyberstalking, Internet pornography and hacking a feminist analysis renders aspects of the phenomenon explicable. This, then, points the way to further analyses of other computer ethics phenomena in terms of gender, using appropriate theoretical constructs from feminist theory and elsewhere, and underlines the importance of making such analyses available to a wider audience.

2
Feminist Political and Legal Theory: The Public/Private Dichotomy

Introduction – the links between politics, law and ethics

As the previous chapter outlines, a study which brings feminist ethics to bear on computer ethics must attend to a wide range of feminist theory in the process. This serves to emphasize the ways in which feminism, as an academic discourse, has grown in theoretical and empirical content over the last thirty or more years. Put simply, there is no single body of knowledge labelled 'feminism' to draw upon, and no unitary stand to be taken which could be termed a feminist position in relation to computer ethics. It is doubtful whether there ever was, but the idea of a single feminist view is even more problematic, given the explosion of research and writing on feminism to which I refer. The problem, then, is to choose what is relevant and what will add depth to the analysis that I am constructing.

In addition to the development of feminist ethics itself, which I will describe in Chapter 3, I argue that feminist legal theory and feminist politics are the two most relevant bodies of feminist theory for the present work. This reinforces the point, developed in the last chapter, that ethics, either conceived of as a philosophical discipline or as a practical guide, does not stand apart from other bodies of theory. It overlaps and involves (at least) politics, the law and epistemology. For instance, recent thinking in 'critical ethics' (Robinson 1999) suggests new ways of moral thinking where problems are seen not only as moral, but additionally as social and political, and where power relations may be challenged rather than remaining hidden away in the depths of abstract ethical theory. Intellectual moves, such as Robinson's, serve to reinforce the increasing interconnectedness of, at least, some academic disciplines and also underline the ways in which ethics is moving away from an abstract philosophical position towards an approach which is becoming seen as thoroughly social in inspiration.

There is an obvious sense in which ethics connects to law, in that the body of legislation can be seen as a legislative expression of our moral view of life. Although this conveys it rather simplistically, the law embodies the collective will of a society, or at least the more powerful members of society, towards what is regarded as right and wrong and the ways in which we should treat one another. Ethics is then prior to the law but both the law and ethics are re-interpreted and re-made in the light of one another. Similarly, politics can be seen as the expression of how we choose to govern ourselves. The positioning of political parties along the political spectrum, resulting in specific policies, can be seen as reflecting ethical views of how people should be treated (e.g. care of children, disabled or elderly people). Through the examples relating to data protection law in Chapter 4, we can see these links and where they may break down, in other words where we fail to reflect our moral consensus in the way that we apply the law.

The development of feminist legal theory and feminist politics follows the traditional trajectory of many feminist disciplines. The starting point is the formation of a view that women do not fare equally as well as men in some aspects of life and/or that women's experiences are ignored and hence absent from standard accounts; then a critique of the parent discipline is constructed. Such a critique will expose the way that the universalizing tendency of the parent discipline is based on the experience of men, whilst ignoring or marginalizing women's contributions. From this point, as the feminist version of the discipline matures, new feminist versions of theory and practice are elaborated. So feminist disciplines are usually twin pronged affairs, balanced between critique and development of new theoretical and empirical structures. We can see how this plays out in the development of feminist politics and feminist legal theory.

Feminist politics

Politics concerns structures of governance. Frazer (1998) notes that political theory is usually split into prescriptive theory or how governance *ought* to be done and descriptive theory or how it can be done or is done. A traditional approach to governance tends to mean that the public state institutions, for example, of parliament, senate, congress, the legislature, judiciary, and so on, in other words the traditional centres of power, are emphasized. The problem is that these institutions tend to be dominated by men and an emphasis on such institutions inevitably means that political theory becomes a study of masculinity, albeit usually in a tacit way. The places that women inhabit, usually the private domestic sphere of home and family, are generally absent from such a discussion and this is one very substantial way in which women are marginalized from political life and thought. This discussion leads to one of the major planks which feminist political theory rests upon, namely the public/private distinction and the ways in which this distinction serves to reinforce women's exclusion from political life. The following section discusses the implications of the private/public distinction in more detail. Meanwhile I note its centrality within the repertoire of feminist politics.

As Frazer (1998, p. 51) emphasizes, theories of gender are sometimes implicit both in classical and recent political theory, yet they are often quite explicit, as in the work of Rousseau and Mill. However, standard versions of the history of political theory sanitize the accounts of great men, in treating their writings on gender as not part of their real work, hence to be largely ignored. One is reminded of the way in which standard histories of science ignored Newton's vast body of writing on mysticism and alchemy, treating it as an aberration, concentrating, instead, on his mechanical and optical theories. In the same way, if the 'great men' of politics write on gender it is generally seen as an aberration, despite the pervasiveness of gender relations in social life.

This kind of 'rational reconstruction' of history is a traditional enlightenment trick, designed to show a linear progression from some point in history to the present day, peeling off and discarding as erroneous that which has not become part of contemporary theory. For instance, the 'rational reconstruction' approach was prevalent in the history of science in the middle part of the last century, but was challenged by newer social constructivist approaches and eventually by actor–network theory (Adam 1989; Law and Hassard 1999). Similar forces are at work in other spheres of intellectual life. But what has not been so obvious in critiques of rational reconstructionism, is the importance of the gender element. Although rationally reconstructing the history of a subject, particularly a subject like the physical sciences, is often seen as protecting the purity of the highest form of knowledge, free from taint of error or bias, it also, less explicitly, protects the purity of the *makers* of knowledge. In political theory, the musings of the great philosophers on gender relations can be conveniently sidelined and not considered to be part of their real contribution to the subject. However feminist philosophers (Pateman 1989; Phillips 1991) have uncovered this tendency and, in forming their critique, have emphasized that these theories of gender relations are, in fact, central to the formulation of political theory and political institutions. Nowhere is this tendency more evident than in the public/private dichotomy.

The public/private split – 'the personal is political'

If one were to think of a single slogan that encapsulates the spirit of second wave (i.e. 1960s and beyond) feminism it would probably be 'the personal is political' (Frazer 1998). In fact, the phrase has become such a cliché that it seems easy to dismiss it as meaningless nonsense. Yet 'the personal is political' slogan captures much of the tension of political life for women and it continues to be of considerable relevance to women's experiences today. To claim that the personal is political is to argue that not all that is important in politics resides in the public sphere, that is, within the public state institutions detailed above, which are predominantly male preserves. Instead, it is to argue that the private, personal sphere, traditionally women's preserve, is also political and important and has largely been ignored because of the emphasis on masculine, generally public, institutions. 'The personal is political' collapses the distinction between public and private worlds and, at the same time, emphasizes that the personal world is as important as the public world, in political terms.

The split between public and private worlds is of ancient origin. Okin (1998) argues that concepts of public and private spheres are longstanding in Western thought, stretching back to the seventeenth century and with origins in Greek philosophy. Aristotle described the public world, the *polis*, and emphasized that it was separate from the private world of the home and household (Frazer 1998, p. 51). This theme was elaborated in the work of later political philosophers, Rousseau and Hegel. Their emphasis on the split between a world that is political and public and pertaining to the activities of men, and a world that is private, of the home and relating to women, depended on a theory of gender and the proper relations of the two genders. Political philosophers of a more liberal persuasion, such as Locke and Mill, although sympathetic to women's rights, nevertheless mounted no challenge to the traditional public/private distinction, and thus reinforced that very distinction to the detriment of women. As I note in Chapter 4 this is one of the real problems with liberal politics, which at first sight appears to be more palatable to women's interests, but often serves to buttress women's traditional roles, thereby reinforcing their subordination.

As Okin (1998) demonstrates, one problem is that both historically and in contemporary political thought, the idea is perpetuated that it is relatively unproblematic to separate and describe the two spheres. Such a position is hard to maintain when one attends to the writings of various feminist scholars who argue that theories of gender relations demonstrate the complex and entwined relationship of the public and the private. She points out that the distinction between public and private is usually taken to mean a state/society or domestic/non-domestic split, where there is, in fact, a multiplicity of meanings not usually described by traditional political theorists, who ignore the political nature of the family and major elements of gender inequalities (Okin 1998, p. 118).

Separate spheres and divisions of labour

Much of the concern over the public/private dichotomy rests on its implications for gendered divisions of labour. Now one could make a case for a 'separate spheres' argument where women and men inhabit separate but equal spheres and where 'private = women and public = men'. But the problem is that, clearly, the spheres are not equal in status nor are they freely entered into. The masculine, external world of work, state and public institutions is of much higher status than the feminine, domestic world of the home, children, family and housework. Men rule in the public world, yet they also rule in the private world. Hence, there are power relations and structural factors at work which are not made explicit in liberal models of politics; indeed liberalism renders them invisible. Additionally, the spheres are not separate but rest and rely upon one another. One might initially think of the way in which the woman at home with children relies on a traditional male breadwinner – this is an obvious way where one might see the private as depending on the economic fruits of the public sphere. But, perhaps less obviously though just as importantly, the public sphere crucially rests on the private sphere as women traditionally look after the home and family thus freeing men for their work in the public world. Women entering the public sphere of work rarely shed the domestic burden onto a partner the way that most men do, and thus many women feel that they must choose between creative achievement and having a family. As Okin (1998, p. 136) puts it: '… it is exceedingly difficult for a woman to have her work, her children, and her relationship with a male partner all flourishing at the same time.' Those women that do choose to 'have it all', so goes the popular mantra, tend to have the double shift of public, paid work and private, domestic work.

To illustrate this point, Wajcman (1998) notes, in her study of women in management, that, in her sample, 93 per cent of male manager respondents lived with a wife or partner, while 73 per cent of women managers in the study lived with partners or husbands. Hence, the women managers were much more likely to be single. Similarly, two-thirds of the women managers did not have children, while two-thirds of the male managers did have children living with them. Of all respondents with children, 94 per cent of the women as compared to 15 per cent of the men, reported primary responsibility for the children. Several other studies have produced similar results (ibid., p. 139). Such statistics are quite striking. They imply that, whatever we might like to think, regarding the breach of corporate 'glass ceilings', and the introduction of more liberal employment and sex equality legislation from the 1970s onwards, many things have not changed very much. Men who climb the corporate ladder can expect to have a partner who will look after the domestic sphere and children. Women climbing the corporate ladder are much more likely to be single and without children, than are men. When they do combine management careers with having children, they are much more likely to retain primary responsibility for childcare.

These statistics offer some evidence to confirm that the public sphere is still largely associated with men and the private sphere with women. Additionally, although they are in some sense mutually supportive, the public sphere rests on the private sphere. Men often achieve successful entry into the public sphere at least partly because of the labour of women who still look after the private, domestic sphere. Looking after the domestic sphere is important, but as women's labour it is largely invisible work – it is often not treated as work at all. Women who enter the public sphere do so largely without the support of a partner to look after children and the domestic sphere.

Campaigns to push women into the public sphere, into careers in management, science or politics say, can be problematic. When such campaigns are inspired by a liberal, political agenda they are likely to render invisible the importance of the domestic sphere and the fact that it involves real work. The onus then rests on women to juggle their lives – men are not pushed to enter into the domestic sphere where their greater involvement might free up women's time for the public world of work.

For instance, I find myself increasingly irritated by 'Take Your Daughter to Work' day, whereby one day a year we are called upon to take our daughters to the workplace to show them the world of work so that they might be encouraged to join it. My colleagues are baffled when I suggest we hold a 'Get Your Son to Stay Home and Do the Housework' day instead. However, it can reasonably be argued that persuading women to enter the world of work is not the problem, rather it is the sharing out of domestic roles more equitably between men and women.

Feminism and democracy

These considerations reinforce one of the most significant aspects of feminist politics namely women's entry into public life, including their entry into political life and participative democracy. We often forget how recently the struggle for women's suffrage took place. I find it astonishing to think that the first time my grandmother was able to vote was when she was well into her forties. It is even more incredible to think that women only gained the vote in Switzerland in 1971. Pateman (1989, p. 212) notes the way in which women's extensive struggles for the franchise are often forgotten and democracy looks like the sole creation of men. This further underscores women's tenuous relationship with democracy where equality for all citizens may not apply to women if they are not treated as full citizens. Liberalism assumes a blanket sort of equality for everyone whilst ignoring and obscuring the politics of difference, in other words, the material aspects of people's lives that militate against equality. Liberal theorists regard the structure of social relations and implied social inequalities as irrelevant to political equality and democracy. The problem, then, is that when differences are found in man's and woman's estate, they are often defended as representing some natural distinction between men and women, for example, the natural subordination of women to men; the natural place of women in the home.

We might imagine that such views are a thing of the past. However, as Pateman (ibid.) notes, arguments about what is natural for men and women now tend to come dressed up as sociobiology. I noted in Chapter 1, and have argued more extensively elsewhere (Adam 1998) that sociobiological arguments can be very problematic. For instance, as I write, the news media have seized upon a report that men's brains are 'programmed to ignore dust' (Womack 2003). Although this report is full of delicious *non sequiturs* (e.g. men have less oxytocin than women and therefore have more need to be in charge of the remote control in order to flick through sports channels), at the same time it contains the seeds of more doubtful ideas. It contains neurobiological research *and* anecdotes from the author's time as a family therapist. Michael Gurian (2003) wrote his book *What Could He Be Thinking?* to reverse the 'dangerous assumption' that men have become redundant. Hence it is clearly defensive. It argues against the ideas of supposedly liberated women that they were wrong to imagine that men can change – they are just not 'programmed' for it (note the metaphor of brain as computer which reinforces 'natural' scientific arguments). Although such reports make us chuckle, and the media clearly play up to that, they are, at the same time, the thin end of a much more sinister wedge which seeks to argue for the naturalness of men's and women's estates, especially when women are put in a subordinate position, but nowadays couched in scientific terms, although here also clearly influenced by anecdote.

Hence, on the one hand, many feminists might feel that there is nowhere in the world where women participate on a completely equal footing with men. On the other hand, deep structural inequalities are ignored in descriptions of the development of participative democracy. Pateman (1989, p. 212) uses the very apt expression: 'women can be written out of democratic political life', to refer to the way that histories of democracy forget that women only recently gained the franchise, yet they write as though this is just a footnote to the ideal of 'one *man*, one vote' democracies. Relationships between the sexes are not seen as relevant to discussions of democracy. Indeed class inequality often receives more attention than gender inequality.

Although the rise of liberalism and arguments against paternalism, as epitomized by Locke's work on the social contract, suggest that political and paternal power are different, women appear to have been forgotten in the equation. Little is said about the status of the wife in the liberal agenda; her proper place is in the home. Indeed such a division of labour was solidified by the ideal of the non-working, Victorian middle-class wife. The angel of the hearth was taken as the ideal expression of womanhood, although women had always sought paid employment and working-class women continued to do so. They had no choice if they were to feed their families. It is not surprising then that, for all its radical arguments, John Stuart Mill's *The Subjection of Women* was blind to the private/public division of labour between men and women. 'Mill's failure to question the apparently natural division of labour within the home means that his arguments for democratic citizenship apply only to men' (Pateman 1989, p. 217). Mill argued that the legal subjection of women by men was wrong (more specifically wives by husbands) and that it ought to be replaced by a 'principle of perfect equality'. He realized that appeals to custom and nature could be challenged but as he, himself, did not challenge domestic division of labour he undermines his argument for democratic equality. He falls back on the old position of assuming that women's proper sphere is children and the home; whereas men have a wide choice of occupation, women have but one. Of course, it could be argued that Mill, writing in the 1860s was just reflecting the times in which he lived. For middle-class women, unless they had independent means, marriage was the only realistic option. But, as Pateman argues, whilst we might excuse Mill, writing 150 years ago, we certainly cannot excuse contemporary political theorists their assumption of women's natural domain being the domestic sphere. Hence, feminist critiques of marriage and personal life cannot be ignored in theories of democracy.

> The example of the workplace, together with ... other examples ... should be sufficient to show the fundamental importance to democratic theory and practice of the contemporary feminist insistence that personal and political life are integrally connected. Neither the equal opportunity of liberalism nor the active, participatory democratic citizenship of *all* the people can be achieved without radical changes in personal and domestic life. (Ibid., p. 222)

Further implications follow from the public/private dichotomy

The way that the liberal political agenda obscures, to the extent of denying, the implications of gender difference is brought home in what Okin (1998, pp. 120–1) terms 'false gender neutrality'. Many contemporary political commentators (and indeed other academic authors) are now scrupulous in using gender-neutral terminology in their writings as opposed to the old generic use of male pronouns to supposedly stand for everyone. As Okin (ibid., p. 120) points out: 'Gender-neutral terms, if used without real awareness of gender, frequently obscure the fact that so much of the real experience of "persons", so long as they live in gender-structured societies, does in fact depend on what sex they are.'

Feminism vs liberalism

As feminist political theory has developed through second wave feminism, the emphasis has turned to the family and personal spheres as political constructs. Pateman (1989, p. 118) argues that the private/public dichotomy has been such a central plank of the feminist political struggle over the last two centuries that 'it is, ultimately, what the feminist movement is about'.

Patemen sees the feminist response to the split as a fundamental argument against liberalism, the political theory that has reinforced the split for so long. Although both feminism and liberalism rest, ultimately, on views of individuals acting as freely choosing agents unshackled by traditional hierarchies, liberalism is notoriously blind to the differences in possibility for free action that individuals may experience on account of their gender. Although there is not sufficient space to explore this in detail here, this is not to deny the complexities and ambiguities of both liberal and feminist positions on the public/private dichotomy. Nevertheless, the separation and opposition of the public and the private has been a central tenet of liberal theory, and, as feminists have criticized, this opposition has served to disguise the patriarchal nature of liberalism, where inequalities of the private sphere are seen to be separate from and even irrelevant to questions of political inequality. Liberalism is formed by both patriarchal gender relations and class relations and 'the dichotomy between the private and the public obscures the subjection of women to men within an apparently universal, egalitarian and individualist order' (ibid., p. 120). For Pateman, liberalism becomes 'patriarchal-liberalism' and the opposition of the public and private is an unequal opposition between men and women. Liberal theory often excludes women and this goes unnoticed as liberalism holds on to the rhetoric of universalism.

Feminists of different political leanings and in a variety of disciplines have revealed and analysed the multiple interconnections between women's domestic roles and their inequality and segregation in the workplace, and between their socialization in gendered families and the psychological aspects of their subordination. Thus, the family became, and has since remained, central to the politics of feminism and a major focus of feminist theory. Contemporary feminism thus poses a significant challenge to the long-standing underlying assumption of political theories that the sphere of family and personal life is so separate and distinct from the rest of social life that such theories can legitimately ignore it. (Okin 1998, pp. 123–4)

Feminism and the law

Feminist legal theory was born out of a growing recognition in feminist circles that the law did not necessarily serve men and women equally well and that traditional legal theory reflected patriarchal structures of society where women remained subordinate. As Fineman (1991, p. xi) notes, the law has remained relatively unwashed by the tide of postmodern theory, but we are now seeing it more and more subject to critical discussion, amongst which we could include the criticisms mounted from feminist legal theorists. As with all feminist writing, the balance between theory and practice is important. As Smart (1989, p. 71) argues, grand theory does not sit well with contemporary feminism. The attempt to find a best or 'true' feminist jurisprudence can be seen as a form of positivism and a 'totalising tendency'. Feminist theory must be connected to feminist practice; material circumstances must not only be taken into account, they must provide the very focus for feminist theorizing.

Smart's (1989) *Feminism and the Power of Law* pioneered the business of breaking down the rigid divisions of topics within the law, starting from the relevance of feminism rather than traditional topics; it remains one of the most convincing treatments of feminism and law, to date. Adding women to existing frameworks was not the answer as such, yet what she (ibid., p. 1) terms the 'Women and ...' approach was often the only way to get gender relations on academic courses on law and social science. Given the burgeoning feminist literature and tradition, much of her concern lies with investigating why the law has proved so resistant to feminist knowledge and critique and how the law continues to ignore women's experiences.

In particular, Smart (ibid., p. 4) argues that the law exercises a particular power, and in so doing resists and disqualifies other forms of knowledge. Indeed the very act of naming 'the law' makes it appear more unitary than it actually is and this lends it more power to impose its definition on everyday life. The problem is that, as much feminist strategy goes towards debates on emancipation and equality, the debate becomes stuck in discussions of the usefulness of law and, paradoxically, ends up granting more authority to the law which can then be used against women's demands. As Smart (ibid., p. 5) puts it, feminism is 'losing the battle before it has begun'. This implies that non-legal strategies are often a better way forward, rather than expecting that the law itself can change elements of the social order. It is then a question of maintaining a convincing feminist argument in 'deconstructing the discursive power of law'. This is why Smart is equivocal about the whole business of building up a feminist jurisprudence if this were only to challenge the form that law takes rather than challenging the notion that law should take a pre-eminent place in ordering our lives. Smart is proposing something more practical, but, at the same time, more radical. We need to tackle the law at the conceptual level.

Issues of the power of law and how feminism might challenge that are central to Smart's argument. She follows Foucault (1979) in arguing that power is not some tangible right which is inexorably owned by some individuals to exercise over others, but rather is part of a move towards a disciplinary society, where the growth of new knowledges such as medicine, criminology, psychology, and so on, bring new modes of surveillance or of regulating people. Smart developed these arguments before more recent responses to the threat of terrorism, which have resulted in increased efforts at surveillance and regulation. Nevertheless, as Chapter 8 demonstrates, such arguments take on particular relevance in a post September 11th world. So those who do not conform no longer need to be punished in the old way. Now, instead, they need to be watched, regulated and pressed to conform. Foucault (1979) wrote before the development of many later ICTs which are now actively used for surveillance and regulation; indeed Smart's germinal work largely predates these too. Nevertheless, the seeds of the disciplinary, regulatory society have been with us for much longer, and it is to this that we must look to gain a more subtle understanding of the power of law.

In epistemological terms, Foucault (ibid.) sees power as attaching to the notion of truth. Rather than 'truth' being what we discover and accept about the real world, he understands it, instead, in terms of how we regulate the world by means of rules, about how to separate true from false and then power becomes attached to what is taken as true. Foucault talks of the sciences in making this claim but Smart (1989, p. 9) argues that law also holds a similar epistemological position, with its specialized methods, language and systems. Hence, it becomes separate and elevated from other discourses, much in the way that the sciences are epistemologically separate and accorded higher status.

Law sets itself above other disciplines such as psychology, social work and even the sciences, as a scientific 'expert' may be called in to give evidence in a legal case, yet the case is ultimately decided by legal argument. Smart (ibid.) argues that the exercise of power in the law should not merely be understood in terms of its material effects, but also, importantly, in terms of its power to silence or disqualify other discourses. Although, much of law's dominion is every day experiences, witness the way that minute details are turned over in a murder trial, for instance, as it trims and potentially sanitizes the discourse of every day life.

Law appears to add a special rigour to descriptions of the mundanities of every day life, and it sets itself apart and above these. Judges can, and do, pronounce on the natures of men and women as if there is to be no argument about these. In the early 1980s, the British judge,

Lord Denning (1980) was notorious for alluding to a sociobiological determinism to argue that women's main purpose in life is child bearing and rearing and that men are naturally more aggressive than women. It is notable that a scientific argument, with its supposed authority, can be readily pressed into the service of a legal argument, especially so for sociobiological arguments. Although 20 or more years on, such pronouncements are ever harder to swallow, they nevertheless serve to disqualify and silence feminist discourse. At the beginning of the twenty-first century we are less likely to hear such assertions from the judiciary, nevertheless they do resurface from time to time. They are more likely to be found in the 'backlash' rhetoric of writers such as Gurian (2003), who, in arguing against the supposed redundancy of men, draw upon sociobiology to support arguments for the natural estates of men and women.

Reproduction and legal discourse

In looking towards the exercise of a Foucaldian type of disciplinary power relating to women, in terms of the power of law, much of this power is exercised over women's bodies. For instance the question of rape and rape in marriage, surrogacy and abortion have all been subject to litigation. In the UK, the fight of Diane Blood to be inseminated with her dead husband's sperm was the subject of much legal controversy (Dyer 2004). Although her case excited much public, and even legal, sympathy, part of the problem was seen to be the construction of the very legislation which could have helped her, in the hands of Baroness Warnock, a figure in the judiciary clearly sympathetic to women's issues. One of the problems was that the relatively new Human Fertilisation and Embryology Act (1990) had not foreseen cases like this and seemed to explicitly disallow Blood's wishes; her husband's sperm had been extracted whilst he lay dying and unable to give the consent required by the legislation.

Good legislation is by nature 'open-textured' (Twining and Miers 1991) , in other words a legal rule does not define, in advance, all the cases to which it applies. This is because, it is recognized that one cannot know, in advance, all the cases to which it should apply. New cases will always occur and a rule is always open to interpretation in the context of a new case. Case law builds up our interpretation of a legal rule. However, this does not mean that we have a free reign in deciding how to interpret a rule. As well as case law, there is the question of the 'spirit of the law' – the political view of how the class of people to which the piece of legislation was designed for, should be treated. So a good piece of legislation, necessarily open-textured though it will be, should be such that it treats that class of people in the spirit of the way that law was intended. The trouble is, that, the intention to treat a certain category of people in a certain way, as embodied in a piece of legislation, is itself an expression of power relations. In the UK, legislation is enacted by act of parliament, the most powerful of state institutions. Despite growing, usually liberal, attempts at social inclusion, it is by no means necessarily the case that the voices of the less powerful – women, ethnic minorities, senior citizens and those without influence will be heard and therefore represented as they might be in the formulation of law. This returns us to Smart's point (1989) about the form of law, silencing and disqualifying feminist discourse.

Let us see how these considerations apply to Blood's case. There was much sympathy for Blood, and a widespread recognition that her case was tragic. Warnock explicitly stated that when the legislation had been drawn up it had not been foreseen that there could be circumstances where the father could not (as opposed to 'would not' which is quite a different matter) give his consent for sperm to be used – this was seen as a loophole in the law. However, in this case, there was also an overtone (one could not call it an undercurrent – it was much stronger than that) that a baby required a father, that Blood should not 'go it alone'. So, although there is the perfectly reasonable question of a man having the right to decide on the use of his sperm, there is also the question of a woman's right to have a child, and to have that child on her own. In the end Blood took her case to European courts to have it heard under European law and ended up, subsequently, having her two children in a Belgian clinic. She then campaigned (successfully) to have her children's births re-registered with her dead husband's name as the father under the European Convention on Human Rights, as she argued, that having a blank against the father's name in a birth certificate violated her children's rights to private and family life (Dyer 2004).

More recently, a number of cases demonstrating a similar principle have been reported in the British media. The issue here revolves round the question of whether frozen embryos can be used where the father has withdrawn his consent. In one case (Hewson 2004), a number of frozen embryos were stored, when the woman was about to be treated for cancer. The couple subsequently split up. The woman had no chance of becoming pregnant after this, due to her medical condition. Her only chance of (biological) motherhood rested with the implantation of the frozen embryos. She agreed to make no demands on the man, financial or otherwise. The man no longer consented to their use – legally, consent of both parties was required – therefore it appeared that the embryos would have to be destroyed. He was exercising his right to choose not to be a father or at least, not to be a father, at that time, and with that woman. The question was raised as to whether he was seeking revenge on her by denying consent and forcing the destruction of the embryos. Whilst, he was not denied fatherhood for ever, she was denied motherhood for ever.

As (Smart 1989, p. 113) argues, the law has a particular interest in men's sperm and whether legal rights should follow their sperm. The ownership of the produce of women's bodies has also always been the subject of legal interest and the alliance of medicine and law serves to regulate women and subject them to surveillance. 'The law–medicine–women's bodies nexus constitutes a very effective deployment of power which it is increasingly hard for women to resist. It is also a cause for concern that law maintains its traditional approach to women's bodies, seeing the biology of bits of these bodies as encompassing a nature which must be sustained and celebrated even against women themselves' (ibid.).

Understandably, these two tragic cases are far from clear-cut and they deserve extensive consideration. However, at the same time, they demonstrate the type of power relation which Foucault (1979) describes, and we can see how this applies to the power of law. There is a systemic regulation of women's bodies; the women in the preceding examples were not free to do exactly as they pleased with their bodies. Production of children was involved and therefore male consent was required, but there were all sorts of other issues bound up with this. There was the question of women deliberately choosing to bring up children on their own. There was a question of taking something from men without consent; there was the question of producing children, to whose creation their fathers could not or would not assent. There was also the question of the law not doing what we wanted of it, as in the original legal decision on Blood's case, and we see something akin to that in the discussion of data protection law in Chapter 4. In such cases we see the power of different discourses. The law can ally medicine and science, the notion of rights, of the father, mother or unborn child and the notion of the 'best interests of the child'. All these can be mustered into legal arguments which can be used to discipline women.

The legal questions surrounding reproduction are complex. In the remainder of this book I shall not return to this topic, although I shall return to the regulation of women's bodies in Chapters 6 and 8. Rather, my purpose here has been to use the (clearly) gendered topic of reproduction to illustrate how the law embodies moral thinking and policy making and how this may not work out as we intend. Furthermore, the example of reproduction in relation to the law illustrates the way in which women may be subject to regulation, discipline, surveillance and control, increasingly through the use of new technologies.

Feminism, law and pornography

In Chapter 6, I return to the question of Internet pornography in more detail. However, a consideration of Internet pornography requires an understanding of the vociferous debates which have taken place amongst the various stripes of feminists and other activists in regard to pornography in the first place. I hesitate to raise the topic of pornography at this juncture, only to return to it in a later chapter. However, as a topic, it belongs to a discussion of feminism, law and women's bodies. Hence its introduction in this section appears logical, although I ask for my readers' forbearance in waiting until Chapter 6 to consider Internet pornography. Once more it is a question of how the law regulates, or otherwise, women's bodies, although, this time, in terms of sexuality rather than reproduction. Pornography represents a very interesting case for feminist analysis of the law.

As Smart (1989, p. 114) notes, the relationship between feminism and pornography, undoubtedly a major subject for the women's movement, raises great passion but, understandably, no unified position, other than a feeling that something must be done as it will not disappear of its own volition. However, it is not clear that a resort to legislation benefits women and some regard an attempt to legislate as a retrograde step, especially as it requires a compromise from different feminist positions and with positions which are not particularly sympathetic to the broader aims of feminism. Even if legislation enters the statute books it is often unclear whether it helps women. Indeed, legislation designed to ameliorate women's estate, such as women's formal equality expressed through equal opportunities and sex discrimination legislation, can have the effect of making it seem as though women have achieved equality where many women continue to be oppressed in subtle, yet tangible, ways. Therefore, in terms of pornography and many other issues, legislation may prove to be a double-edged sword. As Easton (1994, p. 176) points out, by strengthening the repressive power of the state through further legislation, we may create legislation which further oppresses women.

Smart (1989, p. 116) identifies two main positions in the feminist debate against pornography, 'pornography-as-violence', exemplified in the work of Dworkin (1981) and MacKinnon (1987) and 'pornography-as-representation' as expressed by Kuhn (1985) and Coward (1984).

Although these positions agree that pornography eroticizes domination and power differences, from there onwards they diverge. Dworkin's and MacKinnon's approach, in seeing pornography as violent male (hetero)sexual power, the very epitome of male power over women, demands that something be done. This approach tends towards the idea that any representation of heterosexual activity involves men coercing women.

To date, the most important discussion on the issue of pornography, from the violence position, has crystallized into strong pornography/anti-pornography stances which are variations of long running freedom of speech/censorship debates. These are particularly important in the USA, where freedom of speech is protected by the First Amendment, to the extent that pornography can be regarded as freedom of speech and therefore not subject to censorship. In the USA this debate was brought to the fore by the attempts of anti-pornography feminist Andrea Dworkin's and lawyer, Catharine MacKinnon's attempts to put on the legal statute book laws which would make it possible for women to claim legal redress if they could prove in a court of law that they had been damaged by the use of pornography (e.g. by violence resulting from a third party's use of pornography) (Easton 1994, p. 109). They did this through two Civil Rights Ordinances based on the principle of restitution for specific harms caused to women arising from the use of pornography. Both ordinances failed. The Indianapolis Ordinance was struck down as it was deemed to violate the First Amendment rights to freedom of speech. The story, and the issues involved are complex and long running. Here I describe briefly the points salient to the present discussion and form an initial analysis which will be revisited in Chapter 6, in relation to the question of Internet pornography.

First of all it must be noted that Dworkin and MacKinnon were not trying to censor all pornography (Cornell 2000, pp. 3–4). Their proposed ordinance defined pornography in terms of sexually explicit material which subordinates women. A woman working in the sex industry, or indeed any other woman, who was physically harmed by a consumer of pornography and who could show that the harm was inflicted as a result of reading or viewing the pornography could have sued under the ordinance. Dworkin and MacKinnon's ordinance was very controversial, not least amongst many feminists who saw that its initial political success was due to an unlikely alliance with the political right and religious fundamentalist groups.

Smart's (1989) alternative 'pornography-as-representation' approach tries to make a distinction between sexual relationships and representations of sex and is related to the whole way that women are represented in the media. Coward (1984) argues that it is not that these images cause men to commit violent acts but that they smother other representations and make alternative forms of eroticism difficult as they always slide into pornography. An important effect of this approach is to alert us to the more widespread implications of a pornographic outlook and the commodification of women, for example, in advertising, beyond that represented in traditional outlets for pornography.

Whatever one may feel about this chapter in the history of pornography, the question of how far injury is done to women through the use of pornography remains open. Strossen (1995) has been the most forceful exponent of freedom of speech in this respect. In arguing against censorship of pornography, she states the case that no link between sexually explicit materials and violence has been convincingly made. Additionally, there is evidence that sexual violence may decrease with the availability of some materials, for example, sex education in schools. We then have the very blurred distinction between sex education, erotica and pornography to consider. Could it not be the case that some materials may incite some individuals to violence whilst other materials may have the opposite effect? Causal links, and especially negative causal links are notoriously difficult to prove convincingly. If the myriad of literature on the possible link between violence and pornography is inconclusive, and even contradictory, this does not mean that we can dismiss the link as non-existent. Rather, borrowing a useful term from old Scottish law, it is 'not proven'.

However it may well be the case that studies of Internet pornography can begin to offer us better clues as to that link and the means of exploring its nature, especially given the introduction of webcam technology and its use in the online world of pornography. Furthermore this may give us a better sense of the genuine differences between adult pornography and child pornography, as the distinction remains important, given that, in the latter area there appears to be definite evidence of the use of the technology fuelling and exaggerating the paedophile's abusive activities (Panorama 2001). In this way we may hope that further research on Internet pornography may shed light on the long running 'porn wars'.

Feminist jurisprudence

Given continuing concerns about the law's treatment of reproduction, rape, social welfare, child abuse, pornography, sex discrimination and equal opportunities, a groundswell of opinion favouring the development of a distinctly feminist form of jurisprudence has arisen, centred in North America, Western Europe and Australia (Smart 1989; Smith 1993). As noted above, this is problematic as constructing a feminist jurisprudence might be a question of replacing one totalizing discourse with another, and we have already seen how problematic the resort to law has been in connection with pornography. Rather than de-centring law, forming a feminist jurisprudence might confirm law's place in the epistemological hierarchy. Perhaps we need to develop alternative practices to deconstruct law. 'Otherwise feminism may fall into the same trap of presenting itself as the truth, claiming epistemic supremacy and thereby assuming an essentially positivist notion of objectivity, when it should be challenging dogmatism' (Easton 1994, p. 175).

Easton's comment echoes the position of Smart who clearly feels ambivalent about the possibility of a feminist jurisprudence. Many legal reforms have only slightly improved women's position. We must also avoid the attempt at 'grand theorizing' and setting one type of feminism above another. Indeed she criticizes MacKinnon for doing just that, for arguing that radical feminism *is* feminism, for arguing that sexuality is the overarching instrument of male oppression and for arguing that male power is apparently omnipotent (Smart 1989, pp. 76–7). Easton (1994, pp. 176–7) argues that we cannot avoid engaging with law whatever its defects. There have been real gains in narrowing the gap between men's and women's pay, women have become more willing to take cases to industrial tribunals, and there has been heightened awareness on issues of equality and difference. As she suggests, the best strategy may be an alliance of legal measures with other attempts at equality. 'The establishment of women's presence in the media, press and publishing through equal opportunities policies, better employment practices and non-legislative strategies should be pursued in addition to legal measures' (ibid., p. 177).

Conclusion

A consideration of feminist politics raises issues of masculine domination of the state institutions of governance, democracy and the traditional association of women with the private sphere and men with the public sphere. Feminist legal theory extends much of these arguments into a challenge to the law, emphasizing ways in which feminist challenges to the law can cede to the law the power which allows it to disqualify other forms of knowledge, particularly that of women. Smart's Foucauldian analysis (1989) of the changes in the power of law away from regulation towards surveillance is particularly pertinent to women's lives. Women's bodies have always been subject to the power of law. This can be seen in relation to the alliance of law and medicine in reproduction as in Diane Blood's case and the frozen embryos case. Additionally, one of the most important topics for feminism and the law, namely pornography, reveals the complexity of the question of masculine power over women and the ambiguities as to what might be done about it. The uniting themes of the above discussion on feminist politics and legal theory are feminist challenges to masculine power and authority over the institutions of the state – in law and politics – and ways of conceptualizing both these so that oppression and inequalities may be recognized and ways that they may be overcome may be offered.

In this chapter some of the major themes of the book have emerged. The critique of liberalism from feminist politics is focused through a criticism of the public/private split which has ramifications all the way through my discussion of ethical issues relating to gender and technology. Indeed, it appears to be fundamental to almost all discussion surrounding feminist politics.

In my consideration of feminist legal theory, the question of power is central, particularly power which serves to discipline women and women's bodies. Here the example is reproduction, but I return to the more general idea of regulating women through the 'gaze' in later chapters, particularly in relation to cyberstalking, harassment and pornography. The examples relating to reproductive law in this chapter also reinforce the problem, to be emphasized again in Chapter 4, that the link between our moral intuitions and the application of legislation often breaks down. Here it was, at least partly because cases like Blood's were not imagined in advance. There are other ways that this sort of process breaks down, which are especially problematic in relation to ICT law, as Chapter 4 describes. Much of the ground work of the feminist arguments I pick up in later chapters is made through my discussion of feminist politics and feminist law. The next chapter continues to build the argument through a consideration of feminist ethics.

3
Feminist Ethics: Ethics in a Different Voice

Introduction: locating feminist ethics

Ethics is the philosophical study of morality. As Sterba (1998, p. 1) notes there are a number of ethical questions to which philosophers have constantly returned including what is the nature of morality, what are its requirements and justification and what challenges can be made to different systems of morality? These are clearly ancient questions and a consideration of them underscores the way in which ethics is prior to politics and the law – ultimately our systems of governance and legislation rest on our beliefs about how people ought to treat one another, in other words our systems of morality. In this chapter I concentrate on describing the main ethical theories prevalent in Western philosophy and feminist critiques of them. This discussion is followed by an extended consideration of the feminist 'ethics of care' as a potential alternative. Coupled with the discussion of Chapter 2, this prepares the theoretical armoury for the discussion of computer ethics which follows in Chapter 4.

As feminist philosophy had developed apace, over the last twenty-five or so years, it is not surprising to find that feminist ethics is one of the major parts of the new feminist philosophy. Jaggar (1992) has described the rise of feminist ethics, particularly within North American academic feminism, and its search for possible models. Feminist ethical discussion in the 1960s and 1970s focused on grass roots issues such as sexualities and domestic labour, in other words more pragmatic equal opportunities concerns. This strand of research merged with theoretical critiques of traditional ethical theory from about the 1970s onwards. Further research focused on the question of whether there is a distinctively feminine moral experience. These vectors came together in the publication of Gilligan's much quoted work (1982) which mounts the best known challenge, to date, against the idea that women's moral development is somehow inferior to men's.

Feminist ethics has two major roles. The first is to challenge the traditional ethical canon which is seen to be masculine in inspiration; the second to develop theoretical ideas derived, in part, from the challenge to mainstream ethics to develop a new ethics with which to make normative judgements on ethical problems from a wide range of domains, and, in particular, on areas where women assume a subordinate role, or where their experiences have proved negative on account of their gender.

Feminist ethics involves rethinking and revising aspects of traditional ethics which devalue the moral experience of women (Tong 1999). Arguing that traditional ethics fails women, in that it ignores the possibility that their experiences may be different to those of men, at the same time it places an emphasis on traditional masculine ways of ethical reasoning which are based on individual, rationalistic, rule-based ethical models. The overall aim of feminist ethics is '... to create a gender-equal ethics, a moral theory that generates non-sexist moral principles, policies and practices' (ibid.). So, although feminist ethics, in common with feminist thinking in general, starts from the position of acknowledging that women in most walks of life are in a subordinate position to men, in seeking to redress this balance, I believe that it should not confine itself to 'women's issues'. Apart from anything else, in a world where the two genders exist in (almost) equal numbers, nothing can really be a women's issue without its being a men's issue too. For instance, in Chapter 6, it will be argued that the majority of cyberstalking cases involve women as victims and men as perpetrators. It is not possible to attempt a convincing explanation of women as victims without, at the same time, questioning why it should be that the perpetrators are mostly men.

Feminist ethics can help to expose the power inequalities which exist in ethical case studies which mainstream ethics renders invisible in its pursuit of traditional ethical views often resting on individualistic, rationalistic ethical theories. It is this critical edge which has proved appealing to many feminist authors. The challenge is then to harness this energy into a constructive critique of traditional forms of ethics.

Feminist ethics has grown out of long-running debates about the special nature of women's morality which date from at least the time of Wollstencroft's (1988), *A Vindication of the Rights of Women*, in the eighteenth century and Mill's concerns (1970) about the virtue of women in, *The Subjection of Women*, in the middle of the nineteenth century. Arising from an interest on grass roots issues such as sexualities and domestic labour, juxtaposed with more theoretical concerns, the topic of feminine and feminist ethics was firmly put on the feminist agenda by Gilligan's, *In a Different Voice* (1982), which is often thought of as the canonical work of feminist, or at least, women-centred ethics. However, before discussing the extraordinary appeal of Gilligan's work, reactions to and criticisms of it, it will be necessary to describe briefly the difference between feminine and feminist ethics and, following this, the major contemporary ethical theories, with some comment on feminist critique as we go along (the 'challenging the canon' part of feminist ethics). This is done partly to elaborate the background for understanding feminist critiques of standard ethical theories, but it is also useful to set the scene in Chapter 4 where part of the business of thinking about computer ethics involves describing and critiquing its relationship to traditional ethical theories.

Feminine and feminist ethics

In this book I have not made a particular distinction between feminine and feminist ethics, rather I have tended to bracket together as feminist all approaches which broadly look to the experiences of women to transform traditional androcentric Western ethics, and I believe this follows the practice of many, if not most, authors who write on gender and ethics. However Tong (1993, 1999), in particular, distinguishes between the two and, as the differences are both important, in the general sense, and also very pertinent to my study, is well worth rehearsing the distinction here.

Tong (1993, p. 220) argues that a feminine ethics is a women-centred ethics where the ways in which moral behaviours of men and women differ can be identified. Women's moral virtues are celebrated for being at least as good as, if not better than, those of men. Broadly, within feminine inspired ethics, women's values are seen as centring round care, whilst men's centre round justice. The mother–child relationship is seen as the most important source of inspiration informing the, essentially feminine, ethic of care. Tong (ibid., p. 222) classifies Gilligan's work on care ethics and related research on maternal ethics, for example, Ruddick (1989), as part of the *feminine* ethics approach. This is not to denigrate a feminine approach to ethics, as is clear from the discussion below, Gilligan's work (1982) in particular, has been enormously influential in putting the whole subject of feminine and feminist ethics on the moral map.

However, a *feminist* ethics is one which emphasizes the political nature of a women-centred ethics. It is not enough to identify the ways in which women's moral experience is undervalued; there must be active, political opposition to women's oppression. Jaggar (1992, pp. 363–4) contends that the features of a feminist ethics (as opposed to maternal or feminine ethics) are:

(1) to articulate moral critiques of actions and practices that perpetuate women's subordination;
(2) to prescribe morally justifiable ways of resisting such actions and practices;
(3) to envision morally desirable alternatives that will promote women's emancipation; and
(4) to take the moral experience of all women seriously, though not, of course, uncritically.

A feminist ethics must theorize and oppose the structures of women's oppression and seek ways to eliminate it.

Tong (1993) sees it as somewhat problematic that traditional ethics is fairly keen to embrace feminine and maternal approaches to ethics – as if by embracing its less radical sisters it can leave the patriarchal view of ethics relatively undisturbed. A feminist ethics (or even a lesbian ethics) is more radical as it challenges the politics of subordination and domination. Jaggar (1991) argues that feminist ethics should focus on making the world better for women and other vulnerable people and women should not focus on making the world a better place for everyone in general.

I have to admit to having difficulties with the latter point, if, for no other reason that little change is likely in what Oakley (2002) terms the 'sex/gender' system of patriarchy unless men do some changing as well. She contends (ibid., p. 219), that patriarchy does not mean a particular man, or group of men. It is a kind of society in which both men and women participate and not a conspiracy that men impose on women.

... there's no central control room where, particularly at times of feminist challenge, the operations of the anti-feminist brigades are planned with military precision. We can't blame it on the generals this time. It isn't a sex war: it's a place in which we're all stuck, together. (Ibid., p. 220)

Similarly Clare (2000, p. 194) argues:

> The call to us men, at the beginning of the twenty first century, to turn away from violence, to get in touch with our feelings, to express our fears and admit our inadequacies, is a doomed call if it is made, as it tends to be made, predominantly by women. Men, apart from a minority, seem fearful of making the changes that the death of patriarchy demands. Yet that is the scale of the challenge. Men can only save themselves. They cannot rely on women to save them.

Although I entirely agree with the political aims of feminist ethics in recognizing women's oppression and finding measures to counter it, ultimately there must be ways of engaging men with the project and with developing an ethics which, although rooted in alleviating the oppression of one gender, must offer something better for both genders.

Moral relativism

Turning now to consider traditional approaches to ethics, on the face of it, moral relativism, or the idea that ethics is relative to the time and place where it arises (Tong 1993, p. 171) might hold some appeal for feminists as it apparently rejects the kind of totalizing absolutism that is anathema to feminism in recognizing cultural differences and how these make a difference to ethics. But at the same time, commentators (Johnson 2001) from parts of the academy other than feminism, have trouble with moral relativism as it seems impossible to name and criticize oppressive practices under the banner of relativism. So, although feminists may reject absolutism as it does not recognize the material differences which form such an important part of the feminist critique, at the same time, feminists may want to universally condemn some practices as always wrong, for example, rape and violence against women. Tong (1993, p. 173) argues that, in many ways, it is easier to be a traditional relativist than a feminist relativist. A traditional relativist may be able to live without condemning certain cultures' practices whilst a feminist relativist may not. For example, it would be unlikely that a feminist would be persuaded that the practice of female genital mutilation, prevalent in some places in the world, could ever be seen as a non-oppressive practice.

So how can feminist relativists judge the trustworthiness of a culture's moral standards? Tong (ibid., p. 174) sets out the argument as follows. They must dig deeper than the traditional relativist. For example,

Sherwin (1992) considers, as an example, liberal and conservative positions on abortion. Clearly, they do not agree but a moral relativist would argue that they are both morally justified, because they are based on well-established moral thinking they must co-exist without trying to impose limitations on one another. However, as Sherwin (ibid.) argues, such a position is not reflective enough as it does not ask whose interests the different positions serve. The conservative line on abortion might be seen as favouring the rights of foetuses (and perhaps men) over the rights of women. Conservative abortion policies could be seen as interfering with liberals in ways that the liberal position does not interfere with conservatives – hence feminists may argue that the conservative position is less democratic.

Sherwin identifies the crux of the feminist argument, an argument which reappears against all the moral theories we shall examine, namely the question of who gets to make the decisions in a given society.

A feminist moral relativism demands that we consider who controls moral decision-making within a community and what effect that control has on the least privileged members of that community. Both at home and abroad, it gives us grounds to criticize the practices that a majority believes acceptable if those practices are a result of oppressive power differentials. (Ibid., p. 75)

Utilitarianism

Whereas relativism is more properly regarded as an approach towards ethics rather than a theory, utilitarianism and deontology are the two main ethical theories in the Western tradition. Utilitarianism as defined by the nineteenth century British philosopher, John Stuart Mill, is founded on the principle of utility or the 'greatest happiness principle'. This 'holds that actions are right in proportion as they tend to promote happiness; wrong as they tend to produce the reverse of happiness.' (Mill 1998, p. 122). For Mill, pleasure and freedom from pain are the only desirable thing as ends. Johnson (2001, p. 36) expresses the utilitarian principle thus: 'Everyone ought to act so as to bring about the greatest amount of happiness for the greatest number of people.' Utilitarianism is a form of consequentialism, in other words, it is a moral theory which focuses on the consequences of a moral act rather than its internal character, that is, the reasons for performing the act.

On the surface, the notion of the greatest good for the greatest number may seem appealing, yet utilitarianism has been subject to a number of searching criticisms. Importantly, in only attending to the net good, it loses sight of the individual, to the extent that it apparently places enormous burdens of self-sacrifice on some individuals for the sake of others. Imagine a circumstance, for instance, where one individual was sacrificed so that their internal organs could be used to save the lives of several other people (ibid., p. 41). Most people would find such a suggestion distasteful, yet it is consistent with the tenets of utilitarianism. Additionally, imagine a situation where, in an emergency, you had the choice of saving your disabled child or an eminent brain surgeon that you have never met before. Let us imagine that, such is the disability of your child that she will never be able to live and work independently, whereas the surgeon has saved the lives of many people and would continue to do so if allowed to live. Utilitarianism would seem to demand that you save the surgeon, as she makes the greater 'contribution to society'. However, this goes against all our instincts to put those whom we love first, and adroitly underlines one of the problems with a consequentialist ethics, namely that the internal character of an act is not meant to matter; instead we are to coldly tot up the total benefit. Utilitarianism seems extraordinarily uncaring and passionless.

In order to add up the total good, Jeremy Bentham (Tong 1993, p. 16) proposed a 'hedonic calculus' in the early nineteenth century. To this, Mill later added the idea of considering the quality as well as the quantity of happiness or good. As Tong (ibid., p. 16) points out, the idea of a 'mathematics of morality' appears to work better in the abstract rather than in real situations. Nevertheless, a little of the idea of measuring the total good mathematically is carried over into modern life in terms of cost-benefit or risk-benefit analyses. For instance, in the UK, over the last few years in the wake of a number of fatal rail accidents, there has been much consideration of devices to make rail travel safer, and these are sometimes described in cost-benefit terms, for example, a cost of, perhaps, one million pounds for each life saved. As long as we did not feel we were being bullied by the profit motive of large corporations, I argue that many of us would be prepared to accept some level of cost-benefit balancing such as this: at least, we might accept the general principle if not the figures involved. Indeed, legal claims for compensation involve the notion of a calculable financial figure in proportion to the damage suffered by the claimant.

However, it is unlikely that we would be happy with the much more direct weighing up of the value of individual lives, especially in cases which are different to compensation cases, where one life is weighed against another. This is the case in Johnson's example (2001, pp. 42–3) of the early days of kidney dialysis machines. When these were first introduced, there were not enough machines to share round all the people who needed them in the USA. Hence hospital review boards were set up to decide which patients would have access to the machines. These boards weighed up the characteristics of each individual according to how worthy they were alleged to be, with more points for worth of job, number of dependents, lack of criminal record, and so on. Thus it was deemed that those who were more likely to benefit and to contribute to society would receive treatment. Most of us would be troubled, to say the least, that an individual's social utility could be weighed and measured in such a disrespectful way. Yet from time to time we hear of, perhaps less stark yet nevertheless, utilitarian arguments suggesting denial of medical treatment to smokers or to obese people.

As well as the issue of treating people as a means to an end, where the goal is overall social utility, and where individuals may be sacrificed to the overall good, there are further criticisms that can be made of utilitarianism. By focusing purely on the consequences of actions, utilitarianism has nothing to say on the internal character or motivations for an action; as we shall see below, this is the opposite focus of deontological theory. However, in terms of feminist critique, an additional important issue revolves round the question of who gets to make the decisions. For instance, Mill proposed the idea of a set of reasonable and impartial judges who, as *reasonable* people would, *ceteris paribus*, choose a higher good over a lower good.

> But what makes a judge 'reasonable'? When a group of experienced judges identifies Dante reading as a better pleasure than bingo playing is this because Dante reading is indeed objectively better than bingo playing, or is it simply because these judges have enough *power* to transform their personal preferences into universal law? Are Mill's experienced, reasonable judges *impartial* judges, or are they instead *partisan* judges, more than likely propertied and privileged men, intent on affirming the values of the group they call their own? (Tong 1993, p. 16)

The question of who gets to make the decisions is crucial for feminist evaluations of traditional systems of ethics. This mirrors the issue running all the way through traditional forms of philosophy, and particularly in epistemology and ethics, in that the decision maker is abstract and disembodied, in Nagel's terms (1986) it is as if there is a 'view from nowhere'. The problem is, as Lloyd notes (1984), the view from nowhere is really the view of a 'man of reason'. By talking of what is reasonable, what we would all agree to as reasonable people and what is reasonable in our culture, this is a way of imposing a hegemonic position on everyone, without examining whether different groups of people would feel differently, particularly those not in a powerful situation.

Deontological theory

Deontological theory is the ethical theory of duty. Rather than focusing on the consequences of actions it focuses on the motivations for actions and deems them morally worthy if they are done from a sense of duty. Kant's *categorical imperative* holds that we should: 'Act in such a way that you always treat humanity, whether in your own person or in the person of another, never simply as a means but always at the same time as an end' (quoted in Tong 1993, p. 20). This means that we must never treat other people as things or objects, but as people worthy in their own right. Kant exhorts us to seek universalizable laws such as 'do not kill'. Additionally, we must act autonomously as, unless we do so our actions are morally worthless. If someone is forced into obeying a rule they have no moral obligation to obey it, but if they have freely chosen then they have set themselves as under moral obligation to follow the rule.

Tong (ibid., pp. 21–2) points to some problems with the categorical imperative. It is simply not possible to universalize some rules. For instance, there might be situations where one would tell a lie to save a life. Kant has little to offer for resolving the application of universal yet conflicting rules. Finally, there is the question of duty vs emotion. How much better to bring up one's children well because you love them rather than just because you feel it is your duty to do so.

This suggests a serious problem for feminists; duty without love implies a very empty world. As we shall see in the following discussion on feminist ethics, emotionally empty duty jars with several forms of feminist ethics, particularly ethics of care and maternal ethics. Several authors (Gilligan 1982; Baier 1998) emphasize the network of relationships which are necessary for the moral life. This suggests that the idea of duty with no feelings and no connectedness to others would make a strange morality. In addition, the autonomous moral agent implied by Kant's theory is an overly masculine, heroic figure, once again belying the network of relationships within which we exist and within which we make our ethical decisions.

Virtue ethics

In some senses, virtue ethics, as originally developed by Aristotle in classical times, offers an alternative to the other theories described above (Johnson 2001, p. 51). This is because, instead of a primary focus on decision making, its emphasis lies, instead in being good, on character rather than action. Hence we are invited to consider what it means to be a good person, a good citizen, a good IT professional or whatever. The problem is that deciding on a good moral virtue is potentially very controversial. Historically, definitions of male and female virtues have tended to accord higher status to male virtues, where a supposedly masculine value such as justice is held to be better than feminine values such as caring (Tong 1993, pp. 27–8).

With virtue ethics we have the distinct possibility that stereotypical values may be applied to men and women. The virtues of a good woman may look quite different to the virtues of a good man. Furthermore, who gets to choose what stands as appropriate womanly and manly virtues? For instance, looking to the example of the last chapter, was Blood being a good mother, and hence a good woman, by choosing to go ahead with having children in the tragic circumstances in which she found herself? There were clearly some voices, from the conservative end of the spectrum who thought she was not. Some of the rhetoric surrounding her case involved the control that women should have over their bodies, raising the question, once more, of who gets to make moral decisions.

Feminist critiques of traditional ethics

I am conscious that this has been a very quick tour of ethical thought, which can hardly do justice to the many complexities of such theories. Nevertheless I believe that there are some common elements to traditional theories of ethics and the ways in which they have been used, which feminist critiques address.

Nowhere in descriptions of moral relativism, utilitarianism, deontology and virtue ethics do we see issues of power alluded to and yet a feminist argument demands to know who is in a position to make and enforce an ethical decision or judgement and who is not. A feminist moral relativist must feel able to criticize oppressive practices in other cultures especially when these are perpetrated against women and children. In terms of utilitarianism, it is likely to be middle-class professional men who dominate private industry and state institutions where cost-benefit and risk-benefit analyses are drawn up (Tong 1993).

In deontological theory it is not clear that the least powerful members of society are in a position to make the autonomous moral choices which Kant suggests are the mark of rational moral agency. In relation to virtue ethics who will decide the appropriate moral virtues of a good woman? Whichever theory we consider there is a set of disguised power relations at work which are not made explicit and which mean that the less powerful in society may well not be able to take part in moral decision taking. Additionally, this points to the way that, for all of us, our autonomy is circumscribed by the web of relationships which sustain us and within which we learn to act morally; we are not the autonomous moral agents acting dutifully but dispassionately that Kant would like us to be. In the following sections describing feminist ethics we will revisit these and further questions.

Reason and emotion

A discussion of the relationship, indeed the split, between reason and emotion in philosophy and ethics goes much of the way towards explaining the masculine bias of traditional Western ethics and the denigration of women's moral experiences. It also relates to the public/private split, identified as an important aspect of feminist political theory, and its critique of liberalism in Chapter 2, in interesting and important ways.

Several feminist writers (Lloyd 1984; Adam 1998; Held 1998) identify a lengthy association of reason with masculinity in Western philosophy. The rational/irrational dualism has been a long standing theme in Western theories of epistemology. Lloyd (1984) argues that, historically, the association of reason with masculinity extends at least to Ancient Greece and Plato, in a tradition which sees the female gender as passive, corporeal, emotional while the male is taken to be active, rational and incorporeal – involved in mind and thought rather than bodies or emotions. The relation of women to bodily matters and men to mental matters was further reinforced by Descartes' characterization of the mind–body split, where the body became divorced from the higher mental plane of rational thought, the zone of the Cartesian man of reason. We can also see how this maps onto the public/private dualism illustrated in the discussion of feminist politics in Chapter 2. The rational masculine life of the mind belongs to the public sphere whilst the feminine emotional world of looking after bodies belongs to the private world of the home. In terms of epistemology, some feminist writers have suggested that there are women's ways of knowing, different from the masculine norm, more visceral in nature and connected to emotions and the body rather than the life of the mind (Goldberger *et al.* 1996).

I am aware that the above characterization of 'man = rational, woman = irrational' is somewhat stark, and a few paragraphs can hardly do justice to the quantity of writing and thinking on this topic. However, it forms a central plank of the feminist critique of traditional philosophy, both in epistemological terms and also in relation to ethics. If there are 'women's ways of knowing' there may also be women's ways of moral reasoning. We can see how some of these issues are expressed in views about ethical thinking. Held (1998) points to the way that morality is seen as guiding decisions in the public realm whereas behaviour of women in the private realm of the household is seen as natural or instinctive and therefore lying outside morality. Held (ibid., p. 333) quotes Heyd (1982, p. 134) who argues that a mother's sacrifice for her child belongs to the domain of natural relationships and instinct and therefore lies outside the bounds of morality. In the same way, Urmson (1958, p. 202) echoes a common position when he says, '... we are not now considering cases of natural affection, such as the sacrifice made by a mother for her child; such cases may be said with some justice not to fall under the concept of morality'. Similarly Ryan's discussion (1989) of the ways in which humans are *not* rational, calculating animals leaves out the concept of mothering from the equation. With this weight of evidence, Held (1998, p. 333) is forced to conclude:

> Without feminist insistence on the relevance for morality of the experience in mothering, this context is largely ignored by moral theorists. And yet from a gender-neutral point of view, how can this vast and fundamental domain of human experience possibly be imagined to lie 'outside morality'?

At least, part of the reason why ethical theorists ignore motherhood as a primary site of learning moral thinking relates to its location in relation to the public/private distinction and the valuing of the former over the latter. Men's experiences in the public sphere are valued over women's experiences in the private sphere. Mothering is seen as biological, intuitive and emotional and was not taken seriously in moral theory until it was incorporated into feminist ethics.

Held (ibid.) argues that we must counter these images of female experience being seen as naturally irrelevant to morality and of women as clearly deficient in the moral sense in reconceptualizing ethics to take account of women's experiences. We must challenge the position accorded to pure, abstract reason, for instance, as is found in Kant's search for universal, moral principles to guide autonomous rational beings and in utilitarian approaches towards looking for abstract rules to maximize utility. Writing which respects the context in which decisions are made and which recognizes emotions and feelings can be found in the spectrum of research on feminist ethics which emphasizes concrete, embodied experience through an exploration of care (Gilligan 1982; Bowden 1997; Walker 1998), trust (Baier 1998), the experience of mothering and being mothered (Ruddick 1989) and emotions (Jaggar 1991); in turn, these approaches emphasize the interdependence of the self and others rather than the separation of self from others.

Addelson's research (1994) develops the related area of responsibility, which she describes in terms of networks of care rather than in terms of professional responsibility which is often couched in terms of responsibility-as-blame. Hence, although by no means confined to feminist views of ethics (May and Hoffman 1991), an emphasis on collectivist over individualist ethics has arisen, and although this is seen as important in areas such ecology and the green movement it has yet to permeate professional ethics to any significant extent.

Baier (1998) claims that many women philosophers, and some male philosophers too, are much more inclined to work along the lines of Gilligan's approach rather than following the traditional 'game-theoretic' approach to moral theory with its emphasis on artificial moral problems such as the 'prisoners' dilemma'. An examination of the history of ethics shows that ethical theory has been built from a male point of view based on assumptions which are far from gender-neutral (Held 1998). This suggests that feminist explorations of ethics, rather than just incorporating additional insights, often require radical transformation to existing theory to take account of women's experiences.

Gilligan's different voice

As the preceding section suggests, care is a cornerstone of most approaches towards feminine and feminist ethics. Gilligan's *In a Different Voice* (1982) was written to argue against Freud's notion, echoed in Kohlberg's work, that while men have a well-developed moral sense, women do not. Gilligan argued instead that women often construct moral dilemmas as conflicts of responsibilities rather than rights and that, in resolving such conflicts, they seek to repair and strengthen networks of relationships. By Tong's reckoning (1993), Gilligan's research really belongs to the feminine ethics tradition as it attempts to demonstrate the ways in which traditional ethical theory (in the shape of

Kohlberg's analysis) has undervalued women's moral development rather than seeking a more radical attempt to alleviate women's oppression as such.

Nevertheless, it has been immensely influential in spawning the tradition of feminine and feminist ethics with a focus on the ethics of care, mothering and relationships as an approach particularly attached to women's values. This signals a commitment to responsibility rather than rights, the collective social group rather than the individual and an ethic based on caring rather than the supposedly impartial individual reason of the Kantian moral agent. In emphasizing social networks over individuals and how these should be maintained, it is clearly related to the criticisms of traditional ethics described earlier.

This is the basis of an 'ethic of care.' Indeed, the concept of an ethic of care has emerged as a strong theme, if not the strongest theme, in feminist ethics. Jaggar (1992) has termed it 'a minor academic industry'. Other writers who have developed further the concept of an ethic of care include Ruddick (1989) in her book, *Maternal Thinking* and more recently, the extended analyses of Bowden (1997), Tronto (1993) and Walker (1998).

Considerable debate continues to surround Gilligan's work. Although she was criticized and subsequently revised her position, her work has made an enormous impact in the academy beyond the disciplines of ethics and psychology. When it was first published its ideas appeared very radical. On the one hand she does claim that women's moral development is different to men's, but on the other hand, she argues that traditional scholarship on ethical development is not neutral but is designed to favour a masculine, individualistic, rationalistic, justice and rights-based approach to ethics over a feminine, communitarian, care-based approach. In other words, the standard of morality which is valorized as the gold standard is based on a masculine model of ethical reasoning.

Gilligan's work (1982) has been subject to fairly extensive critique and revision (Larrabee 1993; Tong 1993; Koehn 1998). I summarize the salient points for the present discussion.

In her original study, Gilligan (1982) claimed that her empirical research demonstrated that women tended to value an ethic of care which emphasizes relationships and responsibilities while men value an ethics of justice which emphasizes rules and rights. The evidence from a later study (Gilligan 1987) was not so clear-cut as the women in that study focused equally on justice and care while only one man espoused a care ethic. Gilligan saw her work as a refutation of Freud's argument that women are somehow morally inferior to men. As a development of Freud's work, Kohlberg (1981) elaborated a six-stage theory of moral development from Stage 1, as a punishment and obedience orientation up to Stage 6, as an orientation towards universal moral principles as described by Kant. Kohlberg found that women rarely get past Stage 3 (interpersonal concordance) while men usually ascend to Stage 5 (social contract legalistic orientation). Such findings could be used to argue that women are less morally developed than men.

Gilligan (1982) questioned these findings to argue that Kohlberg was really describing male rather than human moral development. In any case, much hinges on the interpretations of Kohlberg's study. His empirical research involved giving subjects hypothetical moral dilemmas to resolve, for example, whether a husband should steal the drug he cannot afford for his dangerously ill wife. Two 11-year-old children, a boy and a girl produced different responses. The boy produced an answer in terms of rights (scoring higher on Kohlberg's scale) while the girl focused on relationships. Gilligan argued that, rather than focusing on a logic of fairness, instead, responsibilities and connection are important and men and women may not achieve moral maturity in exactly the same way, suggesting that the girl was not less morally mature than the boy; rather she was demonstrating a different type of ethical reasoning.

Briefly, Tong (1993, p. 89) describes the main criticisms of Gilligan's work as follows. First, in criticizing Kohlberg's research she may be polarizing his findings as later studies found girls reaching the same level of moral maturity as boys (Greeno and Maccoby 1993). However, as Tong (1993, p. 90) suggests, it may well be that women in the public domain, so-called 'career women' show a more 'masculine', that is, justice-oriented approach to ethics than do women whose primary focus is the home. Further criticisms focus on the notion that the care/justice distinction is not new, that they are complementary and that, in any case justice is a better approach than care. Puka (1993) argues that care is a coping strategy that women adopt to counter sexist oppression. In addition to this there is the question of whether care/justice reasoning really does split along gender lines and whether it is a good idea for women to be too associated with caring and to be always related to 'emotional work'. Tong (1993, p. 99) argues that even if empirical studies do not show that women have a monopoly on care and men on justice there is the whole question of how we attach certain kinds of moral values to different genders. To return to virtue ethics, perhaps care is seen as a feminine virtue and justice a masculine virtue.

'Gendered' moral conceptions guide our social expectations of how 'normal' men and women should talk and act. Men should fight for truth, justice, and the American way. Women should care for their loved ones' physical and psychological needs. What Gilligan may have discovered, then, is something that exists as *value* rather than as *fact* … . (Ibid.)

Whilst accepting many of the criticisms made by feminists of Kantian ethics and utilitarianism, Koehn (1998) has made a number of additional criticisms of the feminist ethics of care. She argues that the feminist ethics of care does not represent a better alternative to the rule-based ethics of which it is so critical. This is because it falls prey to many of the same concerns, including, importantly a failure to respect other people, as feminist care ethics privileges the perspective of the care giver over that of the individuals who are on the receiving end of the caring activities.

Koehn (1998, p. 20) acknowledges that Gilligan's work undoubtedly gave voice to many women's frustrations with traditional ethics. Nevertheless, there are significant problems in relation to care ethics beyond those identified in Tong's analysis (1993). To start with, it is quite difficult to get a definition of care. It appears to be less a concern that something will happen and more to do with being attentive to another's well-being and being willing to act to promote that well-being. Sympathy is not enough, we must feel an engagement with the other.

> for the care ethicist, ethical acts are caring ones of a certain sort. They are those acts in which the caregiver actively concerns herself with attending to the individually expressed needs, feelings and interests of the cared-for and strives to create a shared self with people who are similarly committed to a secure world in which beings are nurtured and given an opportunity to realize fully their individuality. (Koehn 1998, p. 26)

Overall, Koehn argues that there are acts that can be ethical without being caring. The care ethic assumes that physical needs are always the most urgent but this need not always be true. In any case it is not always obvious when someone is in need of care. We may well end up limiting someone's freedom by assuming that they need care (e.g. by having someone admitted to hospital). Her analysis points to further problems with a care ethic – it is notoriously difficult to apply and there is no guidance as to how to decide between competing cases. There is also the question as to how to deal with, say, violent terrorists – do they require the care ethic to be applied as much as our children? Care givers may put themselves at considerable personal risk if they try to embrace those who wish them harm. Within this analysis, Koehn (1998, p. 410) cautions against overvaluing the idea of the 'earth mother'. Maternal ethics (Ruddick 1989) has emerged as a significant strand of care ethics yet a caregiver must beware of infantilizing the one being cared for in order for her to feel the pleasure of care giving herself. This also means that it may be difficult for the cared for, for example, children to gain a sense of responsibility and autonomy themselves if they are smothered by too much care. Koehn also takes issue with the related work of Meyers (1994) on an ethic of empathy and Baeier (1998) on an ethic of trust. Feminist ethicists, as much as any other ethicist need to avoid taking a 'god's eye view' and, second, any practical system of ethics needs to supply some principles for judgement otherwise we have no sound reason for action (Koehn 1998, p. 100).

Dialogical ethics

In response to the many problems identified with feminist care ethics, and its close relatives, as they stand, Koehn (ibid., p. 102) offers a dialogical ethic based on the concept of a Socratic dialogue. Here the care giver does not stand in 'god's eye' position over the cared for. Instead, active listening and dialogue are emphasized. It is not needs-oriented, in contrast to feminist care ethics.

> Socrates is able to see the broader picture concerning consequences, though, precisely because he is not committed to any substantive end apart from being as thoughtful as possible. This suggests that any caring or trusting totally focussed on the needs of others paradoxically may turn out to be uncaring and untrustworthy because this focus substitutes for a more general attentiveness capable of disclosing considerations relevant to assessing the agent's action or choice. (Ibid., p. 103)

Feminist care ethics seeks dialogue as it allows individuals to have their say but a dialogical ethics additionally looks for some element of rationality or good reasons to follow one moral course of action rather than another. Consistency is also important as is closure, in other words some agreement about how it is best to act.

Dialogical ethics provides some important principles which revise feminist ethics. It recognizes that not all opinions are equally good, that principles of justice do have a value in focusing human ethical interactions away from the tendency to mirror others' points of view. Some principles and laws must be used so that there are ways out of negative interactions with others. In addition, the integration of care and trust into a larger political and democratic structure is recognized as an important way out of the potential political naiveté and inward looking of feminist care ethics. Contestability is important – we must be able to challenge different positions and these challenges must be respected. So, although some may criticize dialogical ethics as not being feminist enough in inspiration, it recognizes the situatedness of different points of view and enables us to jointly and responsibly confront ethical problems.

Conclusion

The quest for a feminist ethics mirrors the discussion of the previous chapter on feminist legal theory and feminist politics. Feminist ethics is predicated on the political nature of women's oppression and seeks means to overcome it. It is also an important analytical tool in showing both, the ways in which traditional forms of ethics are based on a vision of an autonomous man of reason, and also the ways in which traditional ethics neglects the structures of power which mean that not everyone has the same access to moral decision making. As in the previous chapter men's relationship to the public sphere and women's to the private is crucial. In this chapter I have followed Tong's classification (1993) of feminine and feminist ethics. The ground breaking work of Gilligan (1982) and others on care ethics can be seen more in the spirit of feminine ethics as they argue that women's moral reasoning is based on care and relationships (crucially the mothering relationship) in contrast to the justice- and rights-based style characteristic of a more masculine approach. However, care ethics has been subject to a fairly comprehensive range of criticisms, many from feminist ranks, and it is not at all clear that it can be rescued and applied in a project such as this one in the application and use of ICTs in women's lives. Apart from anything else the possible relegation of women to be for ever locked into stereotypical caring roles, and at the same time, the paradoxically unequal nature of the carer and cared for in ethics of care, implies that care ethics, at least as described by Gilligan is unlikely to fulfil all the requirements of a feminist ethics. However I have no doubt that some care ethics concepts, for example emphasis on caring and the network of relationships can contribute. At the same time Koehn's dialogical ethics (1998) seems to promise a more balanced approach, yet as a relatively new approach, further fleshing out will be required before it becomes clear how it could be used in practice.

In my brief discussion of feminist ethics, what has become clear to me is that I am unlikely to find a single unified theory to lift out and apply to the case studies and examples of the gendered nature of computer ethics problems. This suggests that, rather than viewing feminist ethics as the quest for the best theory, following the discussion above, we would be better regarding it as a more general approach which gives us a set of philosophical tools with which to critique and deconstruct traditional ethics, including practical examples (e.g. as in Chapters 6–8) and also a number of pointers, such as the emphasis on care and relational networks, with which to reconstruct and understand our case studies along more equitable lines.

Despite my concerns with uncovering a suitable feminist ethics to apply to technology case studies, features of the critique of traditional ethics are important and directly applicable to computer ethics. The most salient of these is the exposure of hidden power relations. We are not all equal when it comes to ethical decision making, yet traditional ethical theories and the abstract philosophical language in which they are often couched makes little of this. In Chapter 4 we see many of these concerns relate to the development of computer ethics.

4
The Rise of Computer Ethics: From Professionalism to Legislative Failures

Introduction: situating computer ethics

In this chapter I give an overview of the discipline of computer ethics, its development, its major preoccupations and its potential strengths and deficiencies, especially in relation to the concerns of this book. Much of the chapter focuses on the distinct discipline that has coalesced into the domain of computer ethics, its roots, philosophical stance and relationship to professionalism. However, I also want to consider the wider issue of how computer ethics problems are viewed in contemporary Western societies, through analysing a number of cases where there was a failure in application of an area of ICT law. By means of these cases I hope to substantiate the claim that we need to develop a more sophisticated understanding of computer ethics problems both within the academy and at a wider societal level. This signals that computer ethics is not (just) an esoteric academic domain, rather it is an area of much wider concern to us as we develop ICTs which permit us to hold and analyse huge amounts of data.

I explore steps on the path from ethical position, to policy, to production of legislation, to application of law, and, in the examples here, with the end result of showing where such a process breaks down. In other words, where the results of applying a particular piece of legislation did not match the ethical principles that the legislation was designed to embody. The examples in this chapter show how we try, as a society, to translate our moral intuitions on computer ethics problems and how and why these efforts sometimes fail. My discussion in Chapters 2 and 3 used feminist theory to argue for the relatedness of the subject matter and broad concerns of ethics, politics and law. The feminist umbrella usefully binds these areas together more tightly than is often the case in intellectual life. The discussion on public vs private is raised again as an issue here and the critique of liberalism which I commenced in Chapter 2 is further developed. Similarly the question of who has power to have their voice heard in making ethical decisions, a question raised in Chapter 3's critique of traditional ethical theories is pertinent here. Although there are definite *caveats* in relation to the ethics of care, nevertheless we must look towards incorporating more relational, caring ethics into our dealings with new technologies. Ironically, in the data protection examples I analyse later in this chapter, we face the possibility that aspects of care may be delegated to digital media.

Of course one could argue that the failure of the law I describe through these examples is not peculiar to computer ethics problems. A similar 'failure of translation' from moral views to the application of legislation could also be present in many areas of social life. What makes computer ethics problems, at least potentially, different is partly the newness of the problems, and the whole business of working out whether we wish to treat a given problem as new and therefore to be subject to new ethical analysis or, instead, whether the problem is better treated as a new variant of an old problem and therefore falls within the purview of existing ethical analyses. Engaging in the moral debates that this process implies takes time to sort out and such debates are not uncontroversial. A further complication is found in the way that moral views change over time, sometimes quite rapidly. As examples, witness the abolition of the death penalty in many Western democracies over the last half century (although, of course, not in several states of the USA), and the relaxation of attitudes towards young people's sexuality over the same period and in the same societies.

The question of the apparent speed with which computer ethics problems may manifest themselves is interesting and must be considered in formulating policy and legislation. There is a widespread feeling that the pace of technological change, at the turn of the millennium, has never been greater (Robins and Webster 1999). Castells (2000) refers to a time–space compression where, it is not just the pace of commerce which has speeded up; so too has the pace of culture.

Later in this chapter I discuss, in detail, the perils of technological determinism or the view that technological developments are inevitable and that they drive social developments. Except for the cynical view that new technologies will possibly always be employed for sex and/or crime (Adam 2001c), we often cannot predict how technologies will be used. We may wish to argue against the futuristic pictures that techno-enthusiasts paint for us of a world overrun by new technologies. Yet, at the same time, we often do have a real sense of technological developments happening quickly without our knowing that they would be used in a particular way. Who would have predicted, a few short years ago, the growth and menace of viruses and the extensive use of the Internet for pornography and cyberstalking? Potential ethical problems relating to the introduction of new technologies do, therefore, appear to come to our attention and demand some sort of response quite quickly. Technologies are also inextricably woven through many areas of our social life. For instance, the examples at the end of this chapter relate to privacy of personal data, and the relationship of privacy to ICTs, an overarching theme of this book, and one picked up again in Chapter 8. Privacy becomes more and more entwined with our use of ICTs in contemporary life to the extent where it becomes practically impossible to talk of privacy in Western democracies without a consideration of contemporary technology use.

Turning to the question of where and why computer ethics has arisen as an area of research, education and broader interest; on one level, we can understand the formation of computer ethics as a separate area of enquiry, in terms of the more general 'turn to ethics' which has taken place across a wide spectrum of intellectual life. In literary theory and the humanities there has been renewed interest in ethics as part of the critical project which challenges the legitimacy and certainty of the old order, seeking, instead, new emancipatory forms of life. In science, and especially technology, there is continuing interest in ethics. Some of this may be due to the formation of a distinct Science and Technology studies (STS) discipline, although apart from some interest in the political inscription of artefacts and the design of technologies (Akrich 1992; Winner 1999), STS (especially sociology of scientific knowledge and actor-network theory) has maintained something of a distance from the 'big issues' including ethics. However, some of the interest in technology ethics can be seen as a direct descendant of the radical science movement, which is not so explicitly linked to the academy as is STS, with its original focus on issues such as nuclear disarmament. However renewed interest in science and technology ethics currently revolves around ecological concerns such as global warming and depletion of fossil fuels, biological and medical matters such as the human genome project, cloning and GM foods, animal rights, engineering disasters such as Challenger, and computers and the Internet. There has been much public and media interest in such areas as computer viruses, the dangers of the Internet for children (and indeed adults – note the concern over Internet romances and even cannibalism), hacking and computer fraud.

If the technology ethics/media interest vector represents one strand of computer ethics' lineage there is no doubt that a second strand relates to 'cyberculture,' or the explosion of interest in cultures developing around virtual reality, the Internet and networking, artificial intelligence (AI) and artificial life (A-life) (Adam 1998, p. 166). As I shall argue below, despite its futuristic tone, much cyberculture writing is politically conservative and its radical pretensions disguise an adherence to a problematic liberalism, one of this book's major themes and which is elaborated further in this chapter.

The third major strand in the development of computer ethics is linked to the topic of professionalism. Part of that topic relates to an upsurge of interest in business ethics (although some might cynically regard the terms as an oxymoron), but, more generally it revolves around the pressure within the IT/IS/computing field to professionalize. The move to professionalize is a very important part of understanding the story of the development of computer ethics and it has coloured that story in particular ways as discussed in more detail below. Apart from anything else a professional/business oriented ethics steers ethical discussion down particular avenues which may be quite different from those of an ethics not attached to the interests of industry or business.

Over the last two or more decades and more, considerable interest has developed in the topic of computer ethics, as a new area of enquiry, to the extent that it has been hailed as the most important recent development in the philosophy of ethics in some quarters (Gorniak-Kocikowska 1996). Despite the upsurge of interest in computer ethics, and the quantity and undoubted quality of much new writing on the topic, it would be hard to maintain the view that it has achieved the same level of theoretical development as, say, feminist ethics. However, a direct comparison between feminist ethics and computer ethics is hardly fair as computer ethics is very much an applied discipline, taught as part of computing, software engineering, IT and IS courses and, as suggested above, it is strongly linked to professionalism, professionalization and the world of business. Furthermore, it is a technology ethics with links to ethically neutral STS and a politically conservative cyberculture. This does not give computer ethics a very strong set of philosophical roots, nor indeed a set of very radical roots. Indeed the pull is clearly towards the needs of business when we consider the topic of professionalism. By contrast, as I argue in Chapter 3, feminist ethics developed through a combination of the development of feminist philosophy with its critique of traditional ethical systems and grass roots feminism. Feminist ethics has, therefore, a much more philosophically inclined parentage than computer ethics. It is interesting, although perhaps not surprising, to note that there is almost no sign of an emergent feminist business ethics. For instance, at the time of writing, a 'Google' search under the term 'feminist business ethics' reveals only one article (Ulshofer 2000); although there is much interest in gender and management in the workplace (e.g. see Wajcman 1998), particularly in the field of gender and organization studies.

Therefore the roots and current direction of computer ethics suggests that its critical potential is yet to be substantially realized. Ethics, as a philosophical subject, attends to theories of morality, or theories of how we ought to live. Hence it is normative rather than descriptive and therefore has a political dimension. The position that I argue here is that ethics, particularly an applied ethics, such as computer ethics can be a potentially potent political force as ethical debate feeds into policy and, ultimately, into legislation. As a subject, ethics deals with theorizing the ways in which human behaviour may be deemed desirable or undesirable. This signals a need to find explanations for such behaviour, otherwise policy and legislation designed to regulate human conduct are unlikely to prove effective. Indeed one notes the speed with which statutes which legislate on computer and Internet issues are often developed. As I shall argue in a later section, in relation to the UK Data Protection Act, the way that we do not always make the link between ethics, policy and legislation, or perhaps do not make it quickly enough, is, in itself, an issue. This sometimes results in laws being applied in ways which we did not intend and where the application of the legislation did not match up to our ethical position and policy.

The relatively conservative parentage of computer ethics means that its focus tends to turn away from political issues and it has a conservative tilt, particularly at the popular and professional end of the spectrum. Much of this writing tacitly subscribes to a technologically determinist position (Bott *et al.* 1991; Sterling 1992; Ludlow 1996; Baase 1997; Ayres 1999). This is a concern even for authors who try to sidestep theory altogether (Langford 1999); they may well be disguising, rather than avoiding, a theoretical position. The stance which is often tacitly adopted tends to regard the progress of technology as inevitable and sees technology as driving and determining how society acts rather than, potentially, the other way round, or some more complex technology–society relationship. Consideration of more complex society–technology relationships has often been neglected in writing on computer ethics. A further problem with a view which neglects or ignores the complexities of the technology–society relation is that, accepting the apparent inevitability of technological developments does not promote analysis and critique of such developments (this is something we see in writing in cyberculture as well as in the professionalism literature), and thereby closes off much potential for discussion of political choice in the use and design of technology. A determinist stance also feeds into the problematic liberalism highlighted in preceding chapters, which takes for granted the objectivity of the world and the trajectories of technologies within it. Inequalities are then seen as relatively superficial components of social life which can usually be ameliorated without major change to social structures. Feminists have rightly been wary of the lure of a liberalism which sees inequalities as relatively simple matters which are easy to cure (Pateman 1989).

The discussion later in this chapter points to ways in which the liberal/determinist position, a major vector in much computer ethics writing, deriving from the roots I have described above, can serve to reinforce inequality rather than alleviating it. Indeed, writers such as Winner (1997) argue that technological determinism and extreme liberalism pose serious threats to democracy by promoting radical, self-interest groups which obviate their responsibilities towards promoting true equality. Additionally, as critical discussion of inequality is relatively scarce in computer ethics, it is not surprising to find that there has been relatively little writing on gender and computer ethics. At least partly because it tends to subscribe to the determinist, liberal position outlined above, much current research on gender and computer ethics struggles to explain gender differences and, importantly, struggles to offer convincing suggestions for change to gender inequities. Chapter 5 explores these issues in more detail.

The roots of computer ethics

By recognizing that new behaviours, or at least new forms of old behaviours, are made feasible by the range of information and communication technologies which are becoming available, computer ethics attends to the theories of morality that can be applied to such behaviours. Understandably, as it has arisen at least partly in response to the growing use of information technologies, computer ethics is an applied ethics. Computer ethics considers ways of forming arguments and judgements on particular information technology-related activities, for example, hacking, privacy and software theft. And certainly, through the codes of ethics of professional societies, such as the Association for Computing Machinery (ACM) in the USA and the British Computer Society (BCS) in the UK, computer ethics can be seen as normative in inspiration, that is, it brings a direct message to computer professionals and users of computers that a consideration of behaviour is a central element of the repertoire of the professional.

If computing, IT and IS can be thought of as relatively new disciplines then computer ethics is even newer. It began to coalesce as a distinct area of enquiry around twenty years ago. Moor's much quoted paper (1985), 'What is computer ethics?' argued for the elaboration of a new computer ethics in the face of novel choices about the use of computers and a vacuum of policies surrounding those choices. Mason's identification of privacy, accuracy, property and access (1986) as the big public policy challenges facing computer ethics in the middle of the 1980s was controversial when first published, and yet has been influential in discussions of the significance of computer ethics over the last decade and beyond. From relatively hesitant beginnings a fairly substantial literature has sprung up on computer ethics. This ranges from textbooks on professionalism, more philosophically inclined scholarly works, through to an ever burgeoning collection of popular and semi-popular literature (see bibliography in Tavani 1998).

The spectrum of literature on computer ethics can be characterized as follows. There is a central core of academic computer ethics research, locating itself at the intersection of IT and academic philosophy. This research is fairly autonomous from the world of industry, although not unrelated, as case studies may have an industry related flavour. Even so a fair amount of this research is abstractly philosophical and is, at least one step away, from being applicable in a practical setting. Surrounding this is a large penumbra of more popularly written and less philosophically inclined material which impacts more on the worlds of teaching and a general readership. The penumbra includes works on professionalism given that computer and information ethics teaching often falls under this rubric in computing and IT courses (Bott *et al.* 1991; Ayres 1999). This penumbra also includes works which could be described under the heading of cyberculture but which have a distinct ethical slant (e.g. Ludlow 1996).

As an applied ethics, computer ethics has suffered some neglect by the dominant analytical tradition in Anglo-American philosophy which is not always noted for espousing the value of real-life examples. But it is possible to go too far the other way. It is with the more popular style of computer ethics writing that many of my concerns lie, particularly as a good proportion of this writing is aimed at 'professional studies' teaching in computing courses. One style I shall designate the 'hands-on' view, is encapsulated in Langford's book, *Business Computer Ethics* (1999). As a computer scientist and business person he has no time for irrelevancies and emphasizes ' "real world" issues – especially those issues that may be perceived, by those at the coal face, as dilemmas typically outside the concerns of an ivory-towered academic ...' (ibid., p. xi). Despite an understandable desire to argue for realism and the needs of industry, such an approach is not particularly helpful theoretically as it denies the need to develop a thoroughgoing theoretical position. It is also unhelpful in locating and exposing the power inequalities relating to ethical decision making which I discuss in Chapter 3. We need to fight against anti-theoretical approaches. They are dangerous in education but they may also be dangerous if they find their way into the policy/legislation dimension where we must have sound ethical reasons for adopting a particular approach.

Hands-on computing professionals may well feel that the writings of Kant or Bentham are too distant from their daily practice. Yet when we consider that overtly utilitarian techniques such as risk or cost-benefit analysis are part of the repertoire of corporate life, we realize that we are not so distant from the arguments of philosophers after all. It must be possible to construct arguments which are philosophically sound and yet are rooted in the real world in contrast to the analytical style which has hitherto dominated philosophy and which shies away from real world cases in favour of 'cats on mats' style examples which are often so simple as to be unscalable to real life (Adam and Richardson 2001). Much better is an approach which brings together both solid theorizing with real world examples which is my preferred method. This style of writing is well illustrated in Ladd's analysis (1995) which is particularly useful in exposing and exploring the intellectual and moral confusion surrounding one of the 'sacred cows' of professional ethics, namely the code of ethics. He shows that, contrary to expectation, such codes may serve to protect the professional privilege of a powerful group rather than encouraging ethical behaviour. Such an analysis would be difficult to construct from the 'hands on' approach which eschews the philosophical theorizing necessary to make such an enquiry appropriately critical and therefore convincing.

The perils of technological determinism

The lack of challenge to ethical theory coupled with the view that the development and use of IT is unavoidable, tends to follow the path of technological determinism, especially, as explained above, amongst those writers at the more popular (cyberculture) or professional end of the spectrum and who tend to avoid philosophical theorizing. Technological determinism is the perspective that views developments in technology as driving society; 'impacts' is the term often used. Such impacts are seen as inevitable, the relationship of technology and society is regarded as linear and mono-directional, that is, from technology towards society. This view has been much criticized, and, by now largely abandoned within the social sciences (Winner 1997; MacKenzie and Wajcman 1999). Yet a widespread, almost 'common sense' technological determinism has hitherto tended to prevail in studies of technology which are not strongly situated theoretically. This is particularly evident in studies of ICTs, where the perceived pace of innovation makes it hard to believe that we drive the technology rather than its driving us. The problem with a deterministic view of information technology, and the reason why it should be exposed and analysed, is not just because it offers an impoverished view of ethical thinking in relation to technology as characterized before, but more importantly because it disguises and thereby denies the possibility of political choice in the use of technology. Arguing against determinism and thereby taking an alternative position means that we need not see ourselves as being swept along by a relentless tide of technology; we may, instead, have choices in the way we use different technologies. Hence it becomes an important political act to make explicit, understand and evaluate the potential choices.

How are these concerns played out in computer ethics writing? The clue lies in the suggestion above, namely that studies of technology, whether situated in computer ethics or not, which do not adopt an explicit theoretical stance, are much more likely to fall prey to a tacit, 'common sense' style of determinism. Much of the reason for this is that eschewing theory is also a way of eschewing the need to adopt a critical stance. Authors who write for a professional audience may regard the kind of critical analysis I suggest as an academic irrelevance. One such computer ethics author notes: 'My students are computer scientists and business people; and neither of these groups is noted for its tolerance of irrelevancies' (Langford 1999, p. xi). Yet it could be argued that writing for a business or professional audience may be predicated on a strong need to preserve the *status quo*, to maintain the acceptance of the dominance of big business and professional groups who will be in charge of ethical decision making and the acquisition and use of technology and associated services which are at the heart of contemporary business life. This is the position which Ladd (1995) hints at in his critique of codes of ethics. Who are codes of ethics for – the protection of the profession or the protection of the public? Questioning and criticizing the vector of technology and making explicit the inequalities of power relations could then be part of a too radical critique of the *raison d'être* of the world of business.

At the same time, some of the more popular writing on computer ethics (Sterling 1992) can be identified as being closely related to the 'cyberculture' literary genre (Adam 1998). Although in a rather different way from the professional ethics literature, this style of writing also avoids theorizing and criticizing the vector of inevitable technological development. Briefly, cyberculture is the term often used to describe the movement, mainly a youth culture, appealing to young men and hence often rather 'macho' in style, which has fermented round virtual reality, the Internet and AI, and which is strongly influenced by 'cyberpunk' science fiction (Schroeder 1994). Such writing is predicated on an uncritical acceptance of the gadgetry of computer technology. Although not explicitly writing on computer ethics, members of the academic wing of this movement are fond of making futuristic pronouncements as to the inevitability of certain types of technology, most often the takeover of the human race by robots (Moravec 1988, 1998; Warwick 1997). Essentially the point here is that the rhetoric which fairly closely surrounds popular computer ethics writing, as it charts a course through the choppy seas of cyberculture, is strongly driven by a view which uncritically accepts the inevitability that technologies will be developed and used in certain predetermined ways.

Although the 'cyberculture' style of ethics writing tends to be somewhat uncritically enthusiastic of an acceptance of technological advance, paradoxically it is often sharply dystopian in vision. The original cyberpunk novel, *Neuromancer* (Gibson 1984) paints a distinctly *noir* view of the future. Even 'scientific sympathizers' such as Moravec (1998) and Warwick (1997) collude in the portrayal of a very unfeeling, uncaring future cyborg/robotic/technicist world or, at least, a world that can be interpreted as such by those of us who are to be controlled by the robots of the future. This is interesting as it suggests that enthusiasm for the progress of technology is not necessarily accompanied by enthusiasm for our ability to use it morally. Under this view, moral progress does not attend technological progress, quite the opposite. This is a feature which is rarely discussed in accounts of technological determinism (Smith and Marx 1998). It is as if the vector of technological progress leaves us no choice but to submit to the machine. This implies that technological determinism as an expression of Enlightenment progress does not necessarily carry with it the Enlightenment vector of rational, moral progress. The modern, Enlightenment ideal of progress is inextricably intertwined with science and technology as the engines of progress, which includes in its purview moral progress away from the dark ages of magic and mysticism towards a rational, moral world view. However, the cyberculture world view, although subscribing to technological determinism, steps beyond the Enlightenment ideal of moral progress – morality appears to be an out of date concept to be swept aside as irrelevant.

The problems of liberalism

Having analysed the main strands of computer ethics' relationship to determinism, I now wish to return to one of the more problematic implications of determinism, namely liberalism. Liberalism is a much used, and perhaps abused term and I am conscious that I cannot possibly do justice to the vast range of writing, from politics through philosophy and ethics, which spans the spectrum of liberal thinking in a short space (Gaus 1999). It is also important not to claim that all shades of liberalism are equally problematic. Rather I want to single out those aspects of liberalism which have particular relevance to, and are implied by, the technological determinism embedded in much writing on ethical problems in computing technology. In Chapters 2 and 3, I have described the way that feminist politics, law and ethics have formulated a substantial critique of liberalism, in some detail. I now want to extend the feminist critique to consider, in more detail, the strong link between liberalism and technological determinism and what this implies for the development of computer ethics. To consolidate the analysis of liberalism from preceding chapters, in the present context, a liberal stance is taken to mean a position where inequality and fairness are recognized as key liberal values and there is a will to change that situation within a framework which emphasizes freedom of the individual. However the measures adopted for change implied by a broadly liberal position can be weak and may be little more than a rallying call for equal participation. This is certainly clear in the critique of liberalism from feminist politics. With its focus on the individual and individual liberty, liberalism leaves untouched the social structures which may be the largest contributory factor in causing the inequality in the first place.

Technological determinism and liberalism go hand in hand. Technological determinism assumes the objectivity and inevitability of developments in technology and science which drive societal change. This implies that even where there is a recognition of inequality, the measures offered to improve it are unlikely to include a challenge to the tacitly assumed objectivity of the world. Similarly, and following on from this point, the liberal stance takes for granted the objectivity of the world with which it deals, neither acting upon nor recognizing the structures of that world which may be at the root of the inequalities. Chapters 2 and 3 argue that structures such as the distinction between public and private spheres, which have been the subject of much analysis and criticism by feminist authors, are left undisturbed in the liberal world view (Pateman 1989). Pateman argues that the public/private distinction is strongly gendered. Women's traditional existence in the private world makes their entry and acceptance in public life problematic. So if liberalism sees no need to challenge structures such as the public/private divide this implies that, as a broadly political stance, it does not have enough critical bite to achieve equality.

An example of this lies in the assumption that while women enter the world of work, in the public sphere, they are often still responsible for the private sphere, the home. Thus employers may reinforce inequality by passing over women for promotion, assuming, for example, that they may take time off looking after children. A more balanced, and essentially non-liberal view, would look to ways in which both men and women can assume equal responsibility for home, children and work and would look towards setting up employment rights and structures to reinforce this alternative. A view driven by a liberal agenda looks to a minimum level of change to effect equality. A non-liberal, feminist position looks to a much more active engagement with the world, otherwise, changes will not be forthcoming.

The above discussion implies that liberal ethics may not serve everyone equally well. In particular, those who are already disadvantaged may have their disadvantage reinforced rather than alleviated. This is a perennial problem for feminism. Liberal measures which may seem, on the surface, to ameliorate women's subordinate position may have the effect of making it subtly worse. Concerns with improving inequalities points to the need for a corresponding change in the structures in which that inequality is inscribed, otherwise critics of liberalism see the job as fruitless. This is part of the wider critique of liberalism which finds a particularly clear expression in feminist theory and feminist analyses of technology which has the potential to be applied more widely to other liberal positions on equality, participation and access (Phillips 1991; Henwood 1993).

Cyberlibertarianism

Winner (1997) forcefully points up the problems of liberalism in regard to ethics on the Internet and related technologies. He argues that the link between technological determinism and liberalism has serious implications for democracy. He identifies 'cyberlibertarianism' as a dominant view in popular discussions of computers and networking. This is akin to my characterization of liberalism except that I have interpreted liberalism more generally and have not tied it to either extreme of the political spectrum. But Winner's cyberlibertarianism is an even more problematic variant of liberalism. It is a form of extreme right-wing liberalism in the shape of a libertarianism where no controls are imposed and the workings of the free market are assumed to create egalitarian, democratic societal structures. Although cyberlibertarianism is clearly a stronger, even more extreme version of liberalism, some of its implications are very similar. Indeed looking towards this more extreme form of liberalism makes liberalism's difficult aspects stand out in sharper relief. These include the concept that technological advance is inevitable and that equality arises without the need to examine deeper societal structures. Winner interprets cyberlibertarianism as a much more dystopian position combining extreme enthusiasm for computer-mediated life coupled with 'radical, right wing libertarian ideas about the proper definition of freedom, social life, economics, and politics in the years to come' (ibid., p. 14). Cyberlibertarianism looks much like the 'cyberculture' which I described earlier, but with its right wing liberal tendencies more explicitly identified. There are also certain parallels with the 'hacker ethic' (Himanen 2001) and the open-source movement, where, although one might not wish to ascribe an extreme right-wing position, there are libertarian views present in the ideal that all information should be free and that equality spontaneously emerges from such freedoms. Jordan and Taylor (2004) characterize this outlook, in terms of its relationship more specifically to hacking, as 'techno-libertarianism', strongly linked to the 'hacker ethic' which Chapter 7 discusses. Such a view looks to a society free from regulation, social ties and community obligations. It is a form of 'digital Darwinism' sloping away from human obligation and emotion and connected to the nerdy masculinity of hacking.

Winner (1997, pp. 14–15) identifies a whole-hearted embrace of technological determinism as the most central characteristic of such a view. '... the dynamism of digital technology is our true destiny. There is no time to pause, reflect or ask for more influence in shaping these developments. Enormous feats of quick adaptation are required of all of us just to respond to the requirements the new technology casts upon us each day.' Radical self-interest, rights without responsibilities, free market capitalism and a distrust of social welfare and government intervention are the name of the game. Yet, somehow, at the same time, these conditions are expected to give rise to a global, decentralized, non-hierarchical, non-bureaucratic democracy. He regards 'communities' on the Internet, born from such a libertarian ethic, as but pale variants of the real thing. Real communities involve all sorts of different people of different ages and opinions and with different views; real communities are hard work – they involve rubbing along with people one might not naturally get along with. Online communities involve seeking out-like-minded people with little discussion of what kind of 'democracy' is thereby created. This mirrors Ess's concerns with the naïve views of democracy (1996a) often propagated in computer-mediated communication. Deliberately mixing only with people like oneself gives little opportunity to understand the needs of others and one's responsibilities to them. Before the cyberlibertarianism view becomes solidified in social relationships, Winner argues that we need to understand the more complex communitarian concerns involved in the use of electronic networks.

In summary, juxtaposing my arguments on liberalism with cyberlibertarianism, Winner is making a similar point in regard to the relationship of technological determinism to forms of liberalism, although his version is even more starkly dystopian. This is useful as sometimes it is not easy to see the problems with a position until we see the implications of a more extreme version of it. Views which regard the trajectories of electronic technologies as determined and inevitable go hand in hand with liberal, and especially libertarian, views which see democracy, implying equality of participation and access, as just waiting to happen. Democracy will somehow arise with little or no effort, almost as an emergent property spontaneously generated from computer technology. On the other hand, the alternative view argues that a deeper, and more consciously attempted, understanding of the political structures of our societies in relation to computer networks is needed to foster truly democratic practices.

The notion of emergent properties is interesting here. Emergence is an important concept in descriptions of AI and A-life (Adam 1998). For AI and A-life, emergence relates to the idea of levels of intelligence as an emergent property of certain kinds of architectures. Here we are talking of a different scale, in terms of democracy spontaneously emerging from a community rather than intelligence spontaneously emerging from a machine. Yet both types of emergence are based upon the powers of computer technology to spontaneously create rational order from something that is not ordered. Emergence is a technologically determinist concept – it puts faith in technology to deliver more than the sum of its parts. This reflects a long-standing view in STS that scientific concepts can be expressions of our ways of ordering society (Barnes and Shapin 1979). A view of intelligent order emerging from a machine seems to reflect the way that we expect intelligent order, that is, democracy, to emerge from a society left to itself to organize. But this view has distinctly right-of-centre liberal cast with a 'free market' feel. Just as libertarian economics lets the market decide with a faith in the free market to produce the best solution, so does cyberlibertarian politics let the best solution, in the shape of a supposed democracy, simply emerge. This is quite similar to the 'free market' type of argument which is found in relation to hacker ethics, as Chapter 7 describes, where there are to be no shackles placed upon hackers and their access to information and this is seen as having a direct causal link to their democratic culture.

Professionalism

A further part of the story of the development of computer ethics derives from the impetus of those who work in computing and IT disciplines to achieve professional status. An important step on the way towards becoming a profession involves developing moral standards which apply to the profession's members in their dealing with the public, for example, as in the Hippocratic Oath in medicine. Indeed, university and college courses on computer ethics often focus on professionalism and professional issues according to the dictates of curriculum requirements for accreditation of professional bodies such as the ACM (Association for Computing Machinery) in the USA and the BCS (British Computer Society) in the UK. Although computer ethics textbooks and readers generally contain a section on professional issues (e.g. see Spinello and Tavani 2001) there are a number of textbooks specifically aimed at the topic of professionalism (Bott *et al.* 1991; Gotterbarn 1997; Myers *et al.* 1997; Ayres 1999).

Part of the problem of professionalization for computing and IT lies in the question: 'what kind of profession?' Whether or not computing should be seen as branch of engineering has been a hardy perennial in the IT world. For instance, it is interesting to note the struggle of the BCS to be accredited by the UK's Engineering Council and have suitably qualified members designated as Chartered Engineers (Adam 1998). In the UK, engineering does not enjoy the same level of professional status as, say, law or medicine. Even so, it took much effort, on behalf of the BCS, to have suitably qualified members recognized even as engineers, serving to underline the relatively marginal status of the IT profession. In fact, questions of professionalism in computing are often asked against the discipline's putative status as software engineering. Whereas in many parts of the world one may not practise as an engineer (e.g. civil engineer, mechanical engineer etc.) without an appropriate qualification and accreditation, the same standards continue to evade the software engineering/computing/IT discipline. Indeed the most famous IT entrepreneur of them all, Bill Gates, notoriously dropped out of Harvard without completing his degree.

Computing does not fit the traditional parameters of a profession at all well (Gotterbarn 1997; Johnson 2001). Standard indicators include professional education, usually undertaken over a period of years in higher education, regulation through licensing from an official state recognized body, self-regulation and autonomy, codes of ethics and professional practice, a level of prestige and respect and usually a higher than average income. Although there are those working in computing and software engineering who obtain their degrees, join and abide by the regulatory codes of their professional society, it is perfectly possible to enjoy a successful, well-paid career in IT without any of this. This makes it impossible for the IT profession to regulate itself and leaves the feeling that, at least in terms of the traditional markers, IT and computing hardly fit at all.

Part of the thrust of the topic of professionalism relates back to the construction of, at least some of the subject matter of computing and software engineering themselves. The 'software crisis' or 'productivity paradox' (Willcocks and Lester 1999) are two well-worn expressions which refer to the way that software projects have, historically, often been late and over-budget. From at least the 1970s onwards this has fuelled attempts to find structured techniques to control 'unruly' programmers and improve the quality and timeliness of systems development. Nevertheless IS projects are still late, often over budget and frequently fail completely, such as the disastrous London Ambulance Service project (Robinson 1994). Yet, against the backcloth of a growing recognition of IS failure understood in broader social and organizational contexts (Howcroft and Wilson 2002) there is, nevertheless, a large IT/IS 'success' literature (Adam and Spedding 2004). This focuses, in mathematically minute detail, on IS success factors for the needs of business interests, to the denial that there might exist just as salient 'failure factors'.

Hence, whilst, at least some of the push for developing a computer ethics, derives from the will to devise professional standards, especially in terms of codes of ethics, IT/IS still enjoys a somewhat marginal status, helped, in large part by the way that failure is often seen to attend software projects.

Computer ethics into legislation and possible consequences

As I noted in Chapters 2 and 3, there is a direct link between our ethical and political reasoning and the business of forming legislation, indeed we would hardly expect it to be otherwise. In this section I turn to consider this in relation to ICT legislation. Here I am not specifically addressing the academic discipline of computer ethics, characterized above, although the concerns of the academic discipline are clearly related. Rather I am seeking to make some more generally applicable comments about our moral intuitions on problems relating to the use of ICTs, connecting these with intuitions derived from computer ethics and cyberculture and the relationship of these to the making and applying of legislation.

Against this backcloth there is also the question that ethics does not just address how we *ought* to behave it must also address *why* we behave in particular ways. Legislation based on policy which does not include an understanding of the aspects of human behaviour to which it applies, is unlikely to be effective. This is an argument I develop further in Chapter 6 in relation to cyberstalking. As suggested above, more generally, the question of the speed with which we must often get legislation onto the statute books is problematic. Social attitudes take time to mature and we need time to work out how to respond to a new behaviour or activity. Hence the link between ethics, policy and legislation may be made too quickly, too slowly or, indeed may not be made in the way we intended at all. In particular, the law may be applied in ways which we did not anticipate and where the application of the legislation did not match up to our ethical position and policy. This is not to say that computer ethics problems are any better or worse, in this respect, than other areas of social life. At the same time I do not want to slip into a determinist position of assuming that technology has an inevitable trajectory, that it determines our behaviour and that we must pedal furiously to keep up with its inevitable advance. However, as I argued at the beginning of the chapter, at least partly because of the pace with which we feel forced into making ICT legislation, unintended consequences may follow. An example illustrates these points.

The UK Data Protection Act

The Data Protection Act (DPA) became law in the UK in 1984 and was subsequently superseded by the 1998 DPA which broadened the scope of the original act, which originally applied only to digital media to include data held by any means of storage. The DPA is designed to achieve fair and lawful processing of personal information. Although its reach is not just confined to data held on computer, its introduction was prompted by the recognition that the use of computer technology offers unprecedented opportunities for the storing, processing and possible abuse of data. That it was revised relatively quickly from its original form is an indication of how quickly our ethical and legal judgements must move in response to the use of computer technologies. Additionally this illustrates how much our conceptions of key concepts such as privacy are shaped by our use of new technologies as the 1998 act includes paper storage of personal data while the 1984 act did not. This signals the role of data protection legislation in influencing our conceptions of personal data and the need to protect individual privacy in relation to data whether or not that data is held digitally. The DPA's application to personal data and its subsequent amendment to apply to non-computerized data serves to underline my claim that new technologies, with their moral implications, quickly become entwined in our social existence. Additionally, but without wishing to fall prey to determinism, this reinforces the argument that I elaborate in Chapter 8, namely that our conception of key ethical concepts, here the concept of privacy, is revised and renewed through our experiences of using technologies.

The situation in regard to treatment of personal data is very complex. There is an age-old tension between freedom of information and privacy. This is compounded by recent legislation for the prevention of terrorism, notably in the USA and the UK, which we might note was already in train before the events of 11 September 2001. In the UK, the original Prevention of Terrorism Act reached the statute books in 1974 and was developed in relation to IRA and related terrorist activity. The power it gave to hold suspects without trial in Northern Ireland was extremely unpopular and a number of miscarriages of justice were laid at its door (Woffinden 1987). The later UK Terrorism Bill became law in 2001 but was subsequently amended after 11 September, to allow for indefinite detainment of non-UK nationals suspected of terrorist activities and for unprecedented levels of state surveillance of its citizens. Similarly, the US Patriot Act, rushed through Congress less than two months after September 11, allows for surveillance of personal data even to the level of an individual library borrower's record. Hence we have the paradox that, whilst the need to provide protection for personal data may have grown in the digital age, the USA and the UK at least, have substantial powers to access personal data in the name of prevention of terrorism. Fear is one way of controlling the populace and the various shades of terrorist alert mean that individuals are much more fearful of say, international air travel and visits to big cities. But surveillance of personal data can allow a government to exercise a high level of control over its citizens and others where the possibility of dissent and legitimate protest now carries with it the possibility of unlimited detention without trial. We return to privacy and the disciplinary power which can be exerted through surveillance in more detail in Chapter 8.

The UK DPA applies to personal data and this recognizes that individual data privacy is important and must be protected and that individuals have a right to know what data is held on them with the concomitant right to have the data changed if it is in error. Importantly, personal data should not be held longer than is necessary. Although the human rights aspects of protection of personal data are paramount, there is no doubt that much of the impetus to put data protection law onto the statute books relates to the requirements for free flow of information across borders for the promotion of electronic commerce.

Leaving aside terrorism and electronic commerce for the moment, I want to concentrate on a set of three tragic, high profile cases which have arisen in the UK in the last five years. The common features of these cases relate to the way that they involve vulnerable members of society, young children and elderly people, whose need for protection and just treatment is uncontroversial. Second, the three cases I discuss all involve a failure to share personal data, about the individuals involved, with other appropriate agents who might have ensured their protection, signalling, to a greater or lesser extent a failure to understand and apply data protection law appropriately. Although, in general, personal data about individuals must not be shared with other organizations, there are exemptions for potential criminal activity, terrorism and the protection of vulnerable people.

In the UK, non-payment of a gas or electricity bill may result eventually in disconnection of electric power or gas. However elderly persons should not have their supply of gas or electricity disconnected. This reflects a moral view that non-payment by an elderly person is likely to reflect an inability to pay. Second, elderly persons are particularly at risk from cold weather and must be able to heat their houses properly. British Gas told an inquest into the deaths of two pensioners whose gas had been disconnected in the winter of 2003 that they had not alerted social services for fear of breaching data protection law (Dyer 2004).

Victoria Climbie was sent by her parents in Nigeria to live with an aunt in the UK, in the hope of securing a better life for her. She lived a life of unspeakable cruelty at the hands of her aunt and died in 2000 at the age of eight. Although she was known to the social services and several other authorities, at least part of the reason for this tragic outcome, was the failure to share personal data about her amongst the various authorities.

In August 2002, two 10-year-old girls were murdered in the village of Soham in Humberside in North East England. Their murderer was Ian Huntley, the caretaker at the girls' school and therefore, to them, a trusted adult. When the case was brought to trial it transpired that he had been the subject of a series of complaints about rape, indecent assault and underage sex between 1995 and 1999. When he was employed by Soham College, the mandatory pre-employment checks were made but the details of these past complaints were not uncovered, hence he was employed by the school. In the belief that the DPA obliged them to delete the files, Humberside Police had erased them.

Without wishing to simplify the complexities of these three tragic cases, there are important similarities and differences. Their overall similarity involves a failure of appropriate organizations to retain and/ or share personal data in circumstances where the normal expectation of privacy of personal data should be set aside because potential harm to vulnerable people was involved. The DPA clearly allows protection of data to be overridden where a crime might be involved. In the case of the elderly couple, we see neglect rather than criminal intent. In the Climbie case up to 14 different authorities, including hospitals and social services, were involved before her death. Lack of data sharing was a clear issue here. In the Soham case it appears that lack of appropriate data retention was a serious issue.

In the wake of the Climbie and Soham cases there has been a move, in the UK, to set up a national database for children (Room 2004). As Room (ibid., p. 1) notes:

> Now that we are about [to] embrace national databases the time is ripe to consider whether there are any flaws in the emerging belief that the duty of care in the area of child protection can be satisfied by the creation of large scale databases of personal information and increased data sharing.

A range of measures were introduced, in UK legislation, in the wake of Victoria Climbie's tragic death, culminating in the Children's Bill which was passed by the British parliament in March 2004. The Bill proposes a number of measures to enhance the welfare of children but one of its most revolutionary aspects is the provision for the creation of a national database for children (under the age of 18) and the appropriate provision for tracking, referral and data sharing. Of the 11 million or so children of that age group, 50–100 children per annum die of abuse or neglect. Naturally, as a society, we would want to do everything in our power to prevent these tragic deaths.

A database for children

A number of implications run from the implementation of a children's database. Once again we must consider the public/private split and how to handle the ethical dilemmas that follow. Bringing up children is often seen as a private matter where the state is reluctant to step in. But the recognition that abuse and/or neglect often occurs in the private sphere of the home gives the state the right to interfere. In contemporary life, children are no longer seen as the property of their parents or carers. However it is vital that data in such a database is accurate. In the UK there have been some high profile cases of carers being wrongly accused of murder or abuse (Bell 1988). Wrong accusations can be devastating for a family. The blunt instrument of a gigantic database cannot ensure that data is accurate, nor that it will be interpreted in a fair and reasonable way. Such a database cannot get round some of the issues that have dogged tragic cases where authorities have not acted to save the child involved, where lack of resources, inadequate training and overstretched staff may outweigh the positive benefits of a database. Finally, it is difficult to see how the Soham tragedy might have been averted by such a database as information retention of data on those who might harm children, rather than on the children themselves, was required here. At the same time we must ensure the accuracy of such data and that it is shared with appropriate authorities.

If one child's life is saved through the development of the children's database it might seem completely inappropriate to criticize the concept. However I have argued that part of the problem is our failure to translate a moral imperative into a workable legal solution. Might not liberal values, of the sort described above, be at work here? Are we assuming that care is an emergent property of such a database, much in the way that democracy is often held to be an emergent property of Winner's (1997) cyberlibertarian communities? If so, then we have come full circle.

In this chapter I have argued that computer ethics can be seen as a relatively conservative academic discipline, where the perils of a technological determinism and liberalism coupled with the conservative effects of cyberculture tend to militate against more radical approaches. There are important implications for a nascent IT/Computing profession which needs to demonstrate allegiance to identifiable moral parameters. From that position I have argued that concern with computer ethics problems should be of much wider interest to a larger audience outside the academy and the IT profession. Indeed the three cases I discuss illustrate how important it is that our moral concerns concerning the application of digital technologies are translated into legislation and procedures for protecting the most vulnerable members of our society. Yet there is now a distinct possibility that we may delegate at least some aspects of our duty of care towards vulnerable members of society to a database. We may be delegating care to a surveillance technology. In the 1980s and 1990s, through the domain of AI (Adam 1998) there was much talk of delegating aspects of our intelligence to a machine. I do not believe that we intend the same metaphor to apply here, nevertheless we must now consider whether we are about to hand over some aspects of morality to a machine.

It is notable that it is the most feminine of moral attributes, namely 'care' that may be subject to such a delegation. This suggests that it is now high time that feminist ethics be pressed into service in computer ethics. Chapters 6, 7 and 8 attempt this in relation to cyberstalking and harassment often deriving from Internet dating, hackers and privacy respectively. However before turning to that I wish to explore how gender issues have been understood and analysed in computer ethics writing to date. My reasons for doing so relate to my concerns with the notion that gender can somehow be added into discussions of computer ethics as an unanalysed variable with two possible values, male and female. As I hope to demonstrate further in later chapters the question of gender in computer ethics is much more subtle and complex than that. But before exploring these complexities further, it is necessary to understand just what is problematic about many contemporary studies of gender and computer ethics, and how we might start to move beyond the constraints of contemporary approaches.

5
Gender and Computer Ethics – Contemporary Approaches and Contemporary Problems

Introduction: The push from 'publish or perish'

I have argued that the topic of gender has been somewhat neglected in computer ethics writing to date. Nevertheless, there is a small body of academic work which takes seriously the point of view that gender has some bearing on computer ethics problems. This chapter critically reviews such research to argue that current directions in gender and computer ethics research are problematic and could benefit from a better balance between statistically based empirical research and approaches which incorporate a more substantial theoretical understanding of gender and computer ethics. This is becoming even more pressing given the arguments of the preceding chapter, namely that the translation from moral position to legislation is often deficient. We now need much more solid efforts to move concepts such as 'care' into computer ethics and ICT legislation from the research arena.

It may appear that I am very critical of the studies that I describe. However my intention is, rather, to be critical of aspects of the 'publish or perish' academic paradigm which those of us who have chosen an academic career necessarily inhabit. In parts of the world, particularly the USA but other places as well, one may not attain academic tenure, effectively a permanent academic job, without the necessary publication record and this typically takes six or more years. Attaining such a record involves publishing in the right journals so one will often hear talk of 'A' rated, 'B' rated or 'B+' rated journals and the necessity of having so many papers in 'A' rated journals for tenure. In business and management schools the pressure and the competition are particularly intense. However, particularly in the private sector, the financial rewards of an academic career in a US university management school are very favourable. The necessity of publishing in particular journals brings with it a strong pressure to conform to the research styles of those journals. In North America the prevalent paradigm for management research is the statistical survey. Mathematical rigour is highly prized (Oakley 2000). The pressures are not quite the same in the UK and other parts of the world, nevertheless, the hegemony of the positivistic, quantitative paradigm for business and management research remains. We need to banish, for good, the notion that universities are ivory towers where academics are free thinking individuals with complete freedom over what to research and how to research it. Universities are becoming more and more prey to the market forces that abound in other walks of life. It is not surprising, therefore, to find that amongst the relatively few published studies on gender and computer ethics decision making, the majority derive from US business schools, and almost all belong within this paradigm. My major criticisms relate to a lack of engagement with feminist ethics and an approach to gender which is undertheorized.

As a contrast, in order to show how empirical research can engage better with feminist ethics I offer some findings from a small study I undertook with a former student, Jacqueline Ofori-Amanfo (Adam and Ofori-Amanfo 2000). Although I accept that, in this study we have not been able to escape all the problems I identify in other empirical research, we do, at least, offer a reading of a computer ethics problem in terms of an ethic of care, demonstrating that it is feasible to bring elements of feminist ethics to bear on an analysis of computer ethics problems.

In this chapter, I characterize two strands of writing on gender and computer ethics. The first focuses on problems of women's access to computer technology; the second concentrates on whether there are identifiable and meaningful differences between men's and women's ethical decision making in relation to ICTs. Although there are some problems with the underlying theoretical position generally adopted in access studies, as suggested above, it is with a set of statistically oriented studies that I take issue. I engage with the latter area of research to argue that there are problems in confining surveys to a student audience, that such studies privilege the result of an ethical decision over the process of arriving at the decision, that they often fall prey to the qualitative/quantitative debate bedevilling much work on ICTs and IS and that they are frequently undertheorized with respect to the concept of gender.

Given my concerns with a statistical approach towards decision making, I report the results of a small study on the gendered basis of computer ethics decision making against a set of scenarios. Although, as a qualitative study, it might be expected that it would escape many of the problems I raise in relation to quantitative studies of ethical decision making, it does, however, raise other issues about whether focusing on ever more detailed and somewhat artificial studies of decision making really captures what it means to act ethically. Furthermore, the ambiguities of my study, coupled with the findings of the statistical studies surveyed, emphasize further the growing concern that there is much more to the question of gender in computer ethics than finding putative differences between men and women making decisions in artificial circumstances. This further underscores the need to develop strong theoretical bases for computer ethics problems such as hacking, privacy, and so on. Additionally, although the link might not be obvious at first sight, this also relates to the questions I raise in Chapter 4 about the chain of reasoning from ethics to policy to law to application of law. The links of this chain are made stronger, and are less likely to break, if we have appropriate theoretical analyses which help us explain why things happen the way they do.

Barriers and pipelines

In this, and the following section, I explore the two main strands of current research in gender and computer ethics. The first strand can be viewed as a spillover from IS and computing research on barriers and 'pipelines' (Camp 1997) which tends to see the gender and ICT problem as one of women's access to ICTs and their continuing low representation in computing all the way through the educational process through to the world of work. Indeed if one talks of women and computing or gender and computing, it is the question of low numbers of women which many people regard as the issue. It is undoubtedly a problem (although, not the only problem) and worthy of serious consideration. Until recently, such research found voice more substantially in the research areas of work, education, psychology (Brosnan 1998) and on the fringes of computing disciplines (e.g. see Lovegrove and Segal 1991; Grundy 1996; Lander and Adam 1997). However papers in this general mould are beginning to appear in ethics journals and computer ethics conferences suggesting that authors are starting to cast the women and computing access/exclusion problem as an explicitly ethical problem although this is not how the area has been traditionally seen in the past (e.g. see Panteli and Stack 1998; Turner 1998; Panteli *et al.* 1999; Turner 1999).

I do not have space to elaborate an extensive commentary on this first strand of research on gender and computer ethics. However I note that studies which discuss the low numbers of women in computing have been criticized in the past for adopting a traditional, liberal position which characterizes the gender and computing problem in terms of educating, socializing and persuading women rather than challenging the subject matter and deeper structures of the subject (Henwood 1993; Faulkner 2000). As Faulkner (2000) notes, gender always appears to 'stick' to women rather than to men so the gender problem in computing tacitly slides into being a problem for women, not for men and women. Apart from anything else, a liberal argument, in leaving the organization of computing unchallenged, does little to offer a means of alleviating women's position in relation to computing education and work and campaigns to attract women based on such a position do not appear to work. In noting that an unanalysed liberalism is a trap for the unwary, I do not want to imply that all the gender and computer ethics research I cite above suffers from it. Interestingly, because such work is beginning to view itself as ethics research it sidesteps some of the criticisms of liberalism because there is a growing realization that deeper, structural issues are involved in the question of women's inequality.

Although the woman and computing problem is not new, it is still there. Numbers of women through all levels of computing remain low, meaning that women are still being excluded from employment in well-paid and interesting careers for whatever reason, and so it is a problem still to be solved. Casting this more as an ethical problem than an access problem starts to make the issue look less like a question of why women are not, apparently, taking up the opportunities being offered to them, and more like an ethical and political problem of exclusion. In other words it moves the onus for change away from women, and their apparent failure to take up challenges, towards the computer industry's failure to examine and change its exclusionary practices. Apart from anything else this work serves to act as an important reminder of how little has changed for women in the computing industry in the last twenty or so years. Hence, casting the problem of women and computing as an ethical rather than purely as an equal opportunities problem has the positive effect of potentially strengthening the political dimension – exclusion is a much more loaded term than equal opportunities.

Alternatives to pipelines

There is a danger of making the existing gender and computer ethics literature appear overly polarized between pipeline literature and statistical studies. However, there is a small body of work which attempts to develop a stronger theoretical position in considering gender issues in computer ethics. Vehviläinen's (1994) discussion of codes of professional ethics argues that such codes serve to enshrine male expertise at the expense of women's voices. Kramer and Kramarae's study of gendered ethics on the Internet (1997) examines metaphors for the Internet and how these either do or do not enfranchize women. The findings of the latter paper are particularly pertinent to the present discussion and I return to them in Chapter 7 in my discussion of hackers.

Kramer and Kramarae (1997) investigate the commonly used metaphors of anarchy, frontier, community and democracy in relation to the Internet. Each of these metaphors has resonances with, but also problems for women. Because Chapter 4's discussion on technological determinism, liberalism and Winner's cyberlibertarianism (1997) opens up the question of what democracy may mean in cyberspace, it is this aspect of their critique which is especially pertinent here. Kramer and Kramarae, following Held (1993), argue that the ethics of liberal democracy emphasizes freedom and absence of interference but these ideas do not work equally well for everyone and, in particular, may not work for women who have traditionally been thought of as dependants without their own autonomy. This ethic supports those who are already favoured by existing social arrangements – they can expect freedom from interference. But if you do not enjoy the basic necessities of life this form of ethics will do little for you. The under-represented on the Internet will not be protected by such liberal democratic ethics. This resonates with the views of feminist political theorists discussed in Chapter 2, namely that democracy may not work as well for women as for men. Similarly, in accordance with Winner's views on communities in cyberspace (1997), Kramer and Kramarae (1997) argue that notions of accountability and responsibility, concepts which can be used to protect minorities and those in less powerful positions, are absent in the anonymous communities of the Internet. Slender though this body of research may be, it raises many important theoretical concerns for a computer ethics informed by feminist theory to explore further – codes and representation, professionalization and professionalism, the masculinity of expertise, experiences of democracy and freedom, accountability and responsibility – and thereby points the way towards a more thorough-going theorizing of gender and computer ethics issues.

Men's and women's decision making in computer ethics

The other major strand of research on gender and computer ethics focuses on concerns more central to computer ethics as a whole, namely the question of whether there are detectable differences between men's and women's ethical decision making in relation to computer ethics (Khazanchi 1995; Mason and Mudrack 1996; McDonald and Pak 1996; Kreie and Cronan 1998; Bissett and Shipton 1999; Escribano *et al.* 1999). I concentrate on analysing these studies in some detail as they reveal important elements relevant to the development of the field of computer ethics and to the ways in which gender issues are understood in the dominant quantitative paradigm of academic business and management studies. One of the problems of academic writing is that research from one discipline often does not reach other disciplines, even when very similar topics are studied. Therefore it is not completely surprising that management and business studies research on gender and computer ethics is relatively untouched by feminist scholarship, particularly, as I suggest above, because of the pressures to conform to the *status quo* in publications for tenure purposes. But, by the same token, academic feminism does not know much about business or computer ethics research. The challenge is to overcome this impasse and bring the best ideas from all the relevant disciplines together.

We now turn to an analysis of research on gender and computer ethics decision making. Broadly speaking, the research methodology can be characterized as follows. A population of subjects (in these studies always a student population) is surveyed by questionnaire and is asked to rate responses either in relation to a set of questions or a set of artificial scenarios. Responses are usually Yes/No or rated against a Likert scale (a scale with a number of points (3, 4, 5 or more) where one end indicates the most positive response and the other end indicates the most negative response). The results are then analysed quantitatively (some using little more than percentages, but mostly using more sophisticated statistical methods) and this may involve splitting out various ethical variables and rating subjects' responses against them. The analysis is then turned back from quantitative measures into qualitative conclusions which are, in some cases, that women are more ethical than men in relation to computer ethics problems, in other cases that there is no discernable difference. Interestingly, none of the studies I cite found that men were more ethical than women. Sometimes these results are related, theoretically to Gilligan's *In a Different Voice* (1982; Mason and Mudrack 1996; McDonald and Pak 1996; Bissett and Shipton 1999) which is still the best known work in feminist ethics, but other prominent studies make no use of feminist or gender based ethics in terms of explanation (Kreie and Cronan 1998). Interestingly, Gilligan (1982) was the only substantive reference to writing on feminist ethics that I discovered in any of these studies. The following paragraphs describe these points in more detail.

Much decision making in relation to computer technologies takes place within the workplace, therefore I claim that gender studies within business ethics and IS are relevant even if ICTs, as such, are not the main focus. This accords with the discussion in Chapter 4 relating one of the roots of computer ethics to professionalism and business ethics. Hence the first three studies briefly outlined here are concerned with more general business ethics decision making in relation to gender. In style and substance they are very similar to the computer ethics studies I describe in more detail below. I include these, both to sharpen my characterization of the style of research methodology being used, to illustrate that results regarding the importance of gender in ethical decision making are quite inconclusive and finally to strengthen my critique of this methodology which follows later in the chapter.

Mason and Mudrack's questionnaire study (1996) of undergraduate and graduate business students in a classroom setting tested gender socialization and occupational socialization theories against a set of ethical variables. Gender socialization theory suggests differences in ethics variables regardless of the employment position of subjects, while occupational socialization theory implies that employees are similar in outlook and gender differences will not figure in ethical decision making. So the first theory argues for an ethics split along gendered lines, while the second argues that occupational experiences tended to override socialized gender positions, suggesting that men and women are likely to have similar ethical preferences in the workplace. Results were analysed using standard statistical measures Their results fitted neither theory. 'Although no significant gender differences emerged in individuals lacking full time employment, significant differences existed between employed women and men, with women appearing "more ethical" ' (Mason and Mudrack 1996, p. 599). The authors commented that the fact they were using students as subjects, albeit students in employment, and noted that this could make their study results more homogeneous than with a more general population.

McDonald and Pak's research (1996) amongst business managers and MBA students (via postal and directly distributed questionnaires) in Canada, Malaysia, New Zealand and Hong Kong studied cultural and organizational differences as well as gender differences in ethical decision making. They focused on the decision making process and noted that there has been relatively little research on the cognitive processes involved. Based on the literature on ethical frameworks they arrived at a framework containing a set of their own ethical elements including self interest, utilitarianism, duty, justice, religious convictions, and so on. A set of ethical scenarios were devised to explore these and subjects were invited to agree or disagree with the scenarios on a five point Likert scale. The results were analysed statistically and were opposite to Mason and Mudrack's findings (1996) in that they found no major difference between male and female business managers in considering ethical business decisions. However a breakdown by country indicated more distinct differences in ethical frameworks used in each cultural location.

Reiss and Mitra's study (1998) of ethical beliefs amongst college students once more used a questionnaire with a Likert scale where students were asked to rate various actions on a 5-point scale from very acceptable to very unacceptable. These authors (ibid., p. 1583) noted that previous studies tend to split equally amongst those that find women more ethical and those that find no difference. Apparently no study finds men to be more ethical than women in relation to business ethics. The authors analysed their results statistically to find partial support for the hypothesis that men tended to find behaviours of a dubious ethical nature more acceptable than did women.

Focusing more specifically on computer ethics, I discuss the studies of Khazanchi (1995) and Kreie and Cronan (1998) respectively. Khazanchi's aim was to understand whether gender differences influence the degree to which individuals recognize unethical conduct in the use and development of IT. To this end a sample of undergraduate and graduate business students was surveyed against a set of seven ethical scenarios and were asked to rate these as to degree of 'unethicalness'. These scenarios reflected categories comprising the ethical responsibilities of IS professionals regarding disclosure, social responsibility, integrity, conflict of interest, accountability, protection of privacy and personal conduct and were derived from earlier research. Subjects were asked to rate the unethical acts in each scenario against a 7-point Likert scale where 1 = 'absolutely not unethical' and 7 = 'absolutely unethical' with no labels for the intermediate range. Khanzanchi then derived an aggregate score of 'unethicalness' and correlated this against gender. Despite concerns as to the external validity of using students in the survey he found that the women of his survey consistently outperformed the men in identifying unethical actions across all his scenarios. 'The present study shows the ability to recognize (and ultimately resist) unethical actions involving IS dilemmas rests in part on the nature of the ethical dilemma and differences in gender of the adjudicator. The findings provide an insight into gender differences in the ethical judgement of future leaders and managers in the management information systems discipline' (Khazanchi 1995, p. 744).

Bissett and Shipton's questionnaire survey (1999) of IT professionals studying part-time used a set of scenarios with respondents rating whether they would undertake similar behaviour on a scale of 'always' to 'never'. They found a small positive correlation between female gender and a tendency to consider the feelings of others. By contrast, Escribano *et al.*'s survey of university students (1999) involved Yes/No responses to a number of questions. They found the women in their survey far more interested in the ethical aspects of information technologies than were the men, despite the fact that they used such technologies much less than the male respondents.

Probably the most prominent of recent studies of gender and computer ethics is Kreie and Cronan's research (1998) which is published in the high profile periodical, *Communications of the ACM*, read by practitioners and academics. These researchers explored men's and women's moral decision making in relation to a set of computer ethics cases. The examples were, by and large, not blatantly criminal but were designed to reflect the situations we are often presented with in the workplace where extensive computer systems and networks are pervasive, for example, viewing sensitive data, making an electronic copy, and so on. The main research method in the study involved asking respondents to rate their responses against a set of influential environmental factors such as societal, individual, professional and legal belief systems. In addition there are so called 'personal values'. The authors proposed these factors to be those that influence ethical decision making. Once again a student population was surveyed and asked to rate whether the behaviour described in a given scenario was acceptable or unacceptable.

Following the survey it appears that some discussions with students helped explain judgements about the various scenarios. Respondents were also asked about their moral obligation to take corrective action and whether knowledge of negative consequences, for example, a fine or reprimand would affect what a person should or should not do. For each scenario the respondents were asked which set of values, for example, personal values, societal environmental, and so on, influenced their decision most. The authors' conclusion was that most people were strongly influenced by their personal values. Kreie and Cronan (1998, p. 76) conclude: 'Men and women were distinctly different in their assessment of what is ethical and unethical behavior. For all scenarios, men were less likely to consider a behavior as unethical. Moreover, their judgement was most often influenced by their personal values and one environmental cue – whether the action was legal. Women were more conservative in their judgements and considered more environmental cues, as well as their own personal values.' Kreie and Cronan (ibid.) make suggestions as to the policy implications of these results: 'From the manager's viewpoint, men may be influenced more effectively through statements of what is legal (or not). Women might be effectively influenced by passive deterrents (policy statements and awareness training of unacceptable ethical behavior).'

Critique of gender and computer ethics studies

Having described a number of empirical studies of gender and business ethics and gender and computer ethics, I now wish to comment on a number of aspects of these studies to argue that these aspects are problematic. Focusing on the minutiae of potential gender issues threatens to take the new topic of gender and computer ethics into a theoretical dead end, as concentrating on ever more detailed statistics obviates the need both to find underlying reasons for difference, if such exist, and also the need to look at the broader context of moral decision making. Current studies appear to be training their analytical microscope on the wrong specimen. Problematic aspects of such studies are described below under the following sub-headings: student population, quantitative vs qualitative research methodology, ethical decisions vs ethical processes and how to get at the latter, and lack of appropriate theory.

Student population

In every one of the studies detailed above, a student population was surveyed. As university teachers it seems we are unable to resist the temptation to utilize that most captive of audiences, our students! (Adam and Ofori-Amanfo 2000). Although, it is clear, that in some of the studies the students also worked or had work experience, the tendency to utilize and then generalize from a student population is still problematic. This is not just because, as Mason and Mudrack (1996) note, this may give a certain homogeneity to the results obtained. There are bigger issues involved. More importantly there is a power relationship between student and teacher which none of these studies has apparently made explicit.

A student and teacher do not stand in the same relationship as a researcher and a member of the public, say. The teacher grades the student's work and gives testimonials for future employment or education. There is a potentially large differential in power. A student may feel unable to opt out of the research, to make their view felt by consciously not taking part as a member of the public might do. Additionally, given that students become very adept at telling their teachers what they think they want to hear under the guise of 'examination technique', there is the question of whether a student will apply the same process to a teacher's research survey, consciously or otherwise. As I argue, this points up the need to be much more aware of power relationships in computer ethics, an area which has hitherto received little attention.

Quantitative vs qualitative research methodologies

All the studies detailed above were similar in approach, in that they all employed questionnaire surveys, either with a binary 'Yes/No' or 5-point or 7-point Likert scale, which could then be analysed quantitatively for statistical significance. I am aware that a number of the studies I discuss are from one journal (*Journal of Business Ethics*) and that these studies reflect the dominant quantitative paradigm of management and information systems. Even so, it is interesting that authors are prepared to use statistically based questionnaire approaches quite so uncritically. There are a number of problems with such an approach. Only the Bissett and Shipton (1999) paper points to the problem of whether what people say they do is the same as what they do in a real-life situation. This may be even more of a problem than usual in the present set of studies as respondents are explicitly asked whether they would behave in some potentially immoral or even illegal way. In other words respondents are not being asked to choose between categories which are anything like neutral. It is naturally tempting to cast oneself as more moral in the questionnaire than one might be in real life.

This is clearly a well-trodden path in all social research, where the quantitative/qualitative or positivist/interpretivist battle continues to rage (Oakley 2000). We should not ignore the power of the academy, especially in the USA, in shaping such matters into a certain type of mould from which it is difficult to escape, at least if one wants a permanent, tenured position. Despite the preponderance of quantitative approaches to gender and computer ethics decision making, the issue of the appropriateness of statistical methods applied to ethics cannot be ignored and points to the need for a wider consideration of the appropriateness of other research methods.

There is also the question of what responses on a numerical scale actually mean and whether subjects can reliably attach meaning to the individual intervals in a 7-point scale. Is 1 = 'absolutely not unethical' the same as 'absolutely ethical' or not and does it differ from 2 = 'not quite so absolutely unethical'? Shades of ethicality would appear to be conceptually clumsy and very hard to define.

It is interesting that none of the authors in these studies proposed interviewing or using ethnographic techniques such as participant observation (e.g. see Forsythe 1993). Participant observation requires an often lengthy period immersed in the culture under study. The observer becomes part of, and participates in the culture (e.g. in Jordan's study of birth in four different cultures (1978), as a woman with a free pair of hands she was called upon to help deliver a baby!). But, at the same time, the observer must retain a degree of strangeness from the culture under study otherwise he/she will begin to take for granted aspects of that culture that need to be analysed and made explicit. For computer ethics, the promise of participant observation lies in the potential to witness ethical reasoning and behaviour as it happens. This may reveal it to be a process with a much more complex and less clear-cut structure and which may not even result in a decision at all, when compared with the instant Yes/No decisions prompted by questionnaires.

One cannot help but note that interviewing, and participant observation are not only much more time consuming techniques but also that their results are much less amenable to rendering into numerical form. Questionnaires can be made to yield numbers which can then be fed into the statistical mill no matter what the validity of the original qualitative assumptions on which they were based. The generalizability from small numbers (some studies report less than two hundred respondents) can also be questioned.

In performing a quantitative analysis of qualitative elements the studies described above appear to be falling prey to the common assumption prevalent in business studies, computing and information systems which I have criticized elsewhere, namely that objective factors are available and that these can somehow be factored out and used, like the factors in a mathematical expression (Adam 1998). Indeed in the Kreie and Cronan (1998) study there is the additional assumption that, even if such factors do have some reality as discrete factors, we can reliably separate out our beliefs and rate them against things such as social, psychological or religious beliefs. Can we do this in such a way that each belief system can be identified in an individual's response and can be treated separately? Apart from questioning the validity of such a factoring process, I argue that it allows authors to hide behind the apparent authority of their statistics obviating the will to develop a more thoroughgoing conceptual, theoretical analysis. In other words numbers cannot replace theoretical, conceptual explanations.

The qualitative/quantitative conundrum, to which the above discussion suggests gender and computer ethics empirical studies are rapidly falling prey, is part of a larger debate between qualitative and quantitative research methodologies. This discussion applies not just to work in gender and computer ethics, although it is starkly visible in the studies I outlined earlier, but is more generally a part of research in information systems and business. Oakley (2000) points out that this debate has been a long running issue in the social sciences. She argues that it is not nearly as clear cut as it appears as it is impossible to be completely qualitative, for example, we talk of 'some', 'more', 'less'. Similarly it is impossible to be completely quantitative as our quantities are quantities of some quality. Despite this, the debate has assumed an unwelcome polarity, a kind of 'paradigm war' (ibid., p. 31). Inevitably one side tends to dominate and in many parts of the social sciences, good research is thought of in terms of quantitative research.

Somewhat belatedly the qualitative/quantitative debate has filtered into business and management, computing and information systems research where the two camps are seen as 'hard' and 'soft', roughly translating into quantitative and qualitative and where the 'hard', or quantitative, enjoys a hegemony (Fitzgerald and Howcroft 1998). I have already alluded to geographical mappings with quantitative techniques favoured in North America, as I suggested earlier, and qualitative approaches more popular in Scandinavia and Europe. Despite these arguments, I do not want to suggest that qualitative research is to be preferred to quantitative research – there are surely good and bad examples of both. However, with the pressure on academics worldwide to publish it is small wonder that readily achieved statistical surveys, with a veneer of objectivity, should predominate in gender and computer ethics research as elsewhere.

All the studies reviewed above used statistical analyses. In the light of the concerns I express as to the reliability of ethical data gathered by questionnaire we need to be wary of conclusions based on results from such methods. Given these considerations there are strong reasons to believe that empirical ethical studies are not at a sufficiently mature research stage to use statistical methods with certainty. There are alternatives. For instance, Gilligan's study of moral reasoning (1982) focuses on a conceptual analysis. This involved interviewing respondents about fictitious ethical scenarios. Analysing both boys' and girls' responses she was able to map both these against Kohlberg's standard account of ethical maturity (1981) and against an alternative theoretical stance of care ethics. At the stage of empirical enquiry currently obtaining in computer ethics I argue that a more conceptual approach is worthy of further exploration in the short term. Indeed I have taken a similar approach to that of Gilligan in the empirical study reported later in the chapter.

Ethical decisions vs ethical processes

Taken together, the above considerations imply that empirical research in this area has not yet got to grips with understanding the process of making an ethical decision, or, indeed, with the possibility that moral behaviour may involve things other than decisions. If we were to focus on the process, rather than the decision, this would make the decision seem less important *per se*, as quite different approaches can arrive at the same decision through different routes. This aspect is well known to computer ethics researchers, for example, as in Johnson's description of act utilitarianism (2001) which likens it to ethical relativism. In any case, part of the problem is that utilitarianism and Kantian theory focus on ethical decision making. An exercise I set my students taking a computer ethics class involves their analysing a set of ethical scenarios according to the tenets of ethical relativism, utilitarianism and Kantian theory, respectively. The point of the exercise is not to arrive at a correct decision; indeed, for a given scenario, the same decision may be implied by more than one ethical theory. Rather it is the process of making a sound ethical argument which is important. It is tempting to suggest that virtue ethics might offer a means of escaping this problem, with their focus on virtues rather than decisions. However, given the concerns I express in Chapter 4 where women, and indeed men, may end up having stereotypical virtues assigned to them, it is not clear that virtue ethics offers a substantially better alternative. Indeed, thinking about the studies discussed above, women almost always turn out to be more ethical. This hints at a tendency to reinforce stereotypical views of men's and women's virtues.

Looking more squarely at processes rather than decisions would also mean that we would have to be much more sophisticated about our theorizing, as I shall suggest later, and stop treating gender as a unitary, unanalysed variable. Apart from any other reason this tends towards essentialism, that is, the assumption that men and women have essential, fixed, natural and even possibly biological, characteristics.

Essentialism is dangerous, for men and women, as it lets in through the back door all sorts of unchallenged stereotypes, for example, that women are less adept at using technology than men, men are more focused on careers than are women, and so on.

Questionnaire techniques focus too sharply on the decision made rather than how the decision was achieved, except insofar as these techniques account for decisions by the kind of factoring process I described earlier. It is no easy matter to find ways of getting at the process of ethical decision making. None of the studies related earlier is substantially reflective on the adequacies of their data gathering methods in this respect. Yet my arguments imply that, in the longer term, if we wish to gather data about real moral behaviour in the field we must turn to more anthropologically inspired methods, in particular, forms of ethnography and participant observation where the observer partici-pates and becomes part of the culture. Such an approach is likely to yield much richer accounts of the ethical decision process than can be gained solely by questionnaire type surveys. Additionally the use of observa-tional techniques is likely to move the focus of ethical behaviour away from decision making as the primary activity in acting morally. The emphasis on decision making is part of a mechanistic, Tayloristic view of management which regards a goal directed decision, achieved through a set of rational steps, as the primary activity of the manager. This puts the position rather starkly; nevertheless, the rationalist view of management decision making has proved extraordinarily tenacious and difficult to challenge. However, a significant alternative approach is now offered through critical management research (Alvesson and Willmott 2003) and if this can be coupled with the feminist research described in preceding chapters then we may look forward to some exciting new research perspectives.

Lack of theory

The arguments of the last three sections taken together suggest that existing work on empirical research on gender and computer ethics is substantially undertheorized both in terms of gender and in terms of moral behaviour in regard to computer ethics issues. Part of the problem is that the field is far more fragmented than I have made it appear in this review. By and large, the studies I discuss here do not appear to 'know' about one another. There is little sense of a tradition where one study builds on another; wheels are continually reinvented. A second aspect of the weak theoretical base of this research is displayed in the way that, for some of the papers reviewed, the authors end up making often unwarranted stereotypical generalizations which do not appear to follow from their research, by way of conclusion. For instance, Kreie and Cronan (1998) conclude from their study that women are more conservative in their ethical judgement than men, and that they might be best served by passive deterrents towards unethical behaviour, while men might require more substantive ethical deterrents.

It is hard to see why women's apparent tendency towards more ethical behaviour should make them more conservative. This does not follow from the research issues involved in these studies but starts to look like a stereotypical judgement about an expectation of men's more 'laddish' behaviour against a 'well behaved' female stereotype where women are seen as guardians of society's morals. It is against just such a stereotypical judgement that feminist ethics seeks to argue. Similarly Khazanchi (1995) concludes that women are better able to recognize 'and ultimately resist' unethical behaviour. However it is not clear why the ability to resist unethical behaviour should go alongside the ability to recognize it. In fact the opposite could well be the case. One is reminded of Oscar Wilde's observation, often attached to cookie jars as a deterrent: 'I can resist everything except temptation.' Once again this conclusion smacks of gender stereotypes of women's 'good' behaviour or moral virtues. Of course, one could argue that it hardly matters that women are seen as more morally virtuous than men. However, what happens if women are penalized for not living up to saintly expectations? A man stepping out of line might be let off the hook, if it is felt that he could not help his manly instincts, much in the way that Gurian (2003) wants to excuse men from housework. Yet there may be harsher sanctions for women who will not stay within the confines of traditional feminine behaviour.

But the most significant aspect of the undertheorizing problem relates to the way that this research makes so little reference to the, by now, quite substantial body of research on feminist ethics which could be used to help explain results. We can regard the citation of Gilligan's *In A Different Voice* (1982) as a kind of minimum level of reference to feminist ethics. Of the research reviewed earlier, only McDonald and Pak (1996), Mason and Mudrack (1996) and Bissett and Shipton (1999) refer to it and, indeed, it is the *only* work of feminist ethics referenced in any of the studies. I have noted the way that academic disciplines so often run on parallel tracks with little intersection. Even so, it is surprising how far these studies avoid feminist research.

Surprisingly, Kreie and Cronan (1998) make no reference either to Gilligan, nor to any other part of the large body of writing in feminist ethics which might have helped them explain their results. Indeed they make no attempt to explain *why* their research apparently reveals differences between men and women. This is all the more surprising given that Gilligan's work is very widely known over a number of domains, unlike other work in feminist ethics. Importantly, had Kreie and Cronan (ibid.) understood the debate surrounding Gilligan's work, which also centred round an empirical study, they would have been able to apply not only her arguments but also the criticism of her arguments to good effect on their own study. On the latter point, Larrabee (1993) notes that one of the criticisms of Gilligan's research was that she asked her respondents to work through a number of artificial case studies rather than observing them making real, live ethical decisions. As I have argued above, this is difficult research to undertake, it requires a time consuming observational approach rather than a survey and it raises unsettling questions as to the focus of so much management research on decision making.

A similar concern with Kreie and Cronan's study (1998) applies. Asking respondents to approve or disapprove of a scenario where software is copied illegally is likely to invoke disapproval in subjects. We all like to be seen as good software citizens. However, just like driving slightly above the speed limit, small scale software copying is rife and this study just does not get at subjects' moral decision making and the processes behind that decision making in real scenarios where they may be faced with the decision of whether or not to copy some desirable and readily available piece of software, where, on the face of it, no harm is done if the copy is made. Clearly questionnaires and interviews are problematic. Researchers can never be sure if people will respond to a 'live' situation in the same way as they have detailed in the questionnaire. Indeed as individual respondents none of us can be sure that we will behave the way we thought we would and the way we may have described, in all good faith, in a questionnaire.

Although these questions always dog social science data gathering there are special reasons why there are particular problems with gathering ethical data. This relates to the gap between 'is' and 'ought'. We may well recognize good ethical behaviour and therefore respond accordingly in a questionnaire, but we may not have the moral fibre to stick to our good intentions when faced with a real life situation. This is likely to be more apparent at the 'petty crime' end of the scale. For computer ethics small-scale software copying provides a good example of something which is not legal yet is endemic and causes perpetrators little loss of sleep.

This is much like the argument in Nissenbaum's 'Should I Copy My Neighbor's Software?' (1995). On the face of it, taking the viewpoint of standard ethical positions, the answer appears to be 'no'. But following Nissenbaum's detailed arguments shows that the answer is not nearly so clear cut when one probes the reasons for copying or not copying in more detail. The binary approval/disapproval in Kreie and Cronan (1998), or scales of approval and disapproval invoked by Likert scale studies, evoke too sharp a Yes/No response. Indeed, there are hints that the researchers found the responses too clear cut in the Kreie and Cronan (ibid.) study where the authors decided to go back and interview groups of students as to how they arrived at decisions. In other words these authors find themselves obliged to go back in order to probe the processes behind the decisions.

Scenarios – an alternative approach and its pitfalls

Against the concerns expressed earlier, Jacqueline Ofori-Amanfo (Ofori-Amanfo 1999; Adam and Ofori-Amanfo 2000) and I undertook a small empirical study in which we initially hoped to avoid some of the major pitfalls identified in statistical survey. (First person plural is used in the remainder of this section to indicate that two of us undertook the study. The interviews were conducted by Jacqueline.) Our pilot study was designed to explore the judgements that men and women make on scenarios relating to computer ethics problems. Given the small scale of the study, given the ambiguities of previous studies and given our increasing concern as to the validity of data gathering and analysis methods we believed that it was unlikely that we would be able to find conclusive evidence of different ethical beliefs amongst men and women respondents. We were not proved wrong. However I argue that the analysis of our study coupled with the concerns I have already raised point the way forward towards developing more considered studies of gender and computer ethics reasoning. In this work we were consciously avoiding a technique which relied on statistical analysis of questionnaires. Instead, we asked respondents to judge a series of ethical scenarios, utilizing a similar technique to that employed by Gilligan (1982).

A set of structured interviews was undertaken with 20 students (ten male, ten female) from a postgraduate IT conversion degree (i.e. designed to convert graduates from disciplines other than computing). Ages ranged from 21 to 40; there was a wide range of first degree subject ranging from engineering to humanities and a wide range of working experience some of which had included significant previous exposure to computers, some not. It could therefore be argued that this group displayed more diversity in age and experiences than, say, within a typical undergraduate population. Interviews lasted between 20 and 60 minutes and involved reading through a set of six fictitious scenarios, judging at the end of each whether the behaviour of the subject in the scenario was acceptable or not. We designed the scenarios so that each focused on a specific computer ethics problem, for example, hacking, obstruction of others' use of computing equipment, professional issues, email abuse and copying software. In designing these scenarios we were influenced by the scenarios of the Kreie and Cronan (1998) study, Gilligan's research (1982) and the examples used for illustration in the second edition of Johnson's computer ethics textbook (1994).

Analysing the first set of results revealed almost no difference between the responses of the interviewees. We could have tried to explain this in terms of the uniformity of the student sample used (after all I have criticized other studies for using a student audience), but, as we have argued above, our sample was much less uniform than is the norm for a student audience. We were tempted to explain it by arguing that our respondents were displaying considerable moral maturity. However a much more obvious reason presented itself. Despite the care with which we had designed the scenarios a number of our respondents pointed out that it was far too easy to spot the right answer! The scenarios we had developed were too black and white, too obviously right or wrong. This implied that it was necessary to revise the scenarios, making them richer and much more ambiguous.

Therefore a second set of more ambiguous scenarios was designed and we sought a wider audience of respondents, particularly interviewees in employment. The scenarios were shorter and there were fewer of them (four) as we were conscious that we were unlikely to have extensive access to busy professionals' time. We had also identified that it was important to find ways of involving the respondents in the reasoning within a scenario rather than having them somehow stand outside and pass judgement as in the manner of an impassively rational Kantian observer which was implied in the first set of examples. This time, rather than judging the actions of a fictitious 'James Hackworth', say, respondents became part of the scenario, in the second person. It appeared to be quite important to involve the respondents in the scenario, to give them a better chance of imagining what they would really do in a given situation. 'You' must decide whether to wipe out George's library fines; 'you' decide whether to lock the terminal to step outside to smoke a cigarette; 'you' decide whether to download software from the Internet.

The first set of scenarios had involved malicious intent and self-profit. The second set was designed to reflect more needy, desperate reasons for morally doubtful behaviour. In most of the scenarios the first person, that is, the desperate subjects were to be friends and relatives, whom the interviewees as second persons were invited to help or hinder, through morally questionable behaviour using computer technology. In one case the interviewee her/himself was to be the needy subject, that is, desperately needing to have a cigarette. Would s/he lock the terminal in a crowded student laboratory so no one else could use it?

The second set of respondents included 12 men and 12 women; all but nine were professionally employed. The employed respondents came from four organizations, one of which was a university and the other computing companies varying in size from less than ten employees to a large international corporation. The nine respondents not employed were research students involved in computing projects. All our respondents had considerable experience of using computers.

The techniques we employed in devising the second set of scenarios paid dividends in terms of separating out opinions amongst our respondents. They were not nearly as clear-cut as the first set. Yet, as expected, we found no clear split on gender lines. In any case, we were extremely reluctant to make any kind of categorical assertion on gender lines for such a small amount of data and for a sample which is tiny and biased heavily towards the ease with which we could obtain willing respondents. However we have found it useful to explore the kind of conceptual analysis which Gilligan makes in her ethical study. We ask whether ethics of care or indeed other ethical stances can be used to explain the responses of the individuals involved in the study. This is offered as an alternative conceptual approach towards analysis of responses, an approach which can complement statistical approaches and importantly can offer a better connection to theory. For reasons of space we focus on the analysis of one scenario.

Analyzing scenario 1 – hacking

'George needed help desperately. He owed the university library £30 in fines. He had got into this mess because he had been under such severe stress from his course that he had forgotten to renew his books. Coupled with this, he was worried about his mother. The bills were mounting up; he needed to buy train tickets to visit his severely ill mother. He couldn't ignore the problem any longer. You are a good friend of George's. He knew you had already broken into the library system to change your own account several times. George wanted you to break into the library computer system and delete the fine on his record making it look as though he had paid the fine. Would you do this?'

Respondents were asked whether they would break into the library system to wipe out George's fine. Five women and three men said 'yes' while seven women and nine men said 'no'. We draw no generalizations from these results in terms of gender. However it is notable that, as Chapter 7 describes, hacking is overwhelmingly associated with men. Kreie and Cronan's research (1998) also confirms the masculine associations of this activity. This was a view confirmed by several of our respondents during the interviews.

Coupled with this, were we to adopt the traditional ethical position towards hacking as in Johnson's textbook (1994) we would see hacking as a kind of masculine, freedom of speech, anti-establishment, anti-hero activity in tune with the more explicit analysis of authors such as Taylor (1999) in terms of implied masculinity. So strong are the masculine associations of hacking that, under such a view, it becomes difficult to explain why *any* women in our study were willing to hack into a computer system. Yet a number of women in our study indicated that, in those circumstances, they were willing to hack into the system. This may not be readily explicable under a traditional view of computer ethics and hacking, however, if we were to offer an explanation in terms of Gilligan's ethics of care, their position becomes more readily understandable.

Utilitarian ethics gives us no reason to prefer those close to us in deciding the greater good of society. We may weigh up the sum of human happiness, and if the balance is right, we may decide to hack into the system anyway, but it will not be on account of our feelings for George. Kantian ethics emphasizes doing the morally correct thing as an independent rational moral agent; feelings neither add nor subtract from the moral worthiness of the action. However under an ethic of care, those who chose to break into the system could be seen as empathizing with George's desperate plight and valuing their relationship with George over abstract moral rules and even concrete library rules or rules about access to computer networks. In other words, they were willing to put their feelings for their friend above the law. The ethics of care philosophy emphasizes thinking about people in moral decision making and the effect that moral decisions will have on others. Responsibilities are seen as more important than rights. Our hacking example has similarities with Gilligan's famous scenario (1982) relating to the question of whether a man should steal drugs to treat his dangerously ill wife. According to Kohlberg's standard scale of moral maturity (1981), respondents who felt that the man should steal the drugs were morally less mature, whereas, according to Gilligan, an ethic of care would imply that this was a more caring type of response. Similarly, in our example, those who chose to hack would score lower on Kohlberg's scale but would, nevertheless, be displaying a high degree of caring empathy.

Continuing with the hacking example for the moment, as in any fictitious example there are flaws that occur in the necessary simplification of the case. We offered our respondents the choice of whether to hack or not to hack but we did not offer them the opportunity to lend or give George 30 pounds. Similarly our own knowledge of university librarians demonstrates that they are rarely so hard-hearted as to ignore the plight of students with family problems.

Our experiences with this study show that with the size and scale of our approach we have been unable to avoid some of the pitfalls which we have found in other studies. Student groups offer a temptingly captive audience for academics supplying too uniform a population, unrepresentative of the workplace, and with a characteristic imbalance in power relationship. Surveys and interviews may not get to the heart of ethical reasoning in relation to ICTs. We were still focusing on ethical decisions despite our reservations about too sharp a focus on decision making. However we maintain that our second set of scenarios does at least offer a more sensitive data production method than the simpler questionnaires and scenarios offered by other studies. Nevertheless we are aware that our empirical study has not got to the heart of one of the questions that I have raised several times, namely that of power. In devising scenarios where we were inviting respondents to empathize with a fictitious person we were asking our respondents to act at a similar 'power level' to the subject with which they were relating. For example in the library example, George is a student and the respondent, as a friend, is probably a student by implication. It may well be difficult to design scenarios which illustrate and explicate power relations whilst at the same time asking respondents to find the necessary level of empathy. Much thought needs to go into the design of studies to explore these issues and a thoroughgoing exploration of power must be left to future studies. In offering an alternative ethic of care reading of a hacking scenario we have at least shown the possibility that feminist ethics can contribute to an analysis and understanding of issues relating to computer ethics. In any case this recognizes that care is part of the story, even though, just as in the examples relating to data protection law, it is not clear how care can be convincingly incorporated into computer ethics as things stand.

Conclusion – a plea for feminist ethics

In this chapter I have characterized two strands of gender and computer ethics research. The first casts women's exclusion from the computing industry as an ethical problem. Although this type of research has sometimes been criticized for its tendency towards liberalism, I argue that it is broadly beneficial to be reminded that the well-known problem of women's low numbers in computing is still very much in evidence. More pertinently, I have focused on empirical survey studies of men's and women's ethical decision making in relation to business ethics and computer ethics. Existing studies are seen to be problematic on several counts. They survey student populations, thus obscuring questions of power differentials between researcher and student; they accept uncritically that quantitative survey analyses of conceptual questions are meaningful; they focus on decisions made rather than the process of making decisions and they are undertheorized conceptually in relation to gender.

Part of the problem lies in the straitjacket which existing research paradigms offer but part also lies in the way that there is, as yet, no real tradition of gender and computer ethics research which builds upon past empirical and theoretical research. To begin to build such a tradition two related things are needed. First, we need to explore alternatives to the survey technique currently employed in so many empirical studies; in particular, I argue that we can expect to be more successful in uncovering the processes of ethical reasoning using observational and interviewing strategies. Second, we need to combine more thoroughgoing empirical studies with theorizing from the burgeoning literature of feminist ethics and related areas, as described in Chapters 2 and 3 to offer alternative readings of issues such as power and privacy. Only then can we begin to see what feminist ethics can offer computer ethics.

A central argument of this chapter is that research on gender and computer ethics is currently undertheorized. Part of this story is a concentration of research on statistical analyses of snapshots of ethical decisions where the focus on establishing gender differences deflects interest on the wider ways that gender is involved in computer ethics. I would like to argue that there are strong reasons to suggest that feminist ethics can be used to offer fruitful readings of gender and computer ethics problems. Despite its flaws, I hope that the small empirical study reported here can be seen as one example of an ethics of care analysis. We need to begin the process of exploring the alternative ethics that feminism can offer computer ethics. This can be used to understand how collectivist approaches to ethics can offer alternative readings of traditional computer ethics problems such as hacking, privacy and online harassment. This is the basis of the analysis offered in the next three chapters.

Second, feminist ethics brings a direct consideration of questions of power which are so often absent in traditional ethical theories. Utilitarianism argues for the greatest good for the greatest number. But who is to decide whether one good is better than another? We do not all have an equal say. Tong (1993) argues that it is powerful groups, usually white professional men, who are the decision makers in contemporary cost-benefit analyses. Questions of power are often disguised but they are crucial to the ethical decision making process. For instance, it was noted earlier that in the empirical studies discussed there is a disguised power relation between the university teachers undertaking the surveys and the students who take part. This suggests that a study of problems relating to Internet pornography and cyberstalking in terms of gender ethics might prove instructive as there are clear power imbalances involved. Issues of power must be rendered visible to make these and other areas understandable.

Finally, given that theories of feminist ethics rest on the hypothesis that women's moral decision making may be different from men's in important ways we need to understand the implications of this for computer ethics. In particular, we need to examine empirical evidence for a different ethical point of view amongst women insofar as it relates to the problems of computer ethics. So far this has barely been attempted in current gender and computer ethics studies.

Categorical claims that gender either definitely does or definitely does not make a material difference to moral reasoning relating to the use of computers somehow miss the point. More important is the question of whether or not the more collectivist 'ethics of care' approach to ethics and other feminist approaches to ethics can offer alternative analyses and perhaps better ways to tackle computer ethics problems.

6
Internet Dating, Cyberstalking and Internet Pornography: Gender and the Gaze

Introduction: feminist approaches to computer ethics problems

Chapter 5 argued for two broad directions in tackling the question of developing more solidly theorized approaches towards gender in computer ethics. One line of study involves undertaking empirical studies and analysing these in terms of theories from feminist ethics as in the empirical study reported in the preceding chapter. Additionally there is a clear need to turn the spotlight onto known problems in computer ethics and to reanalyse these from the point of view of a more thorough gender analysis than has usually been made, grounded in aspects of feminist theory. This is the approach taken in this chapter in relation to Internet dating, cyberstalking and Internet pornography and in Chapters 7 and 8 in relation to hacking and privacy respectively. This direction is particularly pertinent in relation to problems which involve the body, privacy violations physical or otherwise of bodies and bodily spaces, watching of and gazing at bodies. This is because of the long standing tradition, prevalent in Western philosophy, of associating bodily matters primarily with women rather than men. There is a tendency for advocates of cyberculture, from roboticists to cyberpunk science fiction writers, to ignore and even deny the primacy of the body. This reflects a turn to the virtual, which, at its extreme, sees the body as mere 'meat' (Adam 1998). At the same time, the body has become one of the major topics in the wide ranging literature of contemporary feminist writing (Diprose 1994; Gatens 1996). In summary, and speaking broadly, feminist authors have noted the way that the role of the body has been written out of much of Western philosophy where the mind has assumed the primary rational instrument and this further underscores the long running association of masculinity with the mind and reason and femininity with body and irrationality. These views have been the basis of a substantial critique and feminist revision of epistemology (Alcoff and Potter 1993). If the body has been left out of traditional epistemology, it also appears to be largely absent from traditional ethical theories. We are left with the uncomfortable feeling that Kant's moral agents may not have physical bodies. With his emphasis on pure reason, Rumsey (1997) notes that Kant's isolated and self-seeking adult individuals neglect the community and biology. Kant leaves biology and the body to women where his account of human agency is built on women's exclusion.

This suggests that we may have to look to applied ethics to bring the body, its surveillance and violations of its privacy, back into ethical thinking. Health and bioethics are obvious places to look for a more body-centred ethics, yet we should note feminist critiques of the tendency in modern biology, for instance, as evidenced by the human genome project, to reduce the body to a coded, digital expression (Haraway 1991). These concerns are equally important in critiques of science and technology ethics where recent works (Spier 2001) seem to treat the body as a part of biological engineering. They are especially pertinent to computer ethics, which must work hard to reclaim the body that has so often been written out of the script of computer scientists and cyberculture commentators.

If philosophy has a tendency to equate women with the bodily realm, it may well be instructive to look afresh at gender relations to reclaim or reinvent the body, certainly within computer ethics. By arguing that it may be instructive to bring feminist theory to computer ethics problems, as much feminist thinking has centred on the body this may also go some way to reclaiming the body in computer ethics. For instance, in regard to topics such as privacy, we may begin to think in terms of bodily invasions of privacy, where bodies are watched, looked at or subject to surveillance or indeed where bodies are actually violated and the violations are watched online. At the same time we must acknowledge that concepts of privacy may be different for men and women and may vary according to age, class and other cultural and historical variables as discussed in Chapter 8. Therefore my theoretical position involves attempting to weave together a feminist approach to privacy, bodies and the concept of the gaze in relation to the related areas of Internet dating, cyberstalking and Internet pornography, focusing on Internet paedophile rings in the latter area.

An additional area of feminist theory which I wish to bring to the analysis is a feminist notion of the 'gaze'. This must be understood as an embodied gaze rather than as an anonymous 'view from nowhere' (Nagel 1986). It has both a gazer and a gazed-upon subject. Gazing or watching is not neutral; it is a type of surveillance and can imply violation. It is immediately clear that both cyberstalking and Internet paedophile rings have some sense of a gender dimension, for example, most cyberstalkers are men, most victims women. In Internet dating, men and women are involved in putative relationships that can involve the whole spectrum of sexualities. However, as I shall describe shortly, there is evidence to suggest that women, girls and children in general are most at risk from exploitation. Most individuals involved in Internet child pornography are men. However, while the predominance of men as perpetrators is well known and has been adduced in prominent policy documents (Reno 1999), almost nothing seems to be made of this fact by the policy makers who write such documents. Additionally, policy documents fail to address the issue that, in finding the cause of the problem and ways to counter it, the question of gender might be highly relevant. However, if we are to get beyond a simple assertion that most criminal activity is perpetrated by men, we must begin to see how these specific activities can be analysed in terms of the ways in which men are constructed as perpetrators and women and children often constructed as victims.

Given that the activities I describe are deemed at minimum anti-social, and often actually criminal, the intention is that laying the ground for a deeper gender analysis can ultimately inform the construction of policy, although the route might be less than clear at present. This is essentially the bit before the ethics, policy, legislation chain which I discussed in Chapter 4. How do we ensure that a feminist voice is heard, at the beginning of this process, especially in relation to problems in computer ethics, such as those explored in this chapter, and which contain a clear gender dimension which is yet to be adequately explored?

How far can potentially radical ideas be adequately accommodated in a conventional policy setting without losing their force? Ideas appearing too radical will be ignored; watered down, they may be too anodyne for their original purposes. I have no doubt that this explains some of the reasons why a feminist voice, with a convincing gender analysis is seldom heard in relation to policy matters. I expand these arguments with relation to cyberstalking in detail, and Internet paedophile rings more briefly, both of which currently cause much concern in the media. As Internet dating, cyberstalking and Internet paedophile rings all involve violations of privacy this gives a rationale for considering the ways in which different conceptions of privacy can be seen as gendered, and how the gaze can be incorporated into our ideas of privacy. More especially, the ways in which virtual and non-virtual violations of the body enforce authority and reinforce the submission of the victim are woven into a feminist analysis.

Recent feminist thinking argues against a 'victim' mentality, preferring to see ways in which, even if they cannot in many circumstances achieve empowerment, women can become active agents in resisting violations of their privacy. The Foucauldian notion of the 'gaze', and its ambiguity in reinforcing or resisting submission is useful to explore here and the ways in which the return gaze may be incorporated into an ethics of resistance of invasions of privacy, bodily or virtual. Clearly the gaze is used to terrible effect in Internet child pornography cases where the difficulty of finally removing all copies of the images from computer networks means that others may continue to gaze upon the images long after the original perpetrator has been brought to justice. However, whilst the notion of the return gaze may be fruitful to explore with regard to women who have been cyberstalked and women who are involved in Internet pornography, it would seem almost facile to offer the gaze as a means of resistance in cases of child abuse on the Internet. In these cases it is rather the gaze of the police and other authorities in the process of bringing offenders to book, which potentially reverses the power of the abuser's gaze.

Internet pornography, and especially child pornography is rarely the topic of academic discourse. Not surprisingly we are revolted by crimes against children. Nevertheless, it is important that a critical voice is added to the discussion, both to fight against the crime itself, and against knee-jerk 'witch-hunts'. My discussion revolves around the events leading up to the sentencing of seven men in early 2001 for membership of the so-called 'Wonderland Club', an international paedophile ring who traded three-quarters of a million images of child pornography on the Internet (Panorama 2001). In a second example, a media report of a series of arrests of Internet paedophiles after a lengthy police surveillance suggests that there is a problem on a massive international scale (Guardian 2001). This second example involves images on newsgroups which appear to be freely available, even to minors, rather than the apparently more underground activities of the 'Wonderland Club'. A third, more recent and even more substantial example involves 'Operation Ore' (BBC 2003) where over 1,000 arrests were made.

The debate over Internet pornography can, in some senses, be seen as a contemporary reflection of the much longer running debates over freedom of speech vs censorship in relation to a more conventional adult sex industry which I discussed in Chapter 2. Internationally, laws vary as to the legality of adult pornography. On the Internet some authors regard adult Internet pornography as a business, a stimulus to e-commerce whilst others regard it as but an extension of women's conventional exploitation in the sex industry (Lane 2000). Authors such as MacKinnon and Dworkin, from the anti-pornography feminist movement claim a link between pornography and violence, yet some argue that it is not clear that the link has been proved definitively (Lane 2000). However, child pornography is regarded as qualitatively different. It is almost universally illegal and the link between paedophilia and child pornography seems incontrovertible (Guardian 2001), with experts claiming that at least a third of those viewing child pornography are also involved in child abuse. In addition, we now need to confront the possibility that the ease of use and relative anonymity afforded by the Internet leads some individuals to join with pathological Internet communities and acts as a further spur towards their committing terrible crimes. We have the possibility of children being groomed for abuse and abuse taking place online and relayed to others in a video stream.

Internet dating

Using the Internet to find partners is not necessarily always problematic and, judging by the witty titles of some of the self-help guides, for example, *Cast Your Net* (Fagan 2001), it may be profitable in a search for love or whatever else it is one seeks. Not surprisingly, there are few academic studies but those that are available do not paint a very positive picture. A Taiwan study of Internet dating by teenage girls clearly links the phenomenon to sexual abuse and date rape (Hwang and Yang 2004). A US study, which surveyed women over a wider age range, found that there were a number of negative behaviours experienced by some of the women in the study including stalking, unwanted phone calls and letters. Jerin and Dolinsky (2001) conclude that while the Internet opens up a wider choice in forming relationships it also offers new ways for women to be victimized. The more women used Internet dating, the more likely they were to be stalked. A 'dangers of Internet dating' website (www.dangersofinternetdating.com, consulted 18 August 2004) relays the perils of mail-order brides and net addiction, contains stories of women who were let down by men they met over the Internet and contains links to a number of stories of rape or murder, almost always relating to women or girls as victims, resulting from meetings arranged over the Internet. It does not make very happy reading. However, to some extent, the perils are those which existed in pre-Internet life – the dangers of trusting strangers, and so on. However there is always a certain irony in the fear we have of strangers, fear that women have and fear for the safety of children. Whether adult or child, one is more likely to be murdered by someone already known, often a family member, than by a stranger. Men are more likely to be attacked by a stranger than are women. Nevertheless we must consider whether there are new behaviours, or new forms of old behaviours, which are especially perilous, linked to Internet dating. One such behaviour is cyberstalking, which I describe in general terms in the following section. After this description I relate cyberstalking to the more general problem of online harassment. Cyberstalking examples are described and subject to a feminist analysis. Following this, I consider third-party cyberstalking and the concept of the 'gaze'. Finally, Internet pornography is considered in terms of the 'gaze'.

Cyberstalking

Cyberstalking is the term which has been coined to describe the online variant of the much older crime of stalking (Meloy 1998). Whilst media reports abound (e.g. see USAToday 1999), until recently, academic discussion has been somewhat thin on the ground (Tavani and Grodzinsky 2001; Adam 2002; Spitzberg and Hoobler 2002). The upshot of this is, first, that, otherwise theoretically sophisticated authors working on the psychological aspects of stalking, fail to understand some of the important ramifications of the phenomenon, for example, in terms of the possibilities for 'third-party cyberstalking' (Meloy 1998) where the perpetrator steals the 'virtual identity' of the victim to incite others to stalk and second, that the gendered nature of the problem has yet to be probed to any depth. Indeed it is surprising what little attention the gendered nature of the problem has attracted.

On the former point, Meloy (ibid., p. 10) an acknowledged expert on stalking, defines cyberstalking thus: 'The Internet as a means of stalking can be used for two criminal functions: (1) to gather private information on the target to further a pursuit; and (2) to communicate (in real time or not) with the target to implicitly or explicitly threaten or induce fear.' However he fails to understand the ready potential of the Internet for third-party stalking, that is, the ability of the perpetrator to use features of the Internet, often to assume the identity of the victim online, to induce others to stalk or harass the victim in some way, a possibility which is much harder in the 'offline' world. Similarly, Spitzberg's and Hoobler's pilot studies (2002) measuring cyberstalking victimization, although including it in their categories of cyberstalking behaviour, do not focus on third-party activity to any level of detail.

Nevertheless, other authors have begun to describe the complexity of the cyberstalking phenomenon, particularly in respect to efforts at legislation. Packard (2000) explores current US state and federal stalking laws and how they relate to cyberstalking. A perennial problem with legislation concerning Internet crime in general is how to apply it across state and national boundaries. Current US federal stalking law is designed to apply only to stalkers who follow their victims across state lines. Clearly this makes little sense in an online environment, hence an amendment to the law prohibits certain forms of communication and protects victims from cyberstalkers who influence others to harass the victims.

The work of Bocij and co-researchers (Bocij and McFarlane 2003; Bocij and Sutton 2004) represents the most sustained research on the phenomenon to date. Some useful concepts are brought to the table through this research which makes it clear that we cannot simply switch off as cyberstalking is every bit as dangerous as stalking. Bocij well understands the capacity of cyberstalkers to use proxy forms of stalking. Some things are different from traditional stalking. Cyberstalkers are far less likely to know their victims than are traditional stalkers, hence they may not display the same obsessions. In any case the Internet affords the opportunity for anonymity. Cyberstalking against organizations is found and this could be seen as a form of 'hacktivism' where an organization is attacked to make a political point (Bocij and McFarlane 2003). Disappointingly, this otherwise detailed research makes nothing of the gender issue in relation to cyberstalking.

Online sexual harassment

The more extreme examples of cyberstalking are best introduced through a brief consideration of the more general behaviour from which it derives. Spitzberg and Hoobler (2002, p. 73), in an analysis which is remarkably gender blind, describe it in terms of its relationship to obsessive relational intrusion (ORI). However, I argue that an analysis from feminist ethics should start from a consideration of online sexual harassment. Apart from my own efforts, to date, only Ellison (2001) seems willing to couch cyberstalking in terms of a gendered form of harassment. The prominent feminist legal theorist, MacKinnon (1979, p. 1) writing in the 1970s, defined sexual harassment as '... the unwanted imposition of sexual requirements in the context of a relationship of unequal power. Central to the concept is the use of power derived from one social sphere to lever benefits or impose deprivations in another.' Such harassment can take place in many environments including the workplace, but also by means of chat rooms and Internet dating contact. Sexual harassment is often understood to involve unwanted explicit sexual attention. However it should be noted that, in a world where power relationships most often place men in a superior position to women it describes, more generally, behaviour by men, often in the workplace, which demeans women or otherwise makes them feel uncomfortable and which arises, at least in some part, because of the differential power relationships between the genders. Of course women can sexually harass men, but it is more usual for men to harass women in this way. For these reasons it would be wrong to treat sexual harassment as somehow purely a women's problem, casting them simply as victims when the issue appears much broader. This also acknowledges that, although at the macro level women may be oppressed in patriarchal structures, at the micro level individual men may feel just as powerless and oppressed as individual women. But the starting point from sexual harassment with its recognition of differentials in power is important. Focusing on ORI, in a gender blind analysis of cyberstalking, fails to heed the issue of power in stalking behaviour.

Empirical studies of online sexual harassment paint a complex and ambivalent picture. On the one hand there is evidence of women feeling empowered by their use of information technology and actively resisting paternalistic protection (Riley 1996). Yet it must be recognized that only relatively few women in privileged positions, with access to education and technology, may take part in this empowerment. To balance this, on the other hand, some distinctly negative experiences are reported. Herring's study of interactions on the Internet (1996) reinforces Winner's claim (1997) that computer-mediated communication does not neutralize gender in the way that cyberlibertarian communities assume. Instead Internet communications reinforce and magnify stereotypical gendered behaviours rather than smoothing them out.

The liberal values encapsulated in Winner's conception of cyberlibertarianism and less explicitly in many traditional accounts of computer-mediated communications (Ess 1996b) start from a position of assuming free and equal interactions and that everyone has equal opportunities on the Internet. Furthermore, they assume the technologically determinist position that the spread of Internet usage is inevitable that we have to take part or be swept aside by the technological tide. If we look to individualistic, traditional ethical theories little additional insight is to be had from their analyses. Although they might condemn online sexual harassment, they offer little hope for understanding why such behaviour occurs as they have no analysis to offer along gender lines. This, in turn, implies that they offer little hope of effective policy measures to counter the problematic behaviour.

Cyberstalking examples

Herring (1996) argues that online sexual harassment tends to mirror the levels of harassment that women often find in real life. However, a more extreme version of online sexual harassment, in the shape of cyberstalking, has recently reached the attention of both the media, government and law enforcement agencies. In discussing this phenomenon, and relating it to women, my intention is not to deny the very real dangers which both stalking and cyberstalking represent for children. However, the focus here is on studying stalking behaviour where women are usually victims. This section outlines three contemporary cyberstalking cases where women were involved. Certain aspects of these cases are compared to an example where a man won compensation after being defamed on the Internet, an example which has certain congruences with the cyberstalking cases described. I will argue that the reactions to cyberstalking in the media and at government level, particularly in the USA, give cause for concern. This is because typical liberal and deterministic views of ethics encapsulated therein offer few paths into the root causes of cyberstalking.

With the onset of interest in activity on the Internet, the term 'cyberstalking' was coined to describe stalking behavior executed by means of some aspect of ICT. It is not always possible to draw too fine a line between digital and traditional stalking as, for instance, the telephone has typically been a tool of the stalker. However, with the advent of Caller Identification on telephone services, stalking, in this case used to locate and attack the victim, has been identified as the most vivid threat to privacy posed by this technology (Case 2000). However cyberstalking more usually involves the use of the Internet to perpetrate some aspect of stalking behaviour. This often includes anonymous impersonation, and therefore defamation, of the victim's character, something which is relatively easy, and anonymous for the perpetrator, on the Internet, given, for instance, anonymous remailers, but more difficult in life offline. The urgency of the perceived problem has prompted a rush of legislation and other interest culminating in former US Vice-President Al Gore's commissioning of a report on the subject by the Attorney General (Reno 1999) in the summer of 1999.

Unfortunately, despite a number of high-profile cases having been reported both in print media and on the Internet, the topic has yet to receive systematic analysis against an appropriate theoretical framework which includes gender as central construct as I note above. An appropriate theoretical framework must include a combination of an understanding of the psychological phenomenon of stalking, an understanding of Internet crime, and an appropriate feminist analysis of privacy which acknowledges that the problem affects women and men in different ways.

Meloy's book (1998) comprehensively covers the topic of stalking. However, in discussing cyberstalking, as noted above, he fails to grasp the potential that the Internet offers for stalking and harassment by impersonation, especially the ways in which others can be enticed into stalking behaviour, in other words the potential for 'third party' harassment and stalking. He concludes instead that the problem is largely confined to bombardment with unwanted email. This seriously underestimates the variety and scale of stalking and harassing behaviours made possible through the use of Internet technologies. In the examples below the extension to invasions of privacy afforded by impersonation in cyberstalking cases will become clear.

Three brief examples illustrate the main features of the problem. Hitchcock's experience of cyberstalking is a paradigm example (Mingo 2000). As an author of children's books she quickly saw the potential of the Internet in her professional life. When she first went online she contacted Woodside Literary Agency who were widely advertised in the Usenet groups in which she participated. Woodside accepted her as a client and then immediately asked for up-front fees. She was immediately suspicious that the organization was of doubtful legitimacy. She began to post warnings to fellow Internet writers on Usenet groups and she was one of several authors to do so. Woodside never responded to the authors' queries but continued to 'spam' its advertisements over the Internet. Although Hitchcock was hardly their only critic, Woodside began posting attacks on her into the 'misc.writing' Usenet group and posted claims that she was a pornographer over various newsgroups. After this, counterfeit messages were posted in her name all over the Internet. These messages of an explicit sexual nature invited people to contact her or come to her house. The phone rang incessantly.

Eventually a friend of Hitchcock's was able to gather enough evidence from the headers of the counterfeit message headers to identify Woodside as the perpetrators, and a lawsuit was filed.

A second case, which bears similarities to the Hitchcock case, involved a man from California who was jailed for six years for offences resulting from cyberstalking (Guardian 1999). Having been spurned by a woman, he assumed her identity and posted personal information about her, including her address, in Internet sex chat rooms where he claimed sado-masochistic fantasies in her name. As a result of this a number of men tried to break into her house. The man thought that his anonymity was preserved on the Internet. He was eventually caught after the victim's father spent hours on the Internet posting messages that he hoped would lure the stalker. When the stalker eventually made contact, the woman's father turned the case over to the FBI resulting in prosecution.

A third example, involves Brail's experience (1996) of harassment bordering on cyberstalking. Her rationalization of what happened does not just include the fact that she was a woman online but also because 'I dared to speak out in the common space of the Internet, Usenet' (ibid., p. 144). Brail became embroiled in a 'flame war' on a news group about underground magazines, having defended another woman who had been verbally attacked by a number of men for her views on an alternative women's publication. She too started to become the victim of anonymous obscene postings. The perpetrator posted her name and details on sex chat rooms and so other people began contacting her. Finally the anonymous stalker threatened to visit her house. Understandably she began to feel fearful for her personal safety. However he had left a loophole in the header of his anonymous email and she was able (after having felt forced to learn both self-defence and UNIX) to trace him and email him back to his address whereupon the threats stopped. The alleged perpetrator was never formally identified nor brought to book.

Third-party cyberstalking

The three cases outlined above illustrate the complexities of what is involved in 'third-party' or proxy cyberstalking. In common with the Internet paedophile cases it also becomes clear that the capabilities afforded by the technology can act as a spur in the perpetrators' behaviour when it is so easy to do and, apparently so easy to remain anonymous.

In all three cases the victim was a woman. In the Hitchcock case the perpetrators appear to be a group of people, one of whom was a woman; in the other cases the perpetrators were male. From the published accounts above we know that the 'third-party' stalkers, those who were incited to contact the victims, were male. It is acknowledged that the majority of cyberstalking perpetrators are male and the majority of victims female (Meloy 1998; Reno 1999). Yet, to date, despite our knowledge of the phenomenon growing more sophisticated through research such as that of Bocij (Bocij and McFarlane 2003; Bocij and Sutton 2004), still commentators seemingly fail to make use of this aspect in their analyses, indeed missing the point that understanding the gendered nature of the phenomenon is crucial to achieving convincing explanations of why it occurs.

Third-party stalking would seem to be a case in point. Given that, as discussed above, we are only just beginning to understand the range of third-party cyberstalking possibilities and given the gender breakdown of first- and third-party perpetrators and victims, I argue that it is vital to construct an analysis of this phenomenon which places gender centre stage. In the following section I begin an analysis of cyberstalking and Internet harassment, more generally before formulating a feminist analysis of third-party cyberstalking.

A feminist analysis of cyberstalking and Internet dating harassment

This section analyses the cyberstalking phenomenon, and issues relating to Internet dating harassment, through an examination of the above examples in relation to feminist ethics and related theory. It should be emphasized that this is intended to point out the potential to form a feminist analysis of computer ethics problems rather than an attempt to draw firm conclusions from what is, as yet, a fairly slender gallery of empirical cases on cyberstalking at least. In all three cases the victim is a woman. In one case the perpetrator is definitely male; in the Woodside case it is a small group of men and women and in the Brail case the perpetrator styled himself 'Mike' and is assumed to be male by the victim. In all the cases the victims and/or friends and associates used some aspect of the Internet to help track down the perpetrator, in other words they were able to use the same technology that had been used to stalk them.

It is notable that both Mingo's article (2000) on the Woodside case and Brail's description of her own experiences (1996) explicitly use the rhetoric of 'frontier justice'. It is important not to overstate this point as, in the examples above, those who chose to go to the police were given help. But there is an element in their rhetoric which points to a suggestion that their cases stood somewhat outside the traditional legal arena. Indeed the notion of frontier, and even 'Wild West' has proved a powerful metaphor for commentators writing on Internet ethics and hacking (Sterling 1992; Brail 1996; Ludlow 1996; Kramer and Kramarae 1997; Jordan and Taylor 2004). But if the Internet is an electronic frontier then, by analogy, the justice meted out therein may have to go beyond the normal notions of justice. The existence of a frontier implies that special measures must be taken against those who attack that frontier and justice, perhaps, may be taken into the hands of those defending the frontier who may be far removed geographically, and here conceptually, from the normal channels of law and order. This position is justified given the efforts of victims' friends and families in these cases. For instance, Hitchcock enlisted the help of a 'volunteer cyberposse'.

Only in the California case is there the traditional 'spurned lover'. The other two cases are unusual in the aetiology of stalking in that the women became victims not as ex-lovers or distant objects of desire but rather because they chose to speak up publicly, on the Internet, about perceived injustices. This does tie in with the way that cyberstalkers are less likely to know their victims than traditional stalkers (Bocij and McFarlane 2003). They then became the victims of those they were criticizing. Indeed 'daring to speak out' is the main thrust of Brail's rationalization of her experiences (1996). This signals something quantitatively different about the ability of individuals to 'speak out' on the Internet and what the effect of their speaking out might be. Offline it is more difficult for individuals to make their voices heard in tradi-tional media such as newspapers. Online one may reach hundreds or thousands of people by the press of a button. Tannen (1992) and Spender (1980) argue that in public forums, such as business meetings, women contribute verbally less than men, and where they do contribute as much as a man they are perceived as doing too much talking. I make the tentative suggestion that this phenomenon may translate into Internet communication and women making strongly worded contri-butions to discussion groups may be seen, by some, as 'talking too much'. This confirms one of the assertions of Bocij and McFarlane (2003) who are anxious that cyberstalking be seen as a qualitatively different phenomenon from stalking. One reason is that cyberstalkers are far less likely to know their victims than are traditional stalkers.

Second, traditional stalking episodes typically last much longer, months into years. Whereas we have a picture of a traditional stalker obsessing about his victim for years Bocij and McFarlane (ibid.) are suggesting that the same sort of profile may not fit the same proportion of cyberstalkers. Could it be that some cyberstalking, at least, can be seen as swift, aggressive male response to women claiming a space and speaking up on the Internet?

Yet, women are not supposed to fight back or to speak up. Thinking of Internet dating, the dangers are portrayed very much in terms of women becoming victims, either in terms of murder, harassment or most commonly being seen and seeing themselves as the victims of 'con' artists, of men who dumped them, or who turned out to be married after all (see examples on www.dangersofinternetdating.com). Of course, this aspect of women being tricked by men is hardly confined to Internet relationships. However, it is possible that we do not see the level of retaliation that I am suggesting sometimes happens in cyberstalking cases by women and their friends and families, in the case of injustices meted out in the Internet dating game as women Internet daters have already put themselves in a vulnerable position by going on an 'Internet date' in the first place. Maybe some women feel that this kind of harassment is all they deserve. In any case the rhetoric of websites that offer advice is very much in terms of how women should protect themselves (we see the same sort of rhetoric in texts relating to protection against cyberstalking) as if there is a tacit expectation that men will always behave badly and that women might just be asking for it unless they take adequate precautions to protect themselves. The responsibility to avoid the problems, therefore, is pushed onto the individual woman rather than being viewed as the responsibility of society at large. And as in real life, when something does go wrong women may blame themselves. However, the story seems somewhat different from the cyberstalking cases I report in this chapter where there is a level of agency in women who fight back.

As cyberstalking cases are reported in the media there is a flurry of response much of it reflecting the 'technology out of control' position, a dominant theme of technological determinism. For instance, in a UK newspaper article (Guardian 1999) Maxey, working for the San Diego anti-stalking strike force is quoted as saying: 'The computer has become the new tool of terror ... It's going to be an uphill battle – and we're going to have to run to catch up.'

A press report (USAToday 1999) quotes former US Vice-President, Gore: 'the Internet has inadvertently become a sinister new avenue for carrying out violence against women' and couches cyberstalking in terms of attitudes towards women and domestic violence. 'These are not just family matters, these are crimes', Gore states. 'As a society, as a country, as a national family, we don't have to put up with this kind of abuse, and we will not' (USAToday 1999).

Clearly men and women can be the victims of conventional stalking and cyberstalking. Within the typology of stalking behaviour (StalkingBehavior 2000) one substantial category involves the obsessive personality who fixates on a figure of authority whom the stalker regards as above them in status, for example, a medical doctor or a media figure. In this case the stalker can be a man but is often a woman fixating on a man. Similarly, Case's descriptions of stalking and murder concerning some aspect of Caller Identification on telephone networks (2000) involved both men and women as victims and perpetrators.

In all three cyberstalking examples above, the perpetrators impersonate the victim in anonymous Internet postings. This is a new twist in the aetiology of stalking, as yet not generally recognized by most existing authorities (Meloy 1998). The effect is not only to defame the victim but, in addition, because the postings contain some kind of porno-graphic invitation, they caused others to display threatening behaviour towards the victim, a phenomenon described above as 'third-party cyber-stalking'. This threatening behaviour is not confined to the Internet, as the victim's telephone number and address are given, unwanted visits and telephone calls are made. So the cyberstalker can hide behind the anonymity of the Internet and, at the same time, can trigger real life stalking behaviour in others, where the stalking activity is magnified as others are encouraged to stalk. At the same time, the victim's identity is being 'stolen' as she is impersonated in chat rooms and user groups.

Considering feminist analyses of privacy, the irony is that whilst these women's privacy was decreased, those perpetrating the behaviour actually enjoyed more privacy than would have been possible in the real world version of stalking. Apart from anything else this further underscores arguments against technological determinism in that we cannot predict, in advance, the ways in which a new technology will be used, even for anti-social ends.

Of course, men can also be the victims of anonymous, defamatory Internet postings, posted in their name. Yet it is interesting to consider a recent case involving a man which shows features which are some-what different from the women's cases above. In this example, a physi-cist, Laurence Godfrey, successfully obtained a small amount of damages but a more substantial amount of legal expenses in a libel case against the Internet service provider (ISP), Demon, in the UK (Yahoo 2000). The Godfrey case is quite complex and long running; he was involved in a number of actions for defamation. He was a contributor to a news group about the politics of Thailand. Anonymous postings containing 'squalid, obscene and defamatory' material were posted in his name. He asked Demon to remove the forged material on several occasions but they did not. Hence he brought the case to court and obtained a token level of damages but also his substantial legal costs of £200,000. He is reported to have taken the action in a bid to force Internet service providers to behave more responsibly. However, the legal situation is complex and it seems very unlikely that he would have won his case in the USA where legislation treats the Internet more akin to a telephone network (i.e. no control over contents), than as a broadcast medium, such as television, where controls may be imposed.

There are important parallels and distinctions to be made between the Godfrey case and the three examples I use above. Godfrey was anonymously defamed over the Internet in a similar manner to the victims in the cyberstalking cases. Yet, although the women were seen and appeared to see themselves as victims in some sense, he is not portrayed as a victim by the media, and there is no evidence that his case was construed as an example of cyberstalking. Indeed we hear little of the first-party perpetrators in the Godfrey case. The story is cast much more in terms of the victory of the individual over the might of the powerful Internet service provider.

It would be wrong to draw concrete generalizations as to men's and women's experiences from these four examples, nevertheless they stand as case studies which can be used to air the issues involved. What the case studies do not, on their own, reveal is that despite the fact that both women and men can be victims of stalking and cyberstalking, the majority of reported cyberstalking cases involve women as victims and men as perpetrators. However, the report of former Attorney General, Reno (1999) which is still one of the major governmental responses to the phenomenon, other than recording this fact, makes virtually nothing more of this, seemingly treating it as an accidental rather than fundamental aspect of such behaviour. The report suggests the following:

> ... the first line of defense will involve industry efforts that educate and empower individuals to protect themselves against cyberstalking and other online threats, along with prompt reporting to law enforcement agencies trained and equipped to respond to cyberstalking incidents. (Ibid., p. 2)

The Reno report advocates that cyberstalking is to be tackled by an industry–law enforcement agencies partnership. Additionally, online providers must educate their customers to avoid unwanted and threatening messages and must respond promptly and effectively when threatening behaviour is reported to them. 'Self-protection' is the term emphasized (ibid., p. 11).

Similarly, policy makers and law enforcement agencies have a duty to ensure appropriate legislation is in place, to enable their own training, to share information across states and internationally, to build up expertise, to work with victims' groups and to co-operate effectively with industry. 'Both industry and law enforcement benefit when crime over the Internet is reduced. In particular, the Internet industry benefits significantly whenever citizen and consumer confidence and trust in the Internet is increased' (ibid., p. 12).

The former Attorney General's report offers a number of traditional, liberal ethical measures. In counteracting cyberstalking, the role of industry is emphasized in constructing a solution in terms of free market economics. When coupled with the last quote, this purveys a strongly utilitarian argument, which looks to the good of the majority rather than the suffering of the individual. The expectation is that industry should help with the problem as it makes good business sense for them to do so, not because we expect them to care about their customers as individuals. Although the report advocates a much more socially responsible position, there are faint echoes of an excessive faith in the free market which resonates with Winner's cyberlibertarianism (1997). Additionally, there are definite resonances with the way that a substantial part of the impetus for getting data protection law onto the statute books derives from requirements for free flow of data for electronic commerce. We could be forgiven for thinking that protection of our privacy must always stand in relation to the needs of business.

Understandably no one would advocate that industry bears no responsibility. As the Godfrey case shows, the Internet service provider was slow in responding to his requests to remove offensive messages when it could easily have done so. Similarly no one would advocate that we should *not* try to protect ourselves against cyberstalking and other threatening behaviour. The three cyberstalking examples above show the various measures that the individuals took in protecting themselves. We would all hope for protection from the law, although in the examples above, the victims and their friends and families seemed to do much work in relation to their cases over and above a reliance on official sources of justice. There are a number of Internet groups such as 'Cyberangels' and WHOA (Women Halting Online Abuse) (Bocij and Sutton 2004) which again suggests that women are organizing to stand up to cyberstalking and abuse. This could imply that this is an area where it is hard to make the claim stick that women's rights are being violated, as per the arguments of feminist legal theory. Just as important is the additional complication that much of the legislation is new and may need further revision as the phenomenon is better understood and as case law is accumulated (Packard 2000).

The official version firmly advocates a mixture of trust in free market utilitarian arguments in relation to industry with a strong measure of self-protection and trust in the law, in other words the traditional forces of capitalism and state. This must also be balanced with free speech, a defining concept of liberalism. In the case of Internet dating, traditional responses also seem to be coupled with the notion of women paying the price if they do not take sufficient safeguards. This parallels the idea of women 'asking for it' if they go out alone late at night. Maybe they are not supposed to go out alone on the Internet. Hence the balance between industry and legislative bodies in the education and empowerment of the individual is seen as the solution to the problem. However it is hard to see how such measures could be effective when the strongly gendered nature of the problem has not been fully understood in the first place. An argument from feminist ethics and related theory could, at least, help us to understand why the behaviour takes place and can begin to suggest policy measures to tackle the problem.

A firm separation between public and private spheres is a cornerstone of the liberal tradition. Historically this can be seen as having important implications for the concept of privacy and how it relates differently to women and to men. For instance, only after a long fight, well into the nineteenth century, did married women win the legal right to property, person and children. But as MacKinnon (1987) points out, in the private sphere, traditionally the domain of women and the family, women may have few rights as the state is reluctant to interfere. Given that the private sphere is not so readily open to inspection it is all the more difficult to see where a privacy violation has occurred. As women have traditionally had few rights to privacy it is not always easy to see when their rights are being transgressed (DeCew 1997). This may partly explain the reluctance of official bodies to see cyberstalking as a problem which affects women especially, and women's privacy, to the extent that it may need special measures to counteract it. Internet dating can be regarded as part of the private sphere – understandably not everyone wants to have it broadcast that they are trying to find a partner that way. Therefore it is not surprising that women's harassment often remains private, and therefore, goes unreported.

A feminist analysis of third-party cyberstalking

What is involved in making an analysis of third-party cyberstalking? First, we should look to appropriate literatures against which to couch such an analysis. In Chapters 2 and 3 I laid out the case for feminist ethics, politics and legal studies. For this phenomenon one might also include violence against women studies (Welsh 2000). A prevailing view is that cyberstalking should be seen as a psychological phenomenon (Meloy 1998). Appropriate psychology literature is clearly one relevant vector, but it needs to include a wider feminist literature. Immediately, the question of a relevant theoretical locus opens up from the purely psychological towards social and cultural dimensions. In other words, it is not just a question of individual psychology but also the wider culture in which individuals exist.

An especially pertinent aspect of cyberstalking, and especially 'third-party' cyberstalking relates to privacy. Although there has been considerable discussion of questions of online privacy (Moor 2001) there has yet to be a similar level of interest in men's and women's differential views and expectations of their own privacy online. However, there is every reason to expect that the online world should mirror the 'real world' in this respect. MacKinnon (1987) has pointed out that the private sphere has traditionally been that of women, yet at the same time women have enjoyed few rights and the state is reluctant to interfere. For instance, witness the ways in which the eruption of domestic violence is often regarded as a lesser crime, than an act of violence directed towards a stranger. DeCew (1997) extends MacKinnon's argument to reason that as women have traditionally had few rights to privacy it is not easy for women, themselves, and others to see when these rights are being transgressed. Thomas and Kitzinger (1997) argue that one reason why sexual harassment took so long to be named (the phenomenon did not have a name until the mid-1970s) was that women were, and still are, reluctant to report it. Reinforcing this sense of 'having to put up with it' as a normal part of life's rich pattern are the so-called 'backlash' writers, such as Roiphe (1993) who attack the concept of sexual harassment as part of a 'victim feminism' mentality. The trouble is that this can further reinforce women's diminished sense of personal privacy and it would be a great pity if this were to be translated into the online world.

Cyberstalking transgresses women's privacy in a direct way. Third-party cyberstalking transgresses women's privacy in the same way and also in a second way. This second notion of privacy transgression relates to the manner in which the original perpetrator becomes a voyeur, someone who invades and transgresses by watching and looking. This further reinforces the power that the perpetrator has over the victim.

Third-party cyberstalking and the gaze

The notion of the 'gaze' as a type of power-laden staring producing and reproducing gendered positions has been a powerful notion for feminist theorists but, as White (2001) indicates, the gaze of the Internet user is still largely unconsidered. Gazing in a virtual world has to be rethought as both the agent and the object of the gaze are not present in the normal visual sense, yet there are distinct ways of observing and watching on the Internet. In many Internet games, for instance, there are direct ways of signifying looking and watching but these are of a different quality than the type of more sinister, voyeuristic gaze identified here that is part of cyberstalking and may also be part of the more negative aspects of Internet dating.

Salecel and Zizek (1996) discuss the idea of an empowered male gaze where the gaze may be fetishistic and voyeuristic but may also be a medium of control which entices the other into submission. We can combine this notion of gaze on the part of third-party cyberstalkers gazing as they entice others to harass the victim with Foucault's (1979) description of state regulated looking, to which I return in Chapter 8. This means that private voyeuristic gazing can open up into surveillance which can then be seen as a type of 'official' gaze. So the voyeur and officially sanctioned surveillance can be regarded as two sides of the same coin. Although much of the contemporary theory of the gaze derives from film theory, it becomes eminently applicable in the scopophilic world of the Internet. Denzin (1995, p. 48) discusses the complexity of the gaze:

> A gaze is not simply voyeuristic. It is regulated, has a trajectory, and evokes emotions and conduct which are differentially reciprocated and erotic. A gaze may be active, or passive, direct, or indirect and indifferent. It will always be engendered, reflecting a masculine or feminine perspective. A gaze may be the gaze of power and domination.

Just as with the Panopticon, where prisoners regulate their behaviour as they do not know when they might be watched, so too may those who are potentially the subject of a gaze on the Internet regulate their activity. Denzin (1995) argues that gazes are always structured by underlying systems of power and gender, the looked-at subject regulates their behaviour to act in a particular way.

Women's gaze in cyberstalking

In this description I have emphasized the gaze, in the context of cyber-stalking, and especially third-party cyberstalking as essentially a mascu-line phenomenon. However there are two senses in which women can appropriate the gaze in cyberstalking. To illustrate the first sense I analyse a relatively rare case of a woman who cyberstalked a man, in particular to describe what is different, in this case, with respect to the cases, described above, where men cyberstalked women. The second sense involves interpreting what happens when women unmask or catch their male perpetrators, which is a feminine reinterpretation of the gaze.

Perhaps not surprisingly, as it is a predominantly masculine activity, detailed reports of female cyberstalking are rare. However Burt (1997) reports a case which presents a distinct contrast to the cases described above and also which gives a further insight into notions of the 'gaze'. This involved a female college student who had been spending about eight hours a day monitoring a male relative's Internet usage using the 'finger' online tool. Given their cultural background a sexual relation-ship would not have been possible. She was able to discover that he fre-quently communicated with a woman from the university where he had just graduated and she phoned the woman and her parents in disguise, although we are not told whether or not these calls could be regarded as threatening. Clearly we could interpret this woman as gazing at her male relative. But her case has different features to the male cases. She experienced considerable shame and guilt over her feelings – she knew that they were wrong in her culture. At the same time she knew that she was suffering from a psychological disorder as she eventually presented at a psychiatric outpatient clinic complaining of depression and severe, compulsive behaviour.

In this case the actor knew that she had a problem, that her behav-iour was not normal and that she wished to have treatment to recover from it. At the same time she seems to have held no intent to harm her relative, nor his woman friend, who probably never knew about her actions. There are, of course, cases where men cyberstalk women, in this way, where the woman has no knowledge, and may not be harmed. However, in the tragic Amy Boyer case (Wright 2000), a man who was obsessed with the young woman in question emailed friends about his obsession and set up a website. She, and her family, knew nothing of his obsession, until he murdered her outside her office.

A further aspect of the woman college student case is that although she had held romantic longings for her male relative for a long time she did not meet the criteria for obsessive compulsive disorder until she had access to the Internet. In this respect, as the quote below reinforces, she displayed similar attributes to men who use the Internet for stalking or pornography. The access to the technology seems enough to tip the balance and trigger this behaviour. A shy, secretive personality and a technical background are also salient factors which are also often to be found in male perpetrators, although, of course, can be found in women too.

This opened an opportunity, a channel for behavior that was congruent with the rest of her psychological makeup, and allowed her to express her obsessive thoughts through a unique, and previously unavailable mode of compulsive behavior. Being shy and secretive but also mathematically oriented and technically skillful she had the appropriate background to use computers in order to manifest previously repressed thoughts and feelings ... she was able to make an intervention, a communication, that she had long longed for, without having to bear the anxiety provoking aspects of a true interpersonal relationship. (Burt 1997)

Women reappropriate the gaze

Although I have characterized the three third-party cyberstalking cases above in terms of the masculine gaze, there are important ways in which we can see the women victims as reappropriating the gaze in order to bring some sort of satisfactory solution to their cases. In this case we can see that these women, rather than being stereotypical passive recipients of the male gaze, were able to assert their authority as active moral agents in gazing back at their perpetrators.

MacCannell and MacCannell (1993, p. 214) make it clear that the gaze is a two way process.

... the figure of authority turning its gaze on the victim and the victim looking back. But in the case of the instrumental gaze it is the 'looking' of authority that is crucial – snooping into the victim's affairs, maintaining an information base in order to maintain the effectiveness of threat, and so on. In the case of identificatory gaze, the victims 'looking up' to authority is crucial – their desire to see themselves in the eyes of authority ...

A feminist reading of the gaze underlines the juxtaposition of public 'state' surveillance and private individual watching in a patriarchal society, the two sides of the same coin. White (2001) has also noted that in Internet games the female version of the gaze is often a submissive one, a 'looking up' to some sense of authority. But it is possible to develop a much stronger feminist reading of gazing where looking up can become instead, looking back or returning the gaze. In these three cases the return gaze is not just crucial in reversing the power balance of the original gaze, but it is also crucial in revealing the identity of the perpetrators of the gaze, who achieved much of their ability to stalk their victims through the anonymity afforded by the Internet. When their anonymity is stripped away through the power of the return gaze, they are either turned over to the authorities or they voluntarily stop their stalking behaviour.

In the Hitchcock case (Mingo 2000), Jayne Hitchcock and her fellow authors gazed back at the offending literary agency, exposed them for others to gaze upon, and ultimately to bring them to justice, although the case is complex and long running. The perpetrator in the spurned lover case (Guardian 1999) had assumed that he was protected by the anonymity of the Internet yet he was lured into a trap, again on the Internet, by the victim's father, where his identity was revealed. The woman here, with the help of her family, was able to gaze back to identify her stalker. Finally in Brail's case (1996), she was forced to increase her technical knowledge of UNIX, whereupon she was able to find the identity of her stalker. As soon as she turned the gaze upon him, by emailing him back to his original email address, rather than one of the aliases which he had used, he stopped harassing her. We have a picture of women defiantly returning the stare that is placed upon them.

Although this notion of the return gaze is powerful and it is a potentially powerful concept for women in their response to cyberstalking, it is important not to overstate its relevance. In cases where women are harassed in Internet dating cases, there is, as yet, no concerted effort to return the gaze of the perpetrator, because, as I suggested earlier I believe, that there is some sense of 'asking for it' in cases where women actively seek out romantic contact over the Internet. The challenge then is to bring out of the private sphere and into the public the many ways that women may be harassed and undermined and recast these phenomena as problems belonging to a wider society.

Internet pornography

In this section I briefly describe issues surrounding the question of Internet pornography, focusing on child pornography, in particular. The first issue concerns the psychology of the, usually male, perpetrator and how it can be compared to the perpetrators of cyberstalking. Second, I discuss ways in which Internet pornography can be analysed in terms of the gaze.

My discussion revolves around the events leading up to the sentencing of seven men in early 2001 for membership of the so-called 'Wonderland Club', an international paedophile ring who traded three-quarters of a million images of child pornography on the Internet (Panorama 2001). One of the perpetrators, David Hines, who received a criminal sentence, described how easy it was to obtain images of child pornography on the Internet – within 24 hours of first going online he had found material. He met other paedophiles. As with the cyber-stalking cases, this group of people thought they were protected by the anonymity of the Internet so they traded sexually explicit images of children and talked about them. As a shy, introverted person, again similar to those who perpetrate cyberstalking crimes, he had found an instant set of friends. The problem was not just the trading of images, but also the way that paedophiles had an easy way to contact each other and to reinforce their beliefs that sex with children was not wrong, to promote the ghastly idea that somehow these children were 'in relationships' with adults. Paedophiles shared information about how to 'groom' children for abuse.

With cyberstalking, the availability of the technology has been the trigger for some perpetrators, for example, as in the case of the college student fixated on a male relative. With Internet paedophile rings the technology also seems to act as a trigger. Some members of the Wonderland club abused children themselves so that the images would enhance their status amongst other members of the club. Reports of another recent case seems to reinforce the notion of technology as trigger. A leader in the UK newspaper, the Guardian (2001, p. 23) points out that child pornography used to be rare and hard to find. However in 'Operation Landmark' the police uncovered 60,000 images of children under 16 unloaded and traded on 33 newsgroups. More recently in the UK, 'Operation Ore' netted a huge paedophile ring, including the rock group, *Who*, musician, Peter Townshend (BBC 2003). So large was this operation that it threatened to swamp the judicial services, and prison system, in bringing to justice, all the perpetrators, the vast majority of whom had never been indicted for an offence before.

Pornography and the gaze

In a very chilling sense these people were turning an abusive, adult, authoritative, male gaze upon young children whose very age and innocence made it impossible to mount a defence of themselves in the way that the adult women were able to in cyberstalking cases. Yet, here, the state authorities, the police, actually watched the paedophile ring live, and anonymously, on the Internet, over a period of two years, in order to gain enough evidence to charge and convict the perpetrators. However the UK law under which they were charged (which has subsequently been amended) only allowed for maximum sentences of 18 months. This further underscores the need for Internet legislation to keep pace with criminal activity. Furthermore the responsibility of the Internet Service Providers is called into question. Operation Landmark focused on open newsgroups where the ISP, Demon, allowed the police authorities unprecedented access to newsgroups to monitor them over a period of weeks. Operation Ore accessed details of credit card transactions.

The gaze of the criminals on their victims and the gaze of the authorities on the criminal activity are two obvious senses of the gaze. Yet there is a further sense in which the gaze continues on these children whose lives have been wrecked by such abuse. Many of the children have never been identified and as their images have spread so far on the Internet they may be there for ever gazed upon by others. A quote from a BBC documentary makes this point (Panorama 2001, p. 12):

CORBIN (reporter):	The policemen who patrol the Internet still see the faces of hundreds of Wonderland children. They are out there for ever.
FOTTRELL (police):	A lot of these are the equivalent of movie stars, they're famous, they're celebrities. All their pictures are well known.
CORBIN:	What is the effect on the children of their notoriety?
FOTTRELL:	They are going to be ... their abuse is going to continue for the rest of their life. That documentation of their abuse is going to be part of their life forever.

In these chilling examples it is hard to see how a gaze can be turned back on the abuser by the abused as the power relationship is so imbalanced. However the official state surveillance of the police authorities, often covertly watching activities online for some time, is the gaze which can, in some senses, be turned against the abusers and bring them to justice. At the same time, as the above quote demonstrates, the nature of the technology is such that images of abused children can remain in corners of the Internet for ever, in a sense continuing their abuse indefinitely. There is also an unfortunate twist in the way that the Internet affords a negative sense of anonymity as many of the children whose images have been displayed are never identified.

Conclusion

My aim, in this chapter has been to highlight the way that some current computer ethics problems can be better analysed when they are the subject of feminist analyses which highlight the way that gender is a crucial variable in achieving an understanding of the problems in question. This argument is particularly pertinent for Internet dating, cyberstalking and Internet paedophile rings. As all of these may involve severe violations of privacy and also voyeuristic and abusive aspects, I have found a feminist version of the concept of the 'gaze' and how it relates to bodies and privacy to be useful in my analysis.

It is notable, in the cyberstalking cases I report, that there was a definite thread of women 'not knowing their place' and receiving some of the treatment meted out to them because of the way they spoke up. This does suggest a sense of there being a qualitative difference between cyberstalking and traditional stalking, a difference which would benefit from further research. This reinforces the perennial theme of the 'public/private' split and women's relationship to this divide. Women speaking up on the Internet are transgressing their sphere of the private world by entering the public world and there are clear repercussions. In Internet dating harassment, women often all too readily know their place and it becomes difficult for them to speak up.

The gaze as a power-laden stare is a form of surveillance, albeit a private form of surveillance which threatens to transgress women's and children's privacy and to discipline their behaviour, in particular. Men's and women's different relationship to privacy through technology is a theme which I return to in Chapter 8 where state sanctioned surveillance, in the wake of fears of terrorist threats is discussed in relation to technology and privacy.

7
Hacking into Hacking: Gender and the Hacker Phenomenon

Introduction: hackers and crackers

Hacking is one of the classic topics of any computer ethics course, yet the way that hacking is overwhelmingly seen as a masculine phenomenon is not often discussed in any level of detail. We tend to take for granted the masculine character of its key players and the form of ethics subscribed to by the hacker community. Therefore hacking appears long overdue for feminist analysis. Women hackers, and whether there are any, has proved to be a fascinating topic. This chapter explores the gender dimensions of hacking in terms of the male domination of hacking, the presence or absence of women hackers, the influence of the frontier metaphor and especially 'frontier masculinity'. I explore the central tenets of the 'hacker ethic' (Himanen 2001), including whether hacker communities are more egalitarian than other communities, the equal opportunities, freedom of information and work ethics of the hacker ethic. Whilst these are all problematic in gender terms there are hints that a female version of the hacker ethic, more explicitly political in motivation, is emerging amongst women hackers.

A great deal has been written on the business of hacking; it excites much interest in the media and has also been subject to academic scrutiny (Taylor 1999). It is not my intention to approve or disapprove of hacking activities as such, nor to argue the merits of definitional statements on hacking made by those involved in hacker activities and by others (Raymond 2001). Nevertheless it is clearly useful to recognize that some commentators are at pains to distinguish between those whose activities fall under the banner of 'enthusiast programmer', within the vein of Levy's original definition (1984) of the rise of the movement in the computer centres of MIT and Stanford in the 1960s and 1970s, and the illegal and anti-social activities of others. However, this acknowledges that some of the 'pranks' of the early hackers would clearly not be sanctioned under later legislation and heightened awareness of security infringements.

Furthermore, some activities fall into a grey area between what is legal and what is not. Raymond (2001), High Priest of the open-source software movement and hacker extraordinaire, is keen to emphasize the distinction between 'hacker' as benignly motivated programming enthusiast and 'cracker' as programmer outlaw. Although it is beyond the remit of my analysis to offer an extensive elaboration of the difference, the hacker/cracker distinction must be recognized, as both are of interest in ethical terms, and especially in relation to gender. (It has even been suggested to me that there might be a geographical distinction to be made with 'hacker' the more common term in North America.) Hence the remainder of this account will encompass both categories. Unfortunately the hacker/cracker terminology does not seem to have been widely adopted and, certainly within media reports, 'hacking' is often used for illegal activity; legal hacking appears to be of less interest to the media. This use of the term 'hacking' is not confined to the broadcast and print media as Taylor's recent academic study of hackers (1999) concentrates on the IT underworld. Therefore, in what follows, it appears to be wise to let the sources make their own definitions and to follow these.

Male domination of hacking

As Chapter 5 relates, in relation to 'shrinking pipeline' studies, there is a considerable literature on the relatively low numbers of women present in all aspects of computing and IT, except for office, administrative and secretarial roles where women predominate (Webster 1996). This focus has been so strong that it has tended to dominate research on gender and ICTs to the extent that it is hard to dispel the notion that the gender and ICTs question is largely a numbers game. As Lancaster (2003) explains, assuming that equal numbers of women and men in IT spells equality, is a trap for the unwary. Women may be present in a work or educational setting in considerable numbers (e.g. in offices) and yet may still be in a disadvantaged position as they are at low levels in the hierarchy. This suggests that programmes which attempt to draw women into areas where they are in a minority, for example, science and engineering, are unlikely to be successful if they base themselves on publicity campaigns without understanding the deeper reasons why women are absent in the first place.

Given these concerns it would not be surprising to find that hacking is also dominated by men. As it is strongly linked to identifying with ICTs and technology we should expect to find that it is predominantly a male preserve and thus is borne out by major studies (Taylor 1999; Jordan and Taylor 2004). However, leaving statistics to the side for a moment, I argue that there are additional features of the male dominance of the hacking phenomenon which are just as important in the analysis. It is instructive to characterize women's absence or presence in the world of hacking by comparison with what is written on women in more traditional aspects of computing. This serves to focus the analysis on finding what may be intrinsically different about hacking in gender terms, rather than rehearsing arguments which may be common to gender and ICTs, in general, and therefore, which will not get to the heart of the gender question in the hacker phenomenon. Features of such a comparison include media and academic interest in women hackers and explanations for their presence and absence. Do such explanations differ, in significant ways, from discussions of traditional computing roles? For instance, we could consider media portrayals of women hackers and how these are different from accounts of prominent women in IT, in education and in industry.

A second, less obvious, point for comparison involves comparing the desirability of women entering computing/IT and the desirability of women entering hacking. Much of the discussion on women's absence from computing ultimately leads back to the question of how to attract more women into the discipline. Often the desirability of attracting more women into computing is not examined; it is accepted as fairly obvious that it is desirable to get women into interesting, well-paid jobs which are usually (barring periodic recessions) fairly plentiful and where there is often a shortage of qualified staff. However it should be noted that the argument for getting more women into computing is often made in economic terms, relating much more directly to industry shortages rather than in terms of giving women better career opportunities (Henwood 1993). There is no parallel argument for a shortage of hackers. Hence we would not expect to find similar rhetoric surrounding the idea of getting more women into hacking and yet the merit of more women becoming hackers has indeed been raised (Sollfrank 2002). Exploring these ideas, in terms of women's complex and ambiguous relationships with ICTs, means that we need not subscribe to a stereotyped view of women as technophobes, who must be persuaded and cajoled into using ICTs. This also suggests that we may need to update our views on hacking. Rather than assuming a relatively simple equation of masculinity with technology and femininity with an avoidance or fear of technology, we need more sophisticated ways of exploring men's and women's changing relationships with technology.

The woman hacker – presence or absence compared to IT in general

Taylor (1999) notes the fundamentally masculine nature of hacking. Hacking culture is young, male, technologically oriented, and on the margins of the computing industry. Against one of the major tenets of the 'hacker ethic', namely the assertion that there should be no discrimination on the grounds of 'bogus' criteria (Levy 1984, p. 41) of age, class, race, and so on, Taylor (1999, p. 32) finds the absence of women hackers to be an 'unexplained statistic'. He focuses on the traditional factors discouraging women from computing, namely social stereotyping, masculine 'locker room' environment and gender bias in computing language, and applies these to the hacker phenomenon. Importantly he notes that, even if we take all the traditional deterrent factors into account, given the fraction of women with computing qualifications and therefore with the technical skills to become hackers, statistically we would expect to see more women hackers. So if there are fewer than expected, this suggests that there are further factors at work which are still to be uncovered.

In his empirical study of hackers, respondents found it difficult to identify the reasons why there are fewer women hackers than might be expected, tending to offer arguments based on psychological mastery. Taylor (1999, p. 36) suggests that whilst such arguments can be biologically deterministic, 'they at least offer a succinct explanation for the statistical expectation yet non-appearance of female hackers'. However, he is not totally convinced by simple arguments, pointing instead towards the wild west brand of masculinity portrayed in hacker culture, the misogyny displayed by men who can hide behind the anonymity of the Internet and the association of technology with desire, eroticism and artificial creation. These features are reinforced in his later study of hacktivism (Jordan and Taylor 2004), where the feeling of power adduced by the 'hack' is particularly appealing to young men. These are certainly arguments which other authors have drawn upon in their analysis of gender relations in ICTs. For instance, Herring's research (1996) on gendered computer-mediated communications suggests that gendered stereotypes are often magnified in electronic communication with men more likely to 'flame' and women more likely to use supportive styles of speech. Chapter 6's discussion of cyberstalking suggests a link between women speaking up on the Internet and their being subject to abuse. Furthermore, the link between technology and artificial creation, through AI and A-life, and how this relates to masculinity has been noted by a number of authors (Helmreich 1994; Adam 1998; Kember 2003). The link with artificial creation points to a desire for control, domination and mastery of an artificial world.

I agree that these two points in Taylor's analysis, misogynistic, often anonymous, communication and artificial creation are implicated in gender relations in ICTs. However, given the point, made above, that we need to find what it is about hacking that demarcates it from the 'women in computing' issue in general, it is hard to see how they can act as convincing explanations for the relative absence of women in hacking over and above women's presence or absence in computing in overall terms; there seems to be nothing special to connect them unequivocally to the hacker phenomenon. However, given that the 'Wild West' or frontier spirit does not appear to be a significant metaphor in mainstream computing (most of us do not regard our day at the office in terms of patrolling the Electronic Frontier with a cyberposse, for instance), it would be reasonable to explore the concept of the frontier with the expectation that it may prove a more potent explanatory device.

Frontiers

As I argue above, the romance of the frontier, and more specifically the 'Wild West' frontier is a potent metaphor for Internet commentators who have often conceptualized the Internet as an 'electronic frontier' (Sterling 1992; Rheingold 1993; Miller 1995; Barlow 1996; Brail 1996; Ludlow 1996; Kramer and Kramarae 1997). Hitchcock (Mingo 2000) and Brail (1996), both of whom were stalked on the Internet, explicitly use the idea of the frontier in the description of their stalking cases. The acknowledgement of a geographical frontier may imply that expectations of behaviour might be different there and that normal standards of justice and law might not apply. But if the Internet is an electronic frontier then, by analogy, the special justice of the frontier goes beyond the normal notions of justice. Living on the frontier is different from ordinary life in many ways, not least of all because the frontier may be disputed or even under attack. Special measures must be taken against those who attack that frontier. Normal forms of justice may not apply as one may be geographically far removed from the forces and institutions which could enforce law and justice. Therefore the idea of 'frontier justice' arises with the implication that justice, perhaps, may be taken into the hands of those defending the frontier who may be far away physically, or here virtually, from the normal channels of law and order. It is not clear how far this metaphor can be extended, nor should it be used to excuse hacking activity which is illegal and harmful. Nevertheless some of the victims of cyberstalking, who see themselves very much in terms of living on the electronic frontier have had to take the question of justice into their own hands, for example, as in the Hitchcock case, where she describes enlisting the help of a 'volunteer cyberposse' in order to bring to book those who were stalking her (Mingo 2000).

Barlow, credited with coining the phrase 'Electronic Frontier' and co-founder of the Electronic Frontier Foundation, clearly revels in the parallels between the electronic frontier and the nineteenth century American West 'in its natural preference for social devices which emerge from it (sic) conditions rather than those which are imposed from outside' (Barlow 1996, p. 27). Until the West was 'civilized', he argues, there existed an unwritten code of the West which was fluid and emphasized ethics and understandings over largely unenforceable laws. Justice is seen as an emergent property of the electronic frontier. 'Uncodified or adaptive "law", while as "fast, loose, and out of control" as other emergent forms, is probably more likely to yield something like justice at this point. In fact, one can already see in development new practices to suit the conditions of virtual commerce. The life forms of information are evolving methods to protect their continued reproduction' (ibid., p. 28).

We have already met the idea of emergence in relation to intelligence emerging from the right computer architecture in AI, and democracy emerging from Internet communities. Here we see the idea of justice emerging from life on the frontier. It is no accident that Barlow alludes to virtual commerce. These free market, survival of the fittest arguments look to the power of the market place to spontaneously generate good ways for us to live.

More generally, frontiers and frontier justice, including electronic varieties, resonate with Douglas's classic anthropological work (1966) on boundaries and margins. Much of this work researches the distinction between sacred and profane and the pollution which occurs when the boundary between the two is transgressed. But a second aspect, more relevant here, relates to what happens in the very boundaries or margins themselves. We make boundaries or frontiers to create social order. In making social order we are not just condemning disorder – we are recognizing that disorder is both dangerous and, at the same time, potent (ibid., p. 94). For instance, someone who goes beyond the ordinary limits of society, and who comes back, may possess a power not available to those who have remained in control of themselves and within the bounds of society.

This suggests that those whose position in society is marginal enjoy an indefinable status even though they may be doing nothing morally wrong. Douglas suggests that examples can be found in the unborn child or the perceived transition from childhood to adulthood in some societies. To be in a marginal condition is to be in a dangerous condition but it is also a source of power. So those at the frontier, on the margins, are dangerous and marginal as they are beyond social order; for the US pioneers some were literally 'outlaws'.

People who hold specific offices in society have well-defined powers by dint of that office, but those in the margins may also hold power, albeit of an unconscious and uncontrollable nature. Hence hackers, and those on the electronic frontier have power clearly not because of some well-respected societal position, but rather because of the power and danger imbued in their marginality. The unstructured areas of society contain energy in the margins, albeit of a potentially dangerous kind. Frontiers are, of course, a special kind of boundary. A frontier is a boundary between the known and the unknown where the unknown is a dangerous place. But, at the same time, it is a seductive place.

Kramer and Kramarae (1997) point to the way that anarchy and frontiers have often been linked historically, especially in US history. In the online world the link between these two concepts is demonstrated by hackers' rejection of authority, emphasis on freedom and delight in the 'wilderness and excitement' (ibid., p. 232) of the Internet. Although Taylor (1999) does not elaborate, in detail, why the frontier spirit might serve to exclude women, Kramer and Kramarae point to more specific reasons. Although the US pioneers of the frontier were men and women, 'the prevailing story is that the frontier was conquered by strong white male heroes ... The frontier is the promise of new beginnings. It is male, adventure, boldness, daring, restless energy, independence, rough, violence, strength, heroic exploits, and danger. It is not female, intimacy, caring, vulnerability, meaning in daily customs, or artistic' (Kramer and Kramarae 1997, p. 231). They (ibid., pp. 232–3) argue that, just as historians of the frontier represented women in stereotyped ways, for example, 'Brave Pioneer Mothers' or 'Calamity Janes' without acknowledging their multidimensional contributions in making new societies, so do the documents of the electronic frontier, the popular magazines or 'zines', in representing women as passive sexual stereotypes, deny and obscure present day women's roles in making the new electronic societies. We can see how the valorizing of the frontier spirit can serve to celebrate masculinity and underestimate or render invisible women's contribution in accounts of hacking.

However if we characterize this phenomenon more squarely in terms of the concept, 'frontier masculinity' based on what has been said above on frontiers and borders, we can begin to analyse the forces at work in shaping the culture of hacking in gender terms, without demonizing hackers. Despite the pervasiveness of Wild West and frontier narratives in cyberspace and hacking texts, few authors apart from Kramer and Kramarae (1997) have chosen to explore this myth in gender terms. Miller (1995) argues against the usefulness of the frontier metaphor:

> Just as the ideal of chastity makes virginity sexually provocative, so does the unclaimed territory invite settlers, irresistibly so. Americans regard the lost geographical frontier with a melancholy, voluptuous fatalism – we had no choice but to advance upon it and it had no alternative but to submit. (Ibid., p. 51)

Although we may resist the apparent inevitability of the frontier myth and the brand of masculinity that goes with it, Slotkin (1998) notes the pervasiveness of the frontier myth in the popular imagery of American life. This emphasizes a certain kind of hero, a rugged, hard-headed masculine, white hero who is engaged in a war against nature but is also engaged in a racial war, the war against those who must be civilized in Western terms.

We can see this brand of frontier masculinity at work in popular accounts of hacking, where not only is the hacker's mastery over savage nature (the computer and the program) celebrated but so too is the hacker's disdain for the prevailing norms of society. It is as if societal norms are the culture of a world not civilized in hacker terms, and hackers are celebrated in overcoming these 'uncivilized' norms which include such things as finishing college degrees, sleeping and working at normal times, paying appropriate attention to personal hygiene and appearance and not tampering with the hardware and software of computers, and so on.

If we don an anthropological hat for a moment and regard hacker culture, in preaching the hacker ethic, as the hope of this new civilized world at the frontier, we can regard the old world as 'uncivilized' in hacker terms. This requires us to suspend, or even stand on its head, our belief in how we usually regard the civilized/uncivilized spectrum. The business of making the 'normal' world seem strange can be a useful explanatory device. Those who subscribe to these 'uncivilized' norms then become the 'savages' in the hacker frontier world either ignored or waiting to be civilized. Unsurprisingly many of these will be women as they subscribe to many of the rituals of the non-hacker world. They may be civilized or ignored but are inevitably cast as 'other' in relation to the hacker world. Hence, we can see that the frontier myth with all its ramifications does not serve women well in the electronic world. The idea of the frontier resonates, in some fundamental way, with a heroic view of masculinity. Other than the marginal roles articulated by Kramer and Kramarae (1997), it is not clear how women could carve themselves a similarly important role against the frontier metaphor. Indeed women may not just be marginalized, they may be almost invisible.

The invisibility of women in the hacker world

The use of the frontier myth to make women invisible can be seen at work in Levy's *Hackers* (1984), the earliest substantial work on the hacker phenomenon. It is an eloquent description of the frontier masculinity of the early hacker world and has been immensely important in raising awareness of the history of hacking. Levy was one of the first commentators to question the paucity of women hackers. He notes, 'Even the substantial cultural bias against women getting into serious computing does not explain the utter lack of female hackers'. (ibid., p. 84) Yet, apparently without irony, this quote is juxtaposed with the observation that 'hackers talked strangely, they had bizarre hours, they ate weird food, and they spent all their time thinking about computers' (ibid.) and a long, and unfortunately detailed, description of a male hacker's personal hygiene problems! More importantly, even taking into account women's actual physical presence in hacking activities, Levy is unaware of the way in which his text renders women invisible. The Who's Who at the beginning of the book includes 3 women, 52 men and 10 computers. Some of the computes are described in terms of their relationship to men (e.g. Apple II and Steve Wozniak) but all of the women are someone's wives. Hence women, if they do appear, are defined in terms of their relationship to men, even when they have expert hacking credentials. Women are, therefore, largely invisible.

A description of an episode involving a woman and programming demonstrates how women are cast as 'other', and rendered unimportant.

Despite the fact that this woman, Margaret Hamilton, was an expert programmer, she went on to manage the computers on board the space craft of the Apollo moonshot, she is designated by the pejorative term, 'Officially Sanctioned User' (ibid., pp. 96–7). At MIT, she used the official assembly level language supplied on the DEC machine, not the hacker-written language which had been developed by the MIT hacking group. So, when the hackers of the 'Midnight Computer Wiring Society' altered the hardware of the DEC machine one night to run their own programs, hers failed to work the next day. Naturally she complained and hardware alterations were officially banned, although in practice, eventually tolerated. The episode was designated the 'Great Margaret Hamilton Program Clobber' (ibid., p. 97). Note how the hacker frontier spirit differs from Margaret Hamilton's world. Although she clearly has considerable programming expertise, and therefore could be expected to achieve some measure of respect, she is an official user, thereby belonging to the 'savage' official world which is the antithesis of hacking. She uses the despised official programming language. She keeps daytime hours, rather than joining the nocturnal world of the hackers. Her complaint and the subsequent banning of nocturnal hardware alterations, although initially upheld, gradually reverts to the *status quo*. The hackers are described as 'playful' and the incident is cast as a prank.

This resonates with my earlier discussion of men's and women's virtues. Women are generally seen as more virtuous than men. However men behaving badly can be 'let off the hook'. The above example seems just such an instance where behaviour which seriously inconvenienced a woman user was seen as just a bit of fun and was tolerated; indeed the fact that she was inconvenienced was seen as the major part of their prank.

The hunt for the woman hacker

Rather than purely pondering reasons for their absence, some commentators have deliberately sought out women hackers. Edwards (2003) describes how he initially followed Levy (1984), Weizenbaum (1976) and Turkle (1984) in assuming that hacking was an almost exclusively masculine activity. He argues that the stereotypical masculinity of hacking is beginning to break down with a sizeable female minority in many hacker communities. This is accompanied by portrayals of women hackers in cyberpunk science fiction and as film characters. Partly in the spirit of recovering women's history, which is attempted in other disciplines, such as art and literature (Rowbotham 1973), Edwards (2003, p. 12) sent out an enquiry looking for women hackers on a number of Internet mailing lists and was surprised to get nearly a hundred responses within a few days. He had not defined the term in his initial email; the respondents had identified *themselves* as women hackers. Interestingly Edwards also asked a number of senior male computer scientists for names of women hackers, active in the 1960s, and half a dozen names were immediately forthcoming. In many ways these results seem surprising and Edwards, himself, struggles to explain them. It could be an example of the 'hidden from history' phenomenon (Rowbotham 1973) where women have always been present in some arena, for example, art, literature or science, but where their activities have been suppressed, ignored or attributed to men within the patriarchal structures of public life and where the feminist historian's job is to reclaim women's history. However we also need to consider how we would verify a subject's claims to be a woman hacker if contact is only made through email.

Edwards (2003) hints that the changing material environment of hacking may have made a difference to the presence or absence of women hackers. Early batch processing on large mainframes required presence late at night in the computer centre, 'the graveyard shift', as resources were scarce. This encouraged much face-to-face interaction at strange times of the day, and of necessity in the computer centre, and may have reinforced the tiny communities of hackers as male preserves. However as computing moved into time-sharing and then into fully networked mode these physical factors, which may have previously deterred women, were no longer present. However we need to be wary of assuming that the move to the virtual necessarily opens up hitherto masculine domains to women, as several authors argue that stereotypical male–female interactions can be magnified in virtual interactions (Brail 1996; Herring 1996) and this certainly seems to be the case in my analysis of cyberstalking. This also ties in with the discussion on egalitarian communities later in this chapter. Changes in material conditions may facilitate social changes on some level but they are not enough to bring about changing social relations. Once again we see a variation of the liberal argument at work where underlying social structures are not adequately addressed in discussions of equality.

Sollfrank (1999) sees her search for women hackers as a 'mission to locate subversive women on the net'. In looking for women hackers she attended several hacker conferences; although there were women there they did not identify themselves as hackers. She found it almost impossible to find any at all. Her respondents from law enforcement officials to cyberpunk authors all cited differences in masculine and feminine psychology to explain the lack of women hackers. During this period of research, the only female hacker she came across was Susan Thunders who took up prostitution to fuel her need to buy high-tech equipment for hacking, became a security adviser and then embarked on a career as a professional poker player. As Sollfrank notes: 'Sex, crime and technology all came together in the person of Susan Thunders'. Nevertheless, as she further points out, 'constructing the image of a woman hacker who is actually a whore fits perfectly into the convention of discrediting hackers by referring to their psychological deficiencies and immorality, and by imputing criminal reasons to what they are doing'.

In her first paper, Sollfrank's conclusion (ibid.) is clearly at odds with that of Edwards as she argues that, of all technical spheres, hacking contains fewest women. Sollfrank (ibid.) hints at the potential for women to become involved in politically engaged work through hacking, the kind of work which women often prefer to engage in on a non-technological level. In later papers (Sollfrank 2000; Sollfrank 2002), Sollfrank has made contact with women hackers, persuaded them to give a workshop on 'How to Become a Hacker' at a conference and has consciously made a link between politically inspired cyberfeminism and women hackers. In particular, Clara G. Sopht is an expert in 'Denial of Service' attacks, where networks can be brought down by flooding them with more traffic than they can handle. This sort of activity is termed 'hacktivism' or 'electronic civil disobedience'.

The idea that large corporations or even governments (e.g. as in the case of the Mexican government and the Zapatistas) could be disrupted by such means currently excites much interest on the Internet (Jordan and Taylor 2004). However the notion that women could have a special role to play in this has barely been considered. Jordan and Taylor (ibid., p. 117) suggest that hacktivism may be qualitatively different from hacking and may signal a re-ordering of digital cultures where hacktivism may challenge some of the more masculine aspects of hacking. However they do not have evidence to support this claim at this stage. Instead, we should note Sollfrank's plea (2002) for tactics to '... undermine the fact, that the hacking culture is a purely white male phenomenon, and to populate this environment with loads of dangerous and idealistic women hackers ...'.

A female hacker ethic?

Are hacker communities egalitarian?

The above discussion paints a complex and ambivalent picture with regard to women's involvement in hacking. Clearly the area is still under-researched, particularly with regard to the political dimension and especially areas such as hacktivism (Jordan and Taylor 2004). Nevertheless enough evidence exists to challenge the notion that hacker communities are largely meritocracies where race, gender, and so on, are unimportant. Indeed we might question how such a rhetoric of equality arose in the first place. Part of the answer may lie in the way that hackers cast themselves as a new, alternative political movement challenging the existing order with all its baggage of racism, sexism and repression. However just because a political movement challenges a non-egalitarian orthodoxy, this does not mean that it is free from the instruments of oppression itself. And this would be especially problematic for hackers, where they are so loosely organized along the political dimension. The related notion that democracy is a spontaneous property of new Internet communities has been criticized by a number of authors (Rheingold 1993; Ess 1996b; Winner 1997). Similarly we should note that it has been claimed that new occupational groups escape sexist attitudes because they are not entrenched in old traditions. Indeed this claim has been made in regard to computing and information systems (Igbaria and Chidambaram 1997) but, again has been subject to challenge (Adam *et al.* 2001). The point here is that equality and democracy are not spontaneously emergent properties of new communities whether they be political or occupational groups and it would seem to be more effective if we stopped expecting them to be so.

The equal opportunities ethic

Levy (1984, p. 43) details a central tenet of the hacker ethic. 'Hackers should be judged by their hacking, not bogus criteria such as degrees, age, race, or position'. Interestingly the categories 'gender' and 'able-bodiedness' are absent though it would be reasonable to conclude that 'such as' could include these categories. 'This meritocratic trait was not necessarily rooted in the inherent goodness of hacker hearts – it was mainly that hackers cared less about someone's superficial characteristics than they did about his (sic) potential to advance the general state of hacking'. Levy (ibid.) cites the example of a 12-year-old boy being accepted into hacker circles, though we might note that such an individual is only just outside the college age, white, male category that made up the bulk of Levy's hackers. Indeed just by growing a little older this boy would inevitably fit the standard hacker characteristics in ways in which a middle-aged black woman could never do! This is a typical liberal expression of equality, rather in the vein of the employment adverts which claim equal opportunities regardless of ethnicity, disability, gender, religion, and so on. A statement of equality is seen to be enough to achieve it. This view also tends to dismiss as superficial (here the term used is even stronger 'bogus'), characteristics of people, which are far from superficial but are deeply felt, often regarded as positive, aspects of their identities, and which should be respected rather than diminished or dismissed. Under this 'differences as bogus' view, equal opportunities are then passive instruments, difference and diversity are not identified, and one need do nothing to achieve equality except state a belief in it.

More recent views of equal opportunities which are becoming encoded in legislation in Western countries place a much more active role upon the shoulders of actants. For instance note how a college would now be seen as defaulting if it claimed to offer equal opportunity to disabled students yet its library was a two-floor building without elevators and its lecture theatres contained many steep steps. In addition to ignoring differences in identity, ignoring the material conditions of difference also makes it much easier to claim equality. For instance factors such as some women's inability to work in computer centres late at night because of childcare, persons from ethnic minorities' reluctance to work at night for fear of attacks on dimly lit campuses in seedy areas perhaps where there are undercurrents of racial tension, disabled hackers' inability to use public transport or access buildings without ramps or elevators – all these can be set to one side. It could be argued that some of the material factors I adduce here could have been problematic for early hacking in the 1960s and 1970s, when the hacker ethic was formulated, but are less of an issue in contemporary networked times. Edwards (2003) hints at the idea of hacking becoming more available to women when they no longer had to be present late at night in computer centres. However, as I argue above, making things materially less difficult does not necessarily change the prevailing culture. It may not deter women but it is not an active measure to draw them in. This has been a prevailing theme in feminist ethics (Tong 1993). It also harks back to the idea, described in the previous section, that Internet communities spontaneously become democratic, a myth effectively dispelled by Winner (1997) in his critique of virtual communities.

The freedom of information ethic

'All information should be free.' (Levy 1984, p. 40)

Freedom of information has been a central plank of the hacker ethic since hacker communities began to form in the 1960s. This mirrors the wider emphasis on freedom of speech prevalent in most Western democracies, particularly so in the USA where it is constitutionally enshrined in the First Amendment. It is immediately clear how this ethic could be at loggerheads with feminist concerns when we consider the debates over pornography and censorship, particularly in North America, and mainly in the offline world, though now extending to consider pornography in cyberspace. In feminist legal research, and feminist thinking in general, there has been a long running debate over pornography, crystallizing around deeply felt beliefs over freedom of speech vs censorship. On the one hand Strossen and American Civil Liberties Union (ACLU) defend freedom of expression, seemingly at all costs. On the other, MacKinnon and Dworkin lead the 'anti-pornography' feminist position (Lane 2000). Additionally there is a widespread tacit acknowledgement that pornography is the driver of much of the development of Internet technologies, although due to its underground nature this is difficult to quantify. The debates are complex, far from conclusive and a detailed discussion of the many details is outwith the scope of this book. There are additional concerns about data privacy as described in Chapter 4. Chapter 8 discusses privacy and data surveillance in more detail. The privacy/freedom equation is finely balanced.

However, for present purposes, the salient features of the debate relate to the freedom of information ethic and how it relates to freedom of speech/censorship debates in hacker terms. There is little doubt that organizations such as the Electronic Frontier Foundation and prominent exponents of the hacker ethic and freedom in cyberspace have a political influence. Jordan and Taylor (2004) associate a technolibertarian view with the hacker community where strong libertarian and free market principles are closely allied to the hacker ethic. Additionally there are specific instances of hacker involvement in legislative processes, which do have implications for the freedom of speech/censorship debates particularly insofar as they relate to feminist concerns over pornography. Hackers have been involved in political action, to considerable effect, in relation to Internet legislation. As Raymond (2001, p. 17) notes:

> The mainstreaming of the Internet even brought the hacker culture the beginnings of respectability and political clout. In 1994 and 1995 hacker activism scuppered the Clipper proposal which would have put strong encryption under government control. In 1996 hacker mobilized a broad coalition to defeat the misnamed 'Communications Decency Act' (CDA) and prevent censorship of the Internet.

In fact the 'broad coalition' designating themselves the Citizens Internet Empowerment Coalition (CIEC 1997) consisted of various Internet service providers, broadcast and media associations, civil liberties groups and over 56,000 individual Internet users. Although designed to protect minors from indecent and offensive material on the Internet, the successful challenge was made on the grounds that the CDA failed to understand the unique nature of the Internet and that it was so broad as to violate the freedom of speech protections of the First Amendment. We should also note the subsequent dismissal of the Child Pornography Prevention Act (Levy 2002) which means that virtual pictures of children are not illegal in the USA. This suggests that the hacker position on freedom of information is lacking in an ethic of care which could protect children and minors. Instead, apparently, freedom of speech is promoted as the highest ideal. This resonates with Gilligan's research (1982) where she argues that care and relatedness are more feminine in inspiration rather than the rights-based approach, here the right to free speech, which she attributed to masculine ethical approaches.

This implies that there is now an urgent need to move the feminist debate on pornography and censorship from the offline world, where much has been said and written, to the online world where there has, so far, been little debate. However there is some evidence that a female hacker ethic may differ from the male hacker ethic in respect of aspects of freedom of speech and pornography. Sollfrank (2002) calls for a consciously political cyberfeminism for women hackers. Interestingly some prominent women hackers have explicitly sought to crusade *against* Internet pornography so it is here that we may find the seeds of an alternative female hacker ethic. For instance, Natasha Grigori started out in the 1990s running a bulletin board for software pirates, but has now founded and runs antichildporn.org where hacker skills are used to track down child pornography and pass the information to law enforcement authorities (Segan 2000a). Similarly a women hacker handled, 'Blueberry' set up another anti-child pornography organization, condemned.org (ibid.). Jude Milhon, a hacker who initiated the alternative magazine, *Mondo 2000*, argues that women hackers are more likely to be involved in hacktivism with a political or ethical end than in other areas of illegal hacking (Segan 2000b). Hence there is some, albeit still slender, evidence of the emergence of a different ethic amongst female hackers, one where political activism is to the fore and where explicit stances and action are taken on topics such as child pornography rather than holding to an ideal of freedom of speech at all cost.

The work ethic

Levy's work (1984) on early hackers does not explicitly describe the hacker ethic as a work ethic. Nevertheless from the importance of the adoption of very particular working habits, there is a clearly implied hacker work ethic. This theme has been explored in more detail by Himanen (2001). Himanen argues that the hacker ethic is a new work ethic that challenges the Protestant work ethic of Weber's classic text (1930), *The Protestant Ethic and the Spirit of Capitalism*, which has dominated Western capitalist societies for so long. Here the hacker ethic is a passionate, joyful, playful approach to work where making money is not the driving force and where access and freedom of expression are explicitly enshrined in the ethic. This contrasts with the Protestant work ethic's emphasis on work as moral and, originally, religious duty, where play and leisure are clearly contrasted with work. Hackers' relationship to time is important and different to the 'time is money' ethic of capitalism which has intensified and speeded up in the new information society (Castells 2000). Even leisure becomes work as we 'work out' in the gym and marshal our home lives in tight schedules, as if the whole of our lives have become Taylorized. As Himanen (2001, p. 29) notes, no longer can we just hang out with our children, we are obliged to spend quality time with them! The use of new technology can blur the boundaries of work and leisure, but not always to our advantage. Yet Himanen argues that the hacker ethic advocates organizing for playfulness, a freedom to self-organize time and resists work-time supervision. Some hackers make money through traditional capitalist routes and then, having achieved financial independence, are free to pursue their hacker passions.

The hacker work ethic paints an ideal of freedom from financial worry and the ability to organize one's own work which few, whether men or women, can hope to achieve even in affluent Western democracies. However, from the point of view of the present argument we need to question whether there is a gender dimension, both in terms of desirability and feasibility, lurking within the hacker work ethic. Studies of women, work and leisure (Green *et al.* 1990) suggest that women's access to leisure is different from that of men's; they have less of it. So far it seems that patterns of leisure use of ICTs and the Internet reproduce standard gendered patterns of leisure-time availability rather than breaking them down (Adam and Green 1998). In addition, many women work a 'double shift', that is, they have primary responsibility for home and childcare as well as their paid employment. Commentators on the economy of the household can be surprisingly blind to the contribution that women make by their largely invisible labour of looking after homes, bodies and children (Cudd 2001, pp. 92–4). Those whose life revolves around the computer may not notice the real life bodily care that goes into keeping them fed, clean and organized for their virtual lives within the machine (Helmreich 1994).

We might feel that the accelerated version of the Protestant work ethic is problematic for men and for women. Yet, at the same time, the hacker work ethic is unachievable for many men and women in Western democracies whose material conditions will not permit the freedoms to which hackers aspire. But on top of this the hacker work ethic seems especially problematic for women as women's time is often so circumscribed. The hacker work ethic has no means of acknowledging this and the special position of women's bodily labour in maintaining the machinery of every day life. This suggests that there is another dimension where an alternative female version of the hacker ethic, still to be formulated, but which is, as yet, unimaginable.

Conclusion

In this chapter I have sought to explore the phenomenon of the woman hacker along a number of dimensions. This includes the search for women hackers and why their presence or absence should be of concern. The explanations which have been generated to explain women's relative absence from hacking are more of interest than the actual number of women involved and I have argued that the concept of 'frontier masculinity' is worthy of more attention, particularly as the metaphor of the frontier has proved so appealing for commentators on cyberspace. One of Levy's anecdotes (1984) about a woman programmer is re-read against the frontier metaphor. The few published sources that exist do not yet give us a clear picture of how many women hackers there are and the spectrum of their activities.

Turning more explicitly to the tenets of hacker ethics I have sought to analyse these in terms of the egalitarian claim for hacker communities, the equal opportunities ethic, the freedom of information ethic and the work ethic. The discussion above suggests that all of these have a gender dimension which can be problematic for women in particular. Importantly the supposed egalitarian nature of hacker communities and their claim to be meritocracies which ignore 'bogus' criteria such as age or race tend to repeat the old liberal arguments for equality which feminists and others have discredited as passive instruments which maintain the *status quo* in their denial of difference. Similarly there seems to be little hope that the hacker work ethic has much to offer many men and women, but particularly women whose work and leisure time is so constrained. Within the freedom of information ethic we need a more thoroughgoing exploration of how feminist debates on censorship vs freedom of speech translate into the online world. The hacker 'technolibertarian' freedom of information at all costs approach cuts right across attempts to provide a more caring society which deliberately puts measures in place to protect vulnerable members of society.

But at least here we see some signs of an emerging women hackers' ethic where hacking skills can be put to use for more conscious political ends in hacktivism and anti-child pornography websites and enforcement. In tracking down women hackers we must attend to the latter point especially as there is hope of sowing the seeds of a more inclusive and politically rounded hacker ethic.

8
Someone to Watch Over Me – Gender, Technologies, Privacy and Surveillance

Introduction: the gender–privacy link

The empirical examples in this and Chapters 6 and 7 share a common *leitmotiv*: they are based on privacy and watching and what happens when privacy is breached, where all of these dimensions are to be understood in gender terms. The question of privacy has a strong gender dimension and it is not surprising to find that this is echoed in the digital world. Privacy is a concern not just in terms of ethics; there are also important legal and political dimensions embedded in the concept as the question of whether privacy is different for women and men, and also how this difference can be captured in legislation, continues to be of concern (MacKinnon 1987; DeCew 1997). When we consider privacy we set up a complex ethical equation where the variables of different types of privacy, gender, culture and technologies are all implicated.

Clearly, privacy, and, more specifically, how to understand when women's privacy is being violated, and how to protect women's privacy, is one of the key elements of feminist politics, legal theory and indeed, ethics. Hence it is important to have the necessary theoretical tools to expose and analyse violations of privacy, especially new types of violation which may be occurring in cyberspace. Echoing Kramer and Kramarae (1997), if women have little sense of individual autonomy, it is not always easy to see when their privacy is being violated. Similarly, feminist political theory, in considering the relation between private and public spheres, questions women's and men's unequal participation in democracy and hence their differential access to freedom and privacy (Pateman 1989). These considerations are especially pertinent to the problems raised in this book. Under the larger umbrella of privacy, this chapter turns to an issue which continues to raise much concern, namely surveillance, and questions whether there is a gender dimension to the subject which is currently underexplored. First of all, drawing on the discussion in Chapters 3 and 4, in particular, I consider definitions of privacy, including physical, informational and decisional privacies before going on to discuss, in more detail, the historical, contingent nature of our concept of privacy and the relationship between technology and privacy. This is followed by a discussion of the treatment of surveillance through ICTs and the Panopticon and a consideration of the steps that some Western governments are taking in increasing data surveillance in the wake of increased concerns over terrorism.

Gender and the topic of privacy has long been of interest to feminist writers. The relationship between gender, ICTs and privacy is complex. The discussion in this chapter draws upon my prior analysis of Internet dating, cyberstalking and Internet pornography. I want to avoid the suggestion that women's experience of privacy on the Internet is all negative. Apart from anything else the danger of such a view is that essentialist stereotypes of women's relationship to technology may be unwittingly reinforced. Although there are clearly negative stories to be found, at the same time, women, in the same way that men do, find positive uses for ICTs for networking, work and leisure (Adam and Green 1998). This is as much a part of the story of gender, ICTs and ethics as the more negative aspects. Indeed it is often the inventive, unexpected uses of technologies which demonstrate that we are not driven by technology but have choices in its use.

What is privacy?

Although much of the discussion of previous chapters revolved around privacy in some form or other, I now wish to tackle the subject more directly and to make a start by considering legal and philosophical definitions of privacy. Allen (1998, p. 457) notes the importance of privacy in Western democracies, more or less on a par with liberty and equality as a central liberal value. Although privacy is a central notion in our lives, DeCew (1997) argues that it has only fairly recently been subject to detailed philosophical analysis. As a concept, it is complex, subject to much disagreement amongst commentators, and is historically and culturally contingent. As DeCew (ibid., p. 9) notes, legal protection for privacy in the USA has only developed in the last hundred or so years, despite political writing on the distinction between public and private extending back, at least to Aristotle. In Western societies, the conceptual distinction between public and private, and the assumption and marking of the boundary between them is a fundamental way of ordering our lives. Aristotle identified the *polis* as the public sphere where political activity and the governance of the state takes place. By contrast, the *oikos* is the private sphere of the household. We have already noted the strong identification of both concepts with gender in Chapter 2, and we will explore this, in more detail, in later sections.

In the late seventeenth century, the philosopher John Locke elaborated the distinction between public and private property, and, importantly the notion of owning one's self, one's own labour and the property where one has mixed one's own labour (Kramer 1997). Locke's views can be criticized for example, mixing one's labour with some property could mean one loses the labour rather than gaining the property (Johnson 2001). Nevertheless we can see Locke's approach, to some extent, as marking a move from a medieval view of privacy, where self and property are not necessarily owned by the individual (indeed only very powerful people could achieve such ownership), towards a modern world view where self and labour are regarded as under the ownership of the individual. However, this puts it rather simplistically as, clearly, many people could not achieve ownership of self, labour and property until much later than this and, arguably, many cannot achieve such ownership in the present day, even within Western democracies. For instance, we should note the persistence of slavery in the USA into the nineteenth century and the way that laws allowing married women to own property were only introduced, in the USA and UK from the middle to late nineteenth century so that by 1900, married women had substantial control over their own property in these countries (Lewis 2004). Indeed we should also recall Marx's theories of capital and labour where the ability to own and sell one's labour is the significant feature of modern capitalism. We may not agree with all aspects of Locke's writing on privacy and ownership, nevertheless it is the trend towards differentiation of self, and hence possibilities of privacy which is important in his work.

As Shapiro (1998, p. 277) notes: 'One of the hallmarks of the modern era in the West has been the rise of the individual as a social entity thoroughly distinct from the kinship unit and larger community.' This reinforces Stone's (1977) argument that, in sixteenth-century England, neither privacy, nor individual autonomy were seen as desirable. This was reflected in the design of dwellings which had a single communal, crowded room and only gradually began to be partitioned into separate rooms over time. From our vantage point we often forget just how different the world was for our pre-modern ancestors. Lyon (2001, p. 20) notes that this process of differentiation of the 'sovereign individual' was an important part of the emergence of capitalism and the nation state. 'Persons were distinguished from each other and from family, clan and city so that they might participate freely and effectively in the new democratic order. This is how the discourse of the "individual" appeared. Paradoxically though, the same move entailed the gathering of information on such individuals. Persons were more clearly unique as their individual identities were established but by the same token they became easier to discipline and control. Thus a transition occurred ... in the twentieth century, from knowledge by acquaintance to knowledge by description. Others came to be known by mediated information rather than direct co-presence' (ibid.).

The point, here, is that as a modern concept of privacy emerged along with the concept of the individual so did the notion of informational privacy, as opposed to purely physical privacy. It became feasible to know, not just someone, but to know information about them and to know that information without depending on their physical presence. This is a significant aspect of the historical relationship between technology and privacy, especially between ICTs and privacy, in that these greatly facilitate gathering, processing and disseminating information about individuals, hence offering much scope for informational privacy violation which, once again, must be subject to a gender analysis as we need to build up a picture of the ways in which informational privacy may be different for men and women.

The arguments of the preceding paragraph imply a strong cultural dimension to the development of the concept of privacy. As with many other concepts, it is possible to argue the relationship between cultural and 'biological' conceptions of privacy. For instance, anthropologists argue for some form of privacy as a cross-cultural and cross-species universal, and hence that there are always certain ways of setting distances and avoiding contact to establish physical boundaries for privacy which are common to all cultures. For the purposes of the present argument I believe it does not matter whether some aspects of privacy assume universal status or not, or where the boundary between nature and nurture lies – indeed it probably makes little sense to talk in such terms because we could not unequivocally decide where the boundary lies. The important point is that the evidence makes it reasonable to claim that at least a substantial part of our conception of privacy is culturally and historically contingent and that different groups may benefit or be disadvantaged at different times and, therefore, that an analysis of such variations may be interesting along gender lines.

In legal terms, the right to have control over information about oneself and the right to be let alone, as key concepts, began to crystallize in the nineteenth century. Although we may sometimes regard such thinking as a culture of extremes with regard to the cult of celebrity in contemporary life, the notion that one could be emotionally harmed rather than physically harmed was articulated in Warren's and Brandeis' landmark paper (1890) on the nature of privacy. Hence, as part of the privacy right to be let alone, this established the right of individuals to control publicity about themselves. As DeCew (1997, p. 21) notes the tendency, more recently, in legal cases on privacy, has been to move away from rights-based reasoning towards a utilitarian cost–benefit analysis where the needs of public safety and crime control are given precedence. This is hardly surprising in a world where there is heightened concern for terrorist activity.

In the USA, the concept of privacy has been linked to constitutional rights to freedom and liberty, to the extent that the right to choose whether or not to bear a child without government intrusion has been seen as a matter of privacy. 'This paved the way for using the constitutional right to privacy as a defense for the famous and controversial *Roe v. Wade* abortion decision ...' (Ibid., pp. 23–4)

In terms of legal philosophy there have been two broad views of privacy. Parent (1983) defines privacy as not having undocumented personal information about oneself known by others. He regards privacy as fundamental and unique, culturally contingent and a right from which other rights are derived. Such a view stands in contrast to the position of reductionists who regard privacy as deriving from other rights, such as property rights and bodily security, rather than existing as an independent right in itself.

These narrow legal views often do not express the full range of privacy rights, and potential violations that can occur. As noted above, the possible distinction between physical and informational privacy, and indeed the potential blurring of the two, are important, and, indeed, in my later discussion on gender and privacy it is a crucial distinction. I argue that we must consider whether the intersection of informational privacy and physical privacy is more significant for women than for men. The additional dimension of decisional privacy overlaps with both these and this signals that we must consider how far decisional privacy is problematic for women where women are accorded less privacy than men with regard to autonomy over decisions on their own lives.

Physical, decisional and informational privacies

Allen (1998, p. 458) defines physical privacy as freedom from unwanted physical observation or bodily contact. In Western societies physical privacy is often associated with the home although people expect a level of physical privacy in public places. For instance, they expect certain levels of physical distance from others when walking down a street and expect to be free from physical contact or encroachment of the body.

By contrast, informational privacy involves the confidentiality of information (ibid., p. 459). In the UK, the Data Protection Act (1998) limits what information may be held, and by whom, about individuals and also what may or may not be disclosed. This is one manifestation of the way in which technologies provide the potential for privacy to be invaded. However, we need to be wary of assuming that the important issues relating to privacy in the digital age are purely informational. If we consider topics such as surveillance we may see that concerns over bodily and spatial privacy blend and overlap with questions of digital and informational privacy. This is especially problematic for women as I discuss below.

In addition to physical and informational privacies, we should also note the idea of decisional privacy or the freedom to make and act upon one's own decisions without interference from state or other authorities. For instance it was this principle which was at stake in the USA, Roe *vs* Wade case which established the right to medical abortions (Allen 1988, pp. 90–1). The principle of decisional privacy is controversial; some argue that it is not a form of privacy at all but rather is a more general aspect of autonomy and freedom (Allen 1998, p. 460). Nevertheless as it signals a private realm where individuals may be free to make their own decisions and, as such, is an important part of women's experience of privacy.

Technology and privacy

As suggested above, technologies may make an important difference to our experiences of privacy. Our uses of them may permit us to create social worlds where there are increasing encroachments on our privacy; conversely they may allow us to find other ways of protecting privacy. Different kinds of privacy may be implicated (noting the three kinds of privacy characterized by Allen (1998)) and the relative impact on men and women may not be the same. Not surprisingly we may conclude that ICTs are an important part of the story of gender and privacy.

As the arguments of earlier sections of this chapter imply, culture and time make a considerable difference to our views of privacy and possible violations of privacy. Add to this the widespread view that our interactions with various technologies make a difference to privacy then we have a rich and varied picture of the privacy landscape changing over time (Agre and Rotenburg 1997; DeCew 1997; Shapiro 1998; Allen 2000). Shapiro (1998, p. 275) argues for a long-standing interaction between technologies and privacy, where, particularly for ICTs, the intangible nature of the technology is problematic. Rather than someone physically observing you in your home or somewhere else, aspects of your life may, rather, leak across certain boundaries, particularly the boundary between private and public, often signalled by the boundary between home and the wider world. Indeed technology has historically interacted with the home boundary, sometimes enhancing, sometimes restricting privacy. Even though no single approach can encompass all the issues, the boundary of the home suggests a useful analytical direction for addressing the privacy elements of new information and communications technologies.

The increasing number of ICTs available within the home has implications for privacy and the boundary between public and private that the home traditionally represents (Shapiro 1998). For instance, telecommuting has been a feasible work option for some time. Much has been written as to the benefits and drawbacks of telecommuting (Wilson and Greenhill 2004), and there is now more awareness that it is not the unmitigated benefit to women that earlier claims suggested, as they may, quite literally, be unable to switch off. Telecommuting may provide some level of individual privacy from surveillance by colleagues in the workplace, and control over one's own time, but this is lessened by the potential surveillance that may be exerted through the use of mobile phones and email. At the same time, working from home, using ICTs, may necessitate the setting up of a home workspace and negotiating a private boundary, between this workspace and the competing interests of other family members.

However, before the centralizing of manufacturing labour in the factory during the industrial revolution, the home was the locus of many technologies, but of work and production rather than of information and communication. Ostensibly, the home worker of the pre-factory era had a degree of control over physical privacy, at least in terms of not having work and person monitored by an employer, although workers might lease equipment from small business owners and subsistence living meant that most people had little choice but to work long and hard to scrape a living. Work had to be integrated into home life. In some cases this influenced the design of the dwelling place to a significant degree for example, workers' cottages in and around Macclesfield, the centre of the silk industry, in the North of England differed from the traditional terraced cottage of other textile workers in neighbouring areas in that the Macclesfield houses were built with an attic or 'garret' room with an unusually large window to gather extra light for the operation of the silk loom. This type of house was occupied by a master weaver and his family (Davies 1961). This served to separate the manufacturing technology from the rest of the family's life, perhaps at least partly because weaving was generally a male activity. Men weaved in the garrets, women made buttons in the outlying villages whilst children were employed in tying the silk threads (Feltwell 1990).

In relation to technologies of manufacturing production in the home, women were more likely to combine technology use with domestic chores and therefore had little chance of achieving a level of privacy by and through technology use. However masculine use of technology in the home was more likely to involve the availability of private space free from interference from other parts of family life for example, as with the loom in the garret. One could argue, in economic terms, for the primacy of masculine activities as men traditionally earned higher wages, yet all members of the family, women and children included, were engaged in economic activity. This point also serves to underscore the relationship between privacy, gender and status. Those accorded higher status have always achieved greater privacy by living in large uncrowded dwellings while the lower orders lived in more cramped, crowded conditions – witness the way that the medieval lord of the manor and his family slept in separate apartments while the servants slept all together in the hall.

The relationship between privacy and status, and the ways that technologies may be implicated in preserving both privacy and status can also be read along a gender dimension in that a greater degree of status and privacy often sticks better to masculine rather than feminine activities. This underscores a long-standing relationship between gender, technology and privacy. One could argue that the postulated gender/technology/privacy relationship will readily hold for such older technologies of manufacturing production where a physical artefact, often a fairly sizable artefact in relation to the size of dwelling, is constructed, and when it is the major instrument of the family's income. However, I shall argue below, that there is still a clear relationship between gender, technology and privacy even in relation to modern, much smaller scale ICTs where information, rather than a physical object, may be made or manipulated.

In modern societies there are increased opportunities to gain privacy through economic autonomy (say in comparison to feudal societies) and mobility yet, at the same time there are competing pressures of increased population density, technological advances and increased governmental control (DeCew 1997, p. 13). In the present time when we think about the relationship between technology and privacy, by technology we almost always mean ICTs. DeCew (ibid.) argues for technological advance as a major driver in the incorporation of privacy protection into US law, and as we saw in Chapter 4 this was certainly the spur for UK data protection law. Although social customs necessitated enforcing a certain degree of privacy protection, depending on the culture, things began to change at the turn of the last century.

> From the end of the nineteenth century on, however, the development of widespread communication through newsprint, the growth of mass transportation, and inventions such as the telephone and radio made informal methods of privacy protection both insufficient and ineffective. Development of the microphone and digital recorder, as well as the capacity to tap telephones, added to the technologies that made eavesdropping and electronic surveillance an increasing threat. (Ibid.)

At the beginning of the twenty-first century we might also add to this list, mobile and satellite communications, digital networks and the Internet. The use of electronic ICTs raises issues concerning physical, informational *and* decisional privacy which we now explore in more detail.

ICTs and privacy – electronic surveillance, the Panopticon and power

The question of surveillance is complex, but we start by considering physical privacy and surveillance – the watching of people and property. Technologies have always been an important part of physical surveillance and physical privacy. Lookout towers, ships' 'crows nests', castles on hills, castle windows shaped for firing arrows but not receiving them, telescopes and periscopes – all these are technologies of physical surveillance. However the one that has received most attention from social scientists in recent years is the metaphor of the 'Panopticon'. Although it was never built, the Panopticon was originally devised by the nineteenth-century British utilitarian philosopher, Bentham, as a model for a prison. It was not entirely original as there appear to have been a number of similar ideas in circulation at the time. Nevertheless it is with Bentham that the idea is usually associated. The idea behind the Panopticon is that there is a guard in a central tower surveying the individuals who are in cells in an annular building surrounding the tower (Foucault 1979, p. 200). Each cell has a window on the wall facing the guard and another window on the outer wall of the annular building and cells run the full width of the annular building. This effectively means that the cells are backlit so that the guard may observe the activities of each prisoner. The prisoners are unable to tell when the guard is looking at them, or indeed, whether the guard is there at all. The effect is to ensure that the prisoners discipline their own behaviour. This is the essence of the Panopticon – to isolate the prisoner so that prisoners would not interfere with one another or gang up against the prison guards, to make prisoners visible so that they would gain no privacy from the darkness of a dungeon, and finally, to ensure that the prisoner feels as though he or she is under constant surveillance.

In his landmark work, *Discipline and Punish*, Foucault (ibid.) describes the Panopticon as the classic instrument of power and discipline and his attention to the device has thrust the Panopticon into the consciousness of contemporary social sciences as a metaphor for power and discipline.

> Hence the major effect of the Panopticon: to induce in the inmate a state of conscious and permanent visibility that assures the automatic functioning of power. So to arrange things that the surveillance is permanent in its effects, even if it is discontinuous in its action; that the perfection of power should tend to render its actual exercise unnecessary; that this architectural apparatus should be a machine for creating and sustaining a power relation independent of the person who exercises it; in short, that the inmates should be caught up in a power situation of which they themselves are the bearers. (Ibid., p. 201)

The Panopticon disassociates seeing from being seen, and, importantly, removes the exercising of power from the individual into the technologies – bodies, surfaces, lights, gazes. It does not matter who operates it, nor what their reasons are for operating it. 'The Panopticon is a marvellous machine which, whatever use one may wish to put it to, produces homogeneous effects of power' (ibid., p. 202).

In its original conception, the Panopticon relates to surveillance and physical privacy, disciplining the individual through power relations inscribed within its technologies. The power does not reside with one individual; no one person exerts power over another, rather individuals discipline themselves under a faceless yet potentially ubiquitous gaze. Although Foucault made no mention of ICTs, his work on surveillance and the Panopticon has been immensely influential in recent conceptualizations of electronic surveillance, as part of what Lyon (1994, p. 57) has termed, 'the fashionable flurry of Foucault studies that began in the 1980s'.

Much of the original impetus for theorizing electronic surveillance sprang from the imaginary of Orwell's (1949) *Nineteen Eighty-Four* (Lyon 2001, p. 31). Although Lyon argues that much of the technological apparatus imagined in *Nineteen Eighty-Four* has long been superseded, some aspects of its vision of global electronic surveillance are clearly still relevant perhaps even more so where fear of terrorism grows stronger. However, although Orwell conceived of electronic surveillance in terms of the state, Lyon argues that, today, it is as much to do with the consumer as the citizen. The Panopticon has become the main alterative to 'Big Brother' in providing a model for contemporary electronic surveillance, yet he argues that we need to be cautious in understanding the limitations of the metaphor.

In Foucault's hands, the Panopticon marks the move from punitive to reforming disciplinary practices, in other words it is one of the markers between medieval and modern world views (ibid.). Lyon questions whether the electronic version can be regarded as a postmodern device where the subject has become decentred and sidelined. There is no single force, person or institution which is at the centre of the gaze. Rather, at least potentially, there is a societal panoptic mechanism. In terms of electronic surveillance this works on several levels.

Lyon (1994; 2001) suggests that electronic surveillance is, on one level, the accumulation of codified information, 'dataveillance' which is bound up with the bureaucratic administration, policing and defence of the nation state. Second, he refers to the monitoring of workers in the workplace. Note how some of this mirrors Foucault's discussion of the move from punitive to disciplinary methods of control when we move away from handcuffs to mechanisms such as electronic tagging so people are disciplined and manipulated rather than coerced.

However bureaucratic electronic surveillance is clearly not limited to defence and crime. Gandy (1993) notes that the tax collection authority in the USA, the US Internal Revenue is a major collector of personal data. On the one hand, whilst the instruments of state may be used for monitoring personal data, on the other hand, they may also be used for positive benefits such as administering the welfare state, making the targeting and distribution of welfare benefits much more manageable.

Focusing on the workplace, Zuboff's classic (1988), *In the Age of the Smart Machine*, explores the electronic Panopticon in the work environment. She claims that panopticism lies at the centre of contemporary management techniques. Witness the way that computer information systems allow the most minute level of work to be monitored. She argues that this generates new management styles where employee performance is seen as 'objective' data which may be monitored and may result in a much more vulnerable working environment of workers, who may seek resistance, but more commonly will remain compliant or risk dismissal. Although this is a form of workplace which significantly postdates Zuboff's research, it is notable how much of her analysis can be applied to the contemporary call-centre.

Richardson (2003) has noted the surveillance and disciplinary mechanisms at work in the call-centre through automated CRM (Customer Relationship Management) systems. These automate and manage knowledge and organizational intelligence. CRM systems attempt to codify knowledge and so control customer and other relationships. Through these, the company attempts to capture and standardize sales knowledge and oversee customer service. But they are also a means of monitoring the call-centre worker, recording how many calls are handled in a set time, noting how many breaks are taken, whether the worker follows the set script in making the call or deviates from it and so on. Unsurprisingly, turnover of call-centre workers is notoriously high.

Electronic surveillance through consumerism is another possibility (Robins and Webster 1999; Bartow 2003). A massive level of gathering of transactional information for example, phone bills, credit card transactions, web sites visited (through cookies) all contribute to building up a profile of personal consumer data. Although we may regard consumerist surveillance as containing the seeds of control and manipulation, at the same time, we cannot deny the growth of consumerism as a leisure activity, fuelled, in part, by the ease of financial transactions and electronic shopping.

Although noting the power of the electronic Panopticon metaphor across all these dimensions, Lyon (1994, p. 73) is, nevertheless, wary of extending it into a global societal explanatory device. 'Even if new technology does facilitate not only a novel penetration of the mundane routines of everyday life, but also a blurring of conventional boundaries, it is still not clear that this in itself augurs a general societal panopticism. Electronic panopticism may equally turn out to be a vestigial residue of modernity's – Benthamite – utopian hunger for certitude.'

Lyon also questions how far the panoptic metaphor can be used to explain the creation and maintenance of social order in contemporary capitalist societies. Social skills and economic capacity seduce the population to consume – however this is experienced by the majority as contributing to pleasure not, as the disciplinary coercion of Panoptic metaphor. Indeed, it is becoming increasingly clear that the moral dimension embedded in the original Panopticon metaphor has been subsumed under an instrumental discipline. As many do not experience disciplinary control in terms of imprisonment, Foucault's emphasis on increasingly centralized carceral control does not seem to map well onto this aspect of our experience. Only those who cannot participate fully in the consumer society, through lack of credit, dependence on benefits, and so on may feel the panoptic order as a prison.

These factors suggest that, useful though the panoptic model may be, there is no single metaphor which can capture the richness of the experience of electronic surveillance in contemporary life. Nevertheless, before leaving the topic of electronic surveillance and panopticism, it is useful to note the ways in which the types of privacy, identified by Allen (1998) are blurred through the use of electronic media. Although there has never been a complete separation between the two (as in pre-modern times one could argue that physical surveillance of an individual gave information about that individual, for example, state of health, gender, whether rich or poor), the line between physical and informational privacy is now thoroughly breached in the digital age. For instance, images relating to one's physical location and hence physical privacy are held and processed digitally. Think of the surveillance camera which has become ubiquitous in British towns and cities. It is notable that, although such devices become commonly accepted under the rubric of preserving social order and preventing crime, how often media reports of murders include poignant surveillance camera images of the last moments of the individuals involved; almost as if these can record information about events preceding the awful moment but, at the same time, rendering us powerless to act to prevent the ultimate violation of physical privacy, namely murder.

In the medical arena, the widespread construction of electronic patient records also signals a blurring of physical and informational privacy. The difference between medical, biological, bodily data and informational data is blurred in projects such as the human genome project and the mapping of DNA. The 'visible person' project where the body of a dead convict was sliced into thin sections and the images digitized for scientific study is an extreme example of the blended invasion of physical and informational privacy (Cartwright 1998).

It is the ability to match data to build up a bigger, perhaps erroneous, profile of an individual which marks out the potentially problematic aspects of modern database technology against informational privacy (Johnson 2001). Yet, in this case, there is also a blurring of the boundary between informational and decisional privacy. I have already noted Lyon's argument (1994) on the disciplinary power of electronic surveillance, its impact on consumers and how it is those who are without sufficient economic means who are likely to experience this in disciplinary terms. This is a case where informational privacy seeps into decisional privacy as information, even misinformation, about an individual's creditworthiness impacts significantly their ability to participate in consumer society, to decide to purchase goods, services and holidays. Our informational/decisional privacy is compromised as our movements in cyberspace are tracked, consumer profiles are constructed and we are bombarded with junk mail and spam email.

Surveillance and terrorism

We cannot, of course, leave the topic of surveillance without considering how contemporary fears of terrorist activity have circumscribed different opinions on the need for surveillance and the type of surveillance which might be needed. The rhetoric of the war on terror brings together physical, decisional and informational privacies into one arena as, increasingly, individuals and groups are watched, information about groups and individuals is gathered and the decisional privacy of individuals and groups becomes more tightly constrained in Western democracies under new legislation much of which was rushed through in the wake of the attacks of 11 September 2001. For instance the US Patriot Act permits access to medical and even library records. Under the UK Terrorism Act an individual suspected of terrorist activities may be detained indefinitely. There is a sense in which the panoptic disciplining and regulating of society is achieved through this. As individuals we do not know when our activities are under surveillance so we may regulate them accordingly. The mood is redolent of the Cold War where, especially in the USA, citizens were encouraged to be vigilant against the supposed perils of Communism.

Although we continue to be extremely concerned about terrorism, at the same time, fear of terrorism permits state authorities unprecedented controls over its citizens in Western democracies, as we are persuaded to abrogate our privacy in the cause of the war against terror. This makes it easier to have disciplinary and controlling regimes accepted where a few years ago these might have been unthinkable. For instance, as I write, there is considerable interest in the UK in a national database and individual identity cards. Although, a few years ago, such concepts would never have gained the level of enthusiasm they currently enjoy, there are prominent dissenters. Notably, the Information Commissioner, the 'watchdog' for data protection and the individual responsible for overseeing the enforcement of data protection legislation in the UK, has publicly declared his concerns on the idea of a national database and the possibility of 'function creep' in the amount and type of data held on individuals (BBC 2004).

The fear which terrorism inspires in us is not so distant from the fear that we have over the protection of our children. As Chapter 2 noted, in the UK, moves to set up a national database for children were made in the wake of high profile, tragic cases of child abuse and murder, but cannot replace the need to share data between authorities, to ensure proper training for those involved with children and importantly to foster a climate of care. Similarly, increased data surveillance and regulation of its citizens does not obviate the need for state authorities to take proper heed of intelligence about suspicious activities rather than focusing on the dissent of its citizens.

Hence the disciplinary society engendered by terrorist fears makes political dissent more difficult. For instance, despite widespread protest over the Iraq War there were those, in the USA, who regarded it as unpatriotic not to support the case for war. A further aspect of the war against terrorism can be seen in the way emergency anti-terrorist legislation makes it much easier for state authorities to detain individuals, even if they are subsequently released without charge. In this climate one suspects that those detained in this way are much more likely to be foreign nationals and there is a real concern for the possibility of 'Islamophobia'.

If we do make the analogy between fear of Communism and fear of terrorism we can see a distinct possibility in the rise of racism and far right nationalistic politics, except now, digital technologies promise an array of surveillance technologies unimaginable in the anti-Communism McCarthy era. It would be difficult to argue that women would be directly stigmatized in a backlash against those suspected of having links with terrorism. It is in an indirect sense that we are likely to see adverse effects on women's privacy in a more regulated, disciplined climate where political dissent and speaking up may be tolerated less and less.

Privacy and the gender–technology relation

Given the arguments of preceding chapters it is not surprising to find that men and women may experience privacy differently. Additionally, if, as I have argued above, technologies, and, in particular recent ICTs have a direct bearing on our experiences of privacy, this suggests that a consideration of gender and privacy against the use of ICTs would be a worthwhile analysis.

As Allen (1998, p. 456) points out, feminist research shows considerable ambivalence towards the topic of privacy. Whilst privacy has often been central to feminist critiques of liberal and patriarchal societies, some feminists regard privacy as a barrier to the liberation of women while others regard it as essential. How have these opposing views arisen?

As Chapter 2 discusses, much feminist energy has been channelled into challenging the public/private dichotomy and women's apparently natural association and subordination within the private sphere. The term 'privacy' readily attaches to the private sphere of family and home which has often been the seat of women's subordination and economic dependency. The problem then is that women can be powerless and harm to them can be ignored under the rubric of what is regarded as the private sphere.

Allen (1998, p. 463) classifies feminist critiques of privacy into three categories: the underparticipation critique, the violence critique and the conservative tilt critique. In terms of underparticipation, women's subordination in the home and the domestic sphere, often under the shield of female chastity and modesty, has frequently signalled women's inability to achieve full participation in the societies of which they are members. Women might have participated more in leading roles in work, politics, and so on had they not been confined to maternal and caring roles in the private sphere of the family. The issue of domestic violence, which can be hidden in the private sphere of the home, is still problematic. Although laws exist forbidding spouses to beat one another and forbidding parents to beat children, levels of domestic violence in the private sphere of the home, largely against vulnerable women and children often go unreported and unremediated (Olsen 1984). Finally the 'conservative tilt' approach of legal feminists revolves round the argument that the whole concept of privacy is inherently conservative, has obscured problems of underparticipation and therefore has acted as a brake on the legal processes that could have helped women.

The notion of privacy as a blanket concept deflects public attention away from domestic violence, underparticipation, and so on. Furthermore, conservatives often oppose measures that could offer more freedom to women for example, gay marriage, the right to abortion, welfare benefits, childcare, and so on.

On the other hand, many feminist embrace the ideal of privacy. For instance, in the USA, the right to birth control and abortion were won by arguments concerning the right to privacy and so vital freedoms for women as well as the right to independent decision making are seen as important positive feminist arguments (Allen 1988). In a nutshell, women have too much of the wrong kind of privacy and not enough of the right kind (ibid.). The wrong kind includes an imposed modesty, chastity, domestic isolation and possible even hidden domestic violence. The right kind includes opportunity for individual privacy and private choice. We can see some of this in my argument on cyberstalking. When women stay private that is, not speaking out in public they are not harassed. However, by being subject to cyberstalking when they do speak up on the Internet they are having their rights to privacy whilst acting in a public world violated.

Technology has played an important part in the ways that privacy is conceived and enacted as I discuss above. There are clear gender elements in the access to privacy in terms of the technologies of manufacturing production in relation to the home, as in the silk weaver example where the masculine art of weaving was accorded its own private space in the garret. Chapter 1 outlined the gender–technology relation and the ways in which gender and technology are mutually constitutive. Yet apart from research on gender and ICTs (where there has been some discussion of privacy and gender), there has been surprisingly little direct recognition of the bearing of privacy on the gender–technology relationship. Such commentary as exists tends to approach the topic more tangentially, for instance in considering the role of domestic technology in reinforcing the public/private split (Cowan 1989).

A consideration of gender and technology starts and, indeed, ends in the home. When technologies of manufacturing production still centred on the home, it made little sense to try to distinguish domestic technologies from work technologies as these were thoroughly intertwined and the household integrated into the market economy. However we can see the characterization of domestic technologies *as* domestic technologies through the invention of housework with the coming of the industrial era. As Cowan (ibid., p. 46a) notes, in relation to the USA but applicable elsewhere, before industrialization, all members of the family were involved in production and preparation of food and clothing for the family. With the coming of industrialization at the end of the eighteenth century and the invention of the cast-iron cooking stove or range, automatic flour mills and factory-produced clothes, the family became consumers rather than producers and women began to bear the whole burden of housework, whereas the home increasingly became a place of leisure for men and children. If not actually private in terms of space, men, at least, as the wage earner, could expect to have private time in pursuit of leisure, something that the new housewife could barely enjoy. Of course, it could be argued that as the housewife's domain, she could have expected to enjoy privacy in the space of the kitchen. However this was hardly the case. As the centre of family life, of cooking eating, mending, sitting, and so on, she was always on call for the rest of the family in her domain, the kitchen and so opportunities for privacy were severely curtailed.

Men's (and children's) pre-industrial household tasks of leather working, water carrying, butchery and others virtually disappeared during the industrial revolution (ibid., p. 64). By contrast, although women's relationship to the making of cloth changed when it began to be produced in factories, instead of decreasing their labour the demand for sewing and laundering vastly increased. The availability of cheap cloth signalled an increase in the amount of clothing people expected to own. The move to cotton fabrics (which could easily be washed) and away from rough woollens and linens which could only largely be brushed to be made clean heralded the invention of laundry and the extremely hard physical labour of the weekly wash day. Lack of privacy was even starker for poorer families with crowded living conditions, poor storage and little furniture.

As well as the invention of private time for masculine leisure activities with the coming of industrialization, we should also note that a number of domestic activities became centred on the home instead of becoming centralized. For instance note the idea of the commercial laundry. In the USA it had its heyday in the 1920s (ibid., p. 106), but persisted much longer in the UK as in the 'steamie' of the pre-war Scottish city. The invention of the automatic washing machine, vigorous advertising, increased economic prosperity – all these contribute to push family laundry back into the home and made, as the title of Cowan's book suggests, *More Work for Mother*.

Gender, privacy, ICTs

I have argued for a relationship between technology and privacy which has a significant, although underexplored, gender dimension.

In relation to contemporary ICTs and, in particular, the Internet, potential privacy violations have become increasingly apparent through problems such as spam email, cyberstalking, children targeted in chat rooms, cookies, and so on. This has prompted a flurry of interest, debate and, ultimately, legislation. However, as (Allen 2000), one of the leading US privacy law researchers, has noted, these debates have had relatively little to do with gender.

On one hand men and women may have their privacy violated in cyberspace – they share the same 'leaky boat' (ibid., p. 1176). Why then focus on gender?

> A woman-centered perspective on privacy in cyberspace is vital because only with such a perspective on privacy in cyberspace can we begin to evaluate how the advent of the personal computer and global networking, conjoined with increased opportunity for women, has affected the privacy predicament that once typified many American (sic) women's lives. (Ibid., p. 1177)

Allen identifies (ibid., p. 1178) the reasons why women's privacy is so precarious – they are often regarded as inferiors or of lower status. Double standards apply and this can be seen in the way that much more is often expected of women in terms of modesty and chastity and the way that women are often held more accountable than men for their personal conduct.

On the Internet, both men and women may have too little privacy, in that emails may not be private, personal and financial data may not be kept secret. On the other hand both men and women may suffer from too much privacy as the relative anonymity of Internet transactions can mask harassment, and various other forms of anti-social and, indeed, criminal misconduct as our prior discussions of hacking, Internet dating and cyberstalking demonstrate. Allen (ibid., p. 1177) asks, given that these things can affect both men and women, why problematize gender and privacy in cyberspace?

Women's traditional predicament is too much of the wrong type of privacy, as noted above the imposition of modesty, chastity and domestic isolation (ibid.). On the other hand they do not have enough of the right sort of privacy that is, opportunities for individual privacy and private choice. In particular, women are more vulnerable to privacy problems and they are often held more accountable for their private conduct than are men. However improvements in women's standing in the family and society in general, mean that women have begun to achieve better access to privacy in many countries.

If women are tending to enjoy improved privacy rights it would not be unreasonable to expect that they would enjoy similar privacy benefits and possibly suffer similar privacy violations as men in a newly developed medium such as cyberspace. Similarly the rhetoric that new media and new disciplines will naturally tend to be more egalitarian than older ones is an argument which emerges time and time again (e.g. see Adam *et al.* (2001) for criticisms of this view in relation to the field of IS), the idea being that a new discipline will not have had time to establish old stereotypes of gendered behaviour. However this is a typical liberal argument which fails to recognize the deep structural reasons why women often end up in a subordinate position and why equality is not an emergent property of a new social arrangement. Women do not have the same access to desirable privacy as men do in cyberspace. This is borne out by many of the arguments of preceding chapters in relation to Internet pornography, computer-mediated communication, harassment and cyberstalking. With regard to computer-mediated communication, Herring (1996) argues that gender stereotypical behaviour is often writ large. To this, one might add Allen's comment: 'Some of the worst features of the real world are replicated in cyberspace, including disrespect for women and the forms of privacy and intimacy women value' (2000, p. 1179).

Concern with enhancing privacy, and establishing legal measures to protect it, has steadily grown in the last three decades, at least partly in response to perceived threats connected with computers and surveillance. Cyberspace replicates the traditional spaces in which women dwell and where similar harassment may occur. Interestingly, Allen (ibid., p. 1184) points to the ways in which women may voluntarily give up their privacy on the Internet. There may be such a thing as wanting, as well as having, too little privacy. Feminists may assume that if women could get real privacy they would want it.

> Recent experience in cyberspace suggests, though, that some women, who finally have the ability to demand real privacy and intimacy, are opting for less rather than more of it, using their freedom to abrogate privacy ... While some of the women who bare it all on the Internet are objects of exploitation rather than agents, others are pleasure seekers, entrepreneurs, artists and educators – persons not easily construed as subordinated victims of pornographers and the male entertainment industry. (Ibid., pp. 1185, 1186)

One such example was 'JenniCAM' (Jimroglou 2001) probably the first, and certainly the best known webcam into an 'ordinary' woman's life. Viewers could watch her at home moving from room to room, mainly engaged in mundane activities, but occasionally naked and/or engaging in sexual activities. JenniCAM inspired a huge cult following and it was estimated that the site obtained around 100 million hits per week. Jenny Ringley, the originator of the site, suggested that it was not that she *liked* being watched, rather that she did not *mind* being watched (ibid.). However we should note that as JenniCAM was a pay view site, Jenny Ringley made a great deal of money from exposing her life to the gaze of others.

One can, of course, question how far Ringley's experience mirrors or opposes the experiences of women who deliberately sell their images on the Internet and sites which are clearly part of an Internet pornography industry.

The first mastectomy to be broadcast live on the Internet took place in 1999 (Allen 2000, p. 1188).

> Here we have a woman who did not regard the fact of her surgery as a matter for strict confidence; who was not ashamed to reveal to strangers that she had breast cancer and that her breasts had been removed hoping to cure it; and who was unafraid to disclosed her breasts in public despite the taboo ... Her abrogation of privacy, modesty and shame for the sake of educating the public about an important public health problem is something many feminist would applaud. (Ibid., pp. 1188–9)

Another example of women dispensing with usual privacy can be seen in the weblog or 'blog.' This may satisfy women's traditional desire to keep a diary and, of course, the diarist may remain anonymous. Recently, I was intrigued to find a description of a lecture I had given reported on a woman student's 'blog'. She had not identified herself in the weblog but I was easily identifiable from her description. Although there were no salacious details on her weblog, she described mundane things such as the part-time job she had just acquired, I felt myself at once fascinated and yet intrusive.

Similarly, women may benefit from the opportunities available to network on the Internet, to join virtual communities, to organize romantic and sexual encounters. Although I have emphasized some of the negative aspects of Internet dating, this does not preclude the pos- sibility of positive interactions. Bartow (2003) points to the tension

between women's desire to protect their privacy vs a need to participate fully in online life. For instance, in relation to new interest in
e-commerce, if women continue in their traditional roles as the main
shoppers for families, they may also be disproportionately targeted by
online profiling and therefore be suffering violations of informational
privacy. For instance, Bartow notes how affluent women in various age
groups are seen as a lucrative emerging e-market.

There is clearly a felt need for some women to dispense with normal
standards of privacy in certain circumstances on the Internet. This may
be for commercial reasons such as pornography, exhibitionism or a mixture of the two which may be the case with JenniCAM, or to educate,
such as in the broadcast mastectomy. Increased opportunities for social
and sexual encounters are made possible through the use of the
Internet. Yet, at the same time, there is plenty of evidence to suggest that
many women experience privacy intrusions on the Internet. Chapter 6
detailed problems of harassment, cyberstalking and the use of images of
children in child pornography.

Indeed it is the use of images without consent which constitutes one
of the biggest potential breaches of women's privacy. For instance, film
actors knowingly consent to a certain loss of privacy when they appear
in films intended for mass consumption. Yet, at the same time, many
famous figures regard unauthorized used of their image as a severe intrusion on their privacy. Witness the furore when famous media couples
find unauthorized wedding photographs published. An additional problem is presented with pseudo photographs. Digitally created images of
well-known people can be readily made – these of course can be porno-
graphic. We have already noted, in Chapter 6, the persistence of images
on the Internet. Pornographic images of abused children continue to
circulate years after the images were made. Similarly appropriation of
women's images can occur as can appropriation of identity. 'Third-party'
cyberstalkers deliberately appropriate women's identities in chat rooms
in order to incite others to stalk them. We may have little or no control
over the length of time the tracks left by such cyberstalkers persist
so that women may continue to be harassed by others long after the
original capture of their images or identities.

Conclusion

This chapter has considered privacy, how this may be different for men
and for women and the historical relationship between privacy and technology. This relationship is especially sharpened by the introduction of

ICTs. I note that there are gendered elements to physical, informational and decisional privacy and that these three types of privacy may be helped and hindered for women through the mediation of ICTs.

It may not, at first, be obvious that women's physical privacy should be mediated by ICTs – the mediation is often somewhat indirect, although potentially devastating. It is notable, for instance that a number of the cyberstalking cases outlined in Chapter 6 involved violations of physical privacy, even the ultimate violation of privacy as in the murder of Amy Boyer (Wright 2000). Hence the violations of women's informational privacy which cyberstalking involves may lead to violations of physical privacy. Chapter 6 described instances where women either were visited or feared visits from men encouraged by false postings in chat rooms in their names. Indeed with a heightened awareness of the potential blurring of boundaries between real and virtual we must start to question how far incidents, such as 'cyberspace rapes' are a violation of purely informational privacy or whether physical privacy is not somehow implicated as well.

Cyberstalking and virtual rapes also illustrate the way in which decisional privacy is thoroughly bound up with physical and informational privacy. An example from my own experience illustrates this. I was recently contacted by a woman who appeared to be subject to cyberstalking. When using various Internet facilities she had received anonymous messages. The messages were not, in themselves, abusive, but they indicated she was being watched, that someone knew when she was logged on and what she was doing. She felt she knew her stalker but the police had been unable to help as there appeared to be no 'physical' threat involved. However she indicated that this was interfering with her desire to set up and run a business on the Internet. This was, therefore, a chain of privacy invasion which interfered with her decisional privacy, in her ability to make autonomous decisions about how to run her life. This also involves Allen's point (2000) about good and bad privacy for women. Good privacy involves the ability to keep features of one's life private, including one's ability to make autonomous decisions about one's life. Bad privacy may involve an enforced modesty and chastity for women, limiting them and keeping from the world. But is also means limiting them in the sense of limiting their autonomous choices, especially in terms of their ability to operate on equal terms in the public world of work. This was what was happening to the woman in my example. Her stalker not only invaded her informational privacy but, additionally, had substantially implicated her decisional privacy by compromising her chances of successfully setting up a business on the Internet.

In this chapter my aim has been to reveal the complexities of the concept of privacy, the contingent nature of privacy in historical and cultural terms, the relationship between technology and privacy with its gendered dimension, both in terms of older forms of technologies of production and newer ICTs, the relationship between privacy and gender and, finally, the ways in which privacy may be abrogated or invaded by and for women through the use of ICTs. In this story I want to avoid adopting a technologically determinist position with the concomitant assumption that invasions of privacy are somehow 'caused' by the technology or are inevitable results of utilizing technology. As the above discussion demonstrates, women, and indeed men, have choices about how to use technology and these choices are often inventive and unexpected. Additionally the choices that are made may occasionally force us to revise our stereotypes of gender relations for example, where women voluntarily give up their privacy as in the JenniCAM example. We also need to be wary of assuming that invasion of women's privacy through the use of ICTs is a new issue. As is so often the case with computer ethics we see new variants of old problems, implying that we should, at least, consider old ways of dealing with such problems before suggesting new ways. Nevertheless, we should not underestimate the ease with which ICTs make possible some behaviours and how this impacts on women's lives and privacy.

9
Epilogue: Feminist Cyberethics?

At the start of this project, my original intention was to offer something new to the theoretical debate in terms of a feminist ethics informed by a feminist analysis of computer ethics problems – a 'feminist cyberethics'. In particular, I had grand plans to incorporate care ethics into technology ethics. I have not quite lost sight of the feminist cyberethics project but I now believe my original project is not feasible and probably not desirable, at least in its original form. So the questions remain. Why was the original project infeasible and where does that leave us?

On one level, constructing a feminist cyberethics seems far too grand a plan. If we heed the warnings of Smart (1989) in regard to the problems with constructing a feminist jurisprudence we may end up replacing one totalizing discourse with another. In relation to ethics we have the danger that the very problems that beset traditional ethics, and of which feminists are so critical, may well attend our attempts to construct a new discourse. I am thinking of the question of power and who gets to make ethical decisions and moral policy, a question which was aired in some detail in Chapters 2 and 3. We do not want to end up with a situation where one set of voices is privileged over another. This may not seem a very likely possibility in feminist discourse which is highly attuned to the politics of difference and the ways that women are so often cast in a subordinate position. However, I note Koehn's criticisms (1998) of care ethics where the carer retains power over the cared for. Additionally other traditional seats of feminist moral thinking, for example, mothering and care for others seem to offer levels of control and power to the one doing the caring over those who are cared for, even though a high level of self-sacrifice is demanded of those in caring and mothering roles, at the same time.

For my purposes, at least, the critical potential of feminist ethics has far outweighed the more substantial alternative care ethics currently offered by feminist ethics. Nevertheless, I hope it is clear from my discussions of translating ethics into law, in the data protection examples, cyberstalking and privacy, that I see a more caring, relational form of ethics, where men's and women's experiences are equally valued and where the power relations of ethical decision making are made explicit, as preferable to the individualistic, rationalistic and often emotionless forms of ethics we inherit from the traditional canon.

The perils of a totalizing discourse might be one problem to be avoided but there is a potentially much more substantial limiting factor to my original aim. This relates to the way that there is almost no overlap between the disciplines which I identify as relevant to my project. Of course that was part of the pleasure of the challenge of this work – to make them relevant to each other and to find the overlaps. I have tried to bring them together into the same conceptual room and make them talk. I hope that when I leave the room they will still talk and not slope off to their own rooms. Hence, I have, at least, tried to make a start to this process in this book, but I am conscious that there is much more to be done, not least in terms of further substantial empirical studies informed by wider theoretical concerns.

However, throughout this project, my suspicion has grown that, at least some of the disciplines which I argue need to come together, are too far apart, conceptually, in terms of research method and empirically unless we can successfully undertake more studies of the type I suggested earlier. I alluded very briefly in Chapter 1 to the feminist science and technology literature as being the backcloth against which I have undertaken this project. However, in subsequent chapters I made little explicit mention of this literature, although some of the studies on gender and technology that I reference (e.g. Henwood 1993; Faulkner 2000) and indeed, my own earlier work (Adam 1998) fall very much within that domain. It may appear that I have not used that literature as much as I might have done. This has been deliberate. One reason resonates with Wajcman's point (2004) that traversing the full range of feminist scholarship on technology is now impossible in one volume and that one has to regard one's work as a continuation of earlier projects. For me, the present work is, in some senses a follow on project from *Artificial Knowing*, where I discuss the development of feminist science and technology studies, and related research on women and computing in some detail. Although I am conscious that not all readers of the present work will be familiar with feminist science and technology studies or 'technoscience' research, I have taken for granted some of its findings, namely the association of masculinity with technology and related issues, without spelling these out in great detail.

This is the main reason for not digging too deep into the feminist technoscience literature, at this juncture. Additionally, there is the very real possibility that a study, such as this one, asks much of its readers in terms of taking on board many theoretical strands. There is a danger that we might never get to the punch-line. I felt that bringing feminist law, politics and ethics (already weighty in theoretical terms) to this study was a fairly original approach. It might have been more obvious, although less original to couch it more explicitly against feminist technoscience. It might also have been possible to bring all these disciplines into the equation, but making all the links would have been a book length study in itself.

I hope that the discussion of earlier chapters has made it clear that feminist politics, law and ethics are fairly congruent sub-disciplines, but I am not sure how well feminist technoscience currently fits into this picture. It is not that I feel that feminist studies of science and technology will contradict the findings of feminist politics, law and ethics. Far from it; rather, it is heartening just how much the issues discussed within these disciplines relate to one another, when one examines them in detail and how far they strike a chord with feminist technoscience research. Although this might seem an odd assertion of a discipline which, by any standards, is rarely seen as mainstream, apart from, perhaps the work of Haraway (1991), and research on reproductive and domestic technologies, feminist studies of science and technology are often rather separate from the rest of the feminist academy. This is especially so of engineering, physical sciences and computing and IT. It is as if the absence of women in these areas has mapped onto an absence of feminist studies of the same domains. This means that we generally get little discussion of some topics in more 'mainstream' parts of feminism. For instance, it is notable that a fairly recent, comprehensive feminist collection on pornography makes no mention of Internet pornography (Cornell 2000). It is also surprising to find recent, otherwise comprehensive, surveys of the feminist field which make no mention of technology as a major topic of interest within feminist scholarship (Jackson and Jones 1998).

Most pertinently for the present study, this lack of intersection between relevant feminist domains and feminist technoscience, manifests itself in the way that there has been so little research from feminist ethics in relation to the physical sciences and engineering and, importantly, in relation to IT and computing, from within feminist ethics itself. So, if some of my project involves taking computer ethics to task for not knowing about feminist ethics it should, perhaps also involve taking feminist ethics to task for not knowing about computer ethics.

I have no doubt that were feminist ethicists to take on board some of the issues I raise in this book we might have a different feel to care ethics and maternal ethics. This is where feminist technoscience comes in as the lens which feminist ethics (and the related domains of feminist law and politics) can use in order to create case studies which derive from IT, engineering and physics rather than from women's traditional caring roles in mothering, nursing, and so on. The exciting part of this involves stepping outside some of the stereotypical caring roles where we may be assuming that women will always reside (Koehn 1998), and opening up ethical thinking to new roles for women in science and technology. In any case were we to witness feminist ethics and politics opening up to technology and science more wholeheartedly, this might be useful in countering some of the 'democracy as emergent property of the Internet' which I have criticized in previous chapters. We also find this uncritical view of technology in some approaches to feminist technoscience such as 'cyberfeminism' (Wajcman 2004) which, although celebratory of women's use of IT, tends to belong to the cybercultute genre with its apolitical style and technological determinism.

Furthermore, when we think more specifically of IT and computing, the current state of business ethics is very pertinent. I have noted, in previous chapters, the pressure from big business, in terms of the will of the IT industry to become a profession, the push to make computer ethics not appear too theoretical, the way that 'official' efforts to control cyberstalking can be seen in terms of business needs rather than as part of the duty of a caring sociey and the push for data protection legislation to follow on from the requirements of electronic commerce. I have also noted, particularly in Chapter 5, that the pressure to conform to the research style of academic business research has constrained the relatively few empirical studies on gender and computer ethics that currently exist from within business and management research. This strongly suggests that feminist ethics must tackle business ethics as well.

If the feminist cyberethics project must await further scholarship bringing feminist technoscience into feminist ethics, law and politics, I hope at least, to have made a modest start to the process. The problem of technological determinism is not new. It has received a thorough critique within contemporary science and technology studies

(MacKenzie and Wajcman 1999) and within feminist technoscience research (Wajcman 2004). The relationship between a liberal world view and technological determinism has also been noted before (Winner 1997). However I do not feel that the implications of the link between technological determinism and liberalism have, hitherto, received the attention they deserve, particularly in terms of their relationship to feminist critiques of liberalism. I hope to have shown something of the importance of these links, in relation to a more gender aware approach to computer ethics. In particular, that central plank of liberalism, the public/private split is of paramount importance in understanding debates about privacy in computer ethics and how privacy issues relate so strongly to gender. Once we acknowledge that understanding, I hope that it becomes clear that some computer ethics issues such as cyberstalking can only really be understood if we take gender into account. Similarly if we open up surveillance to inspection, to understand it in terms of the power of the gaze we can understand that women and men, and, importantly, children, may have different access to privacy, that technology has historically been interwoven with our understanding of privacy and continues to be so through our use of ICTs.

The low numbers of women in technological disciplines, including IT, does matter and I concur with Wajcman (2004) that more women in technology would make a difference. This is not because equal numbers of men and women makes equality prevail – a dangerous liberal argument which denies existing power structures which continue to subjugate women. It is rather, as Wajcman suggests, more women involved in the design of technology would be bound to make a difference to the type of technologies which were designed and produced, although not in ways which we would necessarily be able to predict.

Although I do not deny the importance of the lack of women in technology I hope I have made a convincing argument that the relationship between gender and ICTs, especially in ethical terms is much more than a numbers game. For instance, I have been critical of empirical studies which appear preoccupied with the ratio of men and women making certain types of ethical decisions rather than relating their research to feminist ethics. Women's absence can be a presence of another sort as, if they are absent, it is then incumbent upon us to explain their absence. In technological domains this often involves a recognition of the obdurate link between masculinity and technology. Gender can be a very revealing construct even when women are absent. We see this in an analysis of the hacker phenomenon where the ethics surrounding hacking, although seemingly free and open to all, actually reinforces a particular brand of masculinity which serves to exclude women and to marginalize them.

Indeed it is hard to see how we can adopt a more caring, feminist inspired ethics in Internet interactions when 'technolibertarian' views abound where the need to protect vulnerable members of society is subordinated to the freedom of speech ethic. For all the superficial appeal of the 'hacker ethic' it is a dangerously libertarian position.

Although women continue to be harassed on the Internet, there are many examples of women successfuly networking and organizing politically by digital means (Shade 2002). Although they do not grab the headlines in the way more 'macho' hacktivism examples do (Jordan and Taylor 2004), they do, nevertheless, point to a preferable ethics than the hacker ethic.

In calling for feminist ethics to take heed of technology and to join forces with feminist technoscience to construct a more technologically aware ethics to counter the challenges of new technologies and men's and women's relationship to them, I do not wish to lose sight of my initial criticisms of computer ethics. I hope that by showing how alternative theoretical viewpoints, here from feminism, can enrich the subject, I have at least gone some way to show that computer ethics is a subject which should not be regarded just as a rather marginal part of the IT curriculum. Instead, it is a potentially vital part of our critical armoury in understanding both the relationships between ethics, policy and law and also how we may begin to influence that relationship outside the academy, in the wider world, with a feminist voice.

Bibliography

Adam, A. (1989). Spontaneous generation in the 1870s: Victorian scientific naturalism and its relationship to medicine. PhD thesis, Department of Historical and Critical Studies. Sheffield, UK, Sheffield Hallam University.

Adam, A. (1998). *Artificial Knowing: Gender and the Thinking Machine.* London and New York, Routledge.

Adam, A. (2001a). Gender and computer ethics. *Readings in CyberEthics.* R. Spinello and H. T. Tavani (eds) Sudbury MA, Jones and Bartlett: 63–76.

Adam, A. (2001b). Computer ethics in a different voice. *Information and Organization* 11(4): 235–61.

Adam, A. (2001c). Pornography and the Internet: 'the biggest dirty bookshop in history?' *ACM Computers and Society* 31(2): 36–40.

Adam, A. (2002). Cyberstalking and Internet pornography: gender and the gaze. *Ethics and Information Technology* 4(2): 133–42.

Adam, A. and E. Green (1998). On-line leisure: gender and ICTs in the home. *Information, Communication and Society* 1(3): 291–312.

Adam, A., D. Howcroft and H. Richardson (2001). Absent friends? The gender dimension in IS research. *Realigning Research and Practice in Information Systems Development: The Social and Organizational Perspective.* N. L. Russo, B. Fitzgerald and J. I. DeGross (eds). Norwell MA and Dordrecht, Kluwer: 333–52.

Adam, A. and J. Ofori-Amanfo (2000). Does gender matter in computer ethics? *Ethics and Information Technology* 2(1): 37–47.

Adam, A. and H. Richardson (2001). Feminist philosophy and information systems. *Information Systems Frontiers* 3(2): 143–54.

Adam, A. and P. Spedding (2004). Balancing acts: symmetry, impartiality and reflexivity in explanations of IS success and IS failure. Unpublished report, Information Systems Organization and Society Research Centre, University of Salford, UK.

Addelson, K. P. (1994). *Moral Passages: Toward a Collectivist Moral Theory.* New York and London, Routledge.

Agre, P. and M. Rotenburg, eds (1997). *Technology and Privacy: The New Landscape.* Cambridge, MA, MIT Press.

Akrich, M. (1992). The de-scription of technical objects. *Shaping Technology/Building Society: Studies in Sociotechnical Change.* W. E. Bijker and J. Law. (eds). Cambridge, MA and London, MIT Press: 205–24.

Alcoff, L. and E. Potter, eds (1993). *Feminist Epistemologies.* New York and London, Routledge.

Allen, A. L. (1988). *Uneasy Access: Privacy for Women in a Free Society.* Totowa, NJ, Rowman and Littlefield.

Allen, A. L. (1998). Privacy. *A Companion to Feminist Philosophy.* A. M. Jaggar and I. M. Young (eds). Malden, MA and Oxford, Blackwell: 456–65.

Allen, A. L. (2000). Gender and privacy in cyberspace. *Stanford Law Review* 52: 1175–200.

Alvesson, M. and H. Willmott, eds (2003). *Studying Management Critically.* London, Thousand Oaks, CA and New Delhi, Sage.

Ayres, R. (1999). *The Essence of Professional Issues in Computing*. London and New York, Prentice Hall.

Baase, S. (1997). *A Gift of Fire: Social, Legal, and Ethical Issues in Computing*. Upper Saddle River, NJ, Prentice Hall.

Baier, A. C. (1998). What do women want in a moral theory? *Ethics: The Big Questions*. J. P. Sterba (ed). Malden, MA and Oxford, Blackwell: 325–31.

Barlow, J. P. (1996). Selling wine without bottles: the economy of mind on the global net. *High Noon on the Electronic Frontier: Conceptual Issues in Cyberspace*. P. Ludlow (ed.). Cambridge, MA and London, MIT Press: 9–34.

Barnes, B. and S. Shapin, eds (1979). *Natural Order: Historical Studies of Scientific Culture*. Beverly Hills, CA and London, Sage.

Bartow, A. (2003). Women as targets: the gender-based implications of online consumer profiling. Online Profiling Project. Comment, P994809/ Docket No. 990811219-9219-01. http://www.ftc.gov/bcp/workshops/profiling/ comments/ bartow.htm (accessed 30 August 2004).

BBC (2003). Operation Ore: can the UK cope? 13 January 2003 http://news. bbc.co.uk/1/hi/uk/2652465.stm (accessed 30 August 2004).

BBC (2004). Watchdog's 'alarm' over ID cards. http://news.bbc.co.uk/1/hi/ uk_politics/3787971.stm, 8 June 2004 (accessed 30 August 2004).

Bell, S. (1988). *When Salem came to the Boro'*. London, Pan.

Bissett, A. and G. Shipton (1999). An investigation into gender differences in the ethical attitudes of IT professionals. ETHICOMP99, Rome.

Bloor, D. (1976). *Knowledge and Social Imagery*. London, Routledge & Kegan Paul.

Bocij, P. and L. McFarlane (2003). Seven fallacies about cyberstalking. *Prison Service Journal* **149**(September 2003): 37–42.

Bocij, P. and M. Sutton (2004). Victims of cyberstalking: piloting a web-based survey method and examining tentative findings. *Journal of Society and Information* **1**(2). http://josi.spaceless.com/article.php?story = 2000214050558297 (accessed 30 August 2004).

Bott, F., A. Coleman, J. Eaton and D. Rowland (1991). *Professional Issues in Software Engineering*. London, Pitman.

Bowden, P. (1997). *Caring: Gender-Sensitive Ethics*. London and New York, Routledge.

Brail, S. (1996). The price of admission: harassment and free speech in the wild, wild west. *wired_women: Gender and New Realities in Cyberspace*. L. Cherny and E. Wise (eds). Seattle, WA, Seal Press: 141–57.

Brosnan, M. J. (1998). *Technophobia: The Psychological Impact of Information Technology*. London and New York, Routledge.

Burt, T. (1997). Stalking and voyeurism over the Internet: psychiatric and forensic issues. *Proceedings of the Academy of Forensic Science* **3**: 172.

Camp, T. (1997). The incredible shrinking pipeline. *Communications of the ACM* **40**(10): 103–10.

Cartwright, L. (1998). A cultural anatomy of the visible human project. *The Visible Woman: Imaging Technologies, Gender and Science*. P. A. Treichler, L. Cartwright and C. Penley (eds). New York and London, New York University Press: 21–43

Case, D. (2000). Stalking, monitoring and profiling: A typology and case studies of harmful uses of caller ID. *New Media and Society* **2**(1): 67–84.

Castells, M. (2000). *The Rise of the Network Society (2nd edition)*. Oxford and Malden, MA, Blackwell.

CIEC (1997). The Internet is not a television, http://www.ciec.org, (accessed 20 January 2003).

Clare, A. (2000). *On Men: Masculinity in Crisis*. London, Chatto and Windus.

Cornell, D., ed. (2000). *Feminism and Pornography*. Oxford, Oxford University Press.

Cowan, R. S. (1989). *More Work for Mother: The Ironies of Household Technology from the Open Hearth to the Microwave*. London, Free Association Books.

Coward, R. (1984). *Female Desire*. London, Paladin.

Cudd, A. (2001). Objectivity and ethno-feminist critiques of science. *After the Science Wars*. K. Ashman and P. Baringer (eds). New York and London, Routledge: 80–97.

Davies, C. S. (1961). *A History of Macclesfield*. Manchester, Manchester University Press.

Dawkins, R. (1976). *The Selfish Gene*. Oxford, Oxford University Press.

DeCew, J. (1997). *In Pursuit of Privacy: Law, Ethics, and the Rise of Technology*. Ithaca, NY and London, Cornell University Press.

Denning, L. (1980). *The Due Process of Law*. London, Butterworth.

Denzin, N. (1995). *The Cinematic Society: The Voyeur's Gaze*. London, Thousand Oaks and New Delhi, Sage.

Diprose, R. (1994). *The Bodies of Women: Ethics, Embodiment and Sexual Difference*. London and New York, Routledge.

Douglas, M. (1966). *Purity and Danger: An Analysis of the Concepts of Pollution and Taboo*. London and New York, Ark.

Dworkin, A. (1981). *Pornography: Men Possessing Women*. London, The Women's Press.

Dyer, C. (2004). Data act 'often unfairly blamed' The Guardian, 14 January 2004 http://www.guardian.co.uk/soham/story/0,14010,1122553,00.html (accessed 27 August 2004).

Easton, S. M. (1994). *The Problem of Pornography: Regulation and the Right to Free Speech*. London and New York, Routledge.

Edwards, P. (2003). Nerd worlds: computer hackers, unofficial culture and masculine identities, unpublished paper, Program in Science, Technology and Society, Stanford University, Stanford, CA.

Ellison, L. (2001). Cyberstalking: tackling harassment on the Internet. *Crime and the Internet*. D. S. Wall (ed.). London and New York, Routledge: 141–51.

Escribano, J. J., R. Pena and J. Extremeta (1999). Differences between men and women in terms of usage and assessment of information technologies. ETHICOMP 99, Rome.

Ess, C. (1996a). The political computer: democracy, CMC, and Habermas. *Philosophical Perspectives on Computer-Mediated Communication*. C. Ess. (ed.). Albany, NY, State University of New York Press: 197–230.

Ess, C., ed. (1996b). *Philosophical Perspectives on Computer-Mediated Communication*. Albany, NY, State University of New York Press.

Fagan, E. F. (2001). *Cast Your Net: A Step-by-Step Guide to Finding Your Soul Mate on the Internet*. Boston, MA, Harvard Common Press.

Faulkner, W. (2000). The power and the pleasure? A research agenda for 'making gender stick'. *Science, Tehnology & Human Values* 25(1): 87–119.

Feltwell, J. (1990). *The Story of Silk*. Stroud, UK, Alan Sutton.

Fineman, M. A. (1991). Introduction. *At the Boundaries of Law: Feminism and Legal Theory*. M. A. Fineman and N. S. Thomadsen (eds). New York and London, Routledge: xi–xvi.

Fitzgerald, B. and D. Howcroft (1998). Towards dissolution of the IS research debate: from polarisation to polarity. *Journal of Information Technology* **13**: 313–26.

Forsythe, D. (1993). Engineering knowledge: the construction of knowledge in artificial intelligence. *Social Studies of Science* **23**: 445–77.

Foucault, M. (1979). *Discipline and Punish: The Birth of the Prison*. London, Penguin.

Frazer, E. (1998). Feminist political theory. *Contemporary Feminist Theories*. S. Jackson and J. Jones (eds). Edinburgh, Edinburgh University Press: 50–61.

Gandy, O. (1993). *The Panoptic Sort: A Political Economy of Personal Information*. Boulder, CO, Westview Press.

Gatens, M. (1996). *Imaginary Bodies: Ethics, Power and Corporeality*. London and New York, Routledge.

Gaus, G. (1999). Liberalism. The Stanford Encyclopedia of Philosophy (Fall 1999 Edition), E. Zalta (ed.). http://plato.stanford.edu/archives/fall1999/entries/liberalism/ (acessed 24 November 1999).

Gibson, W. (1984). *Neuromancer*. London, Grafton.

Gilligan, C. (1982). *In a Different Voice: Psychological Theory and Women's Development*. Cambridge, MA, Harvard University Press.

Gilligan, C. (1987). Moral orientation and moral development. *Women and Moral Theory*. E. F. Kittay and D. T. Meyers (eds). Totowa, NJ, Rowman & Littlefield: 19–33.

Goldberger, N., J. Tarule, B. Clinchy and M. Belenky, (eds) (1996). *Knowledge, Difference and Power: Essays Inspired by Women's Ways of Knowing*. New York, BasicBooks/HarperCollins.

Gorniak-Kocikowska, K. (1996). The computer revolution and the problem of global ethics. *Science and Engineering Ethics* **2**: 177–90.

Gotterbarn, D. (1997). Software engineering: a new professionalism. *The Responsible Software Engineer: Selected Readings in IT Professionalism*. C. Myers, T. Hall and D. Pitt (eds). London, Springer-Verlag: 21–31.

Green, E., S. Hebron and D. Woodward (1990). *Women's Leisure, What Leisure?* Basingstoke, Macmillan Education.

Greeno, C. G. and E. E. Maccoby (1993). How different is the 'different voice'? *An Ethic of Care: Feminist and Interdisciplinary Perspectives*. M. J. Larrabee (ed.). New York and London, Routledge: 193–98.

Grundy, F. (1996). *Women and Computers*. Exeter, UK, Intellect.

Guardian (1999). Cyber-stalkers make computer new tool of terror. *Guardian*: broadsheet section,13, 29 November 1999.

Guardian (2001). Nine held in net child porn raids. *Guardian*: broadsheet section, 2. 29 November 2001.

Gurian, M. (2003). *What Could He Be Thinking? How a Man's Mind Really Works*. New York, St Martin's Press.

Haraway, D. (1991). *Simians, Cyborgs and Women: The Reinvention of Nature*. London, Free Association Books.

Held, V. (1993). *Feminist Morality: Transforming Culture, Society and Politics*. Chicago and London, University of Chicago Press.

Held, V. (1998). Feminist transformations of moral theory. *Ethics: The Big Questions*. J. P. Sterba (ed.). Malden, MA and Oxford, Blackwell: 331–46.

Helmreich, S. (1994). Anthropology inside and outside the looking-glass worlds of artificial life, unpublished paper, Department of Anthropology, Stanford University, Stanford, CA.

Henwood, F. (1993). Gender perspectives on information technology: problems, issues and opportunities. *Gendered by Design? Information Technology and Office Systems*. E. Green, J. Owen and D. Pain (eds). London, Taylor & Francis: 31–49.

Herring, S. (1996). Posting in a different voice: gender and ethics in CMC. *Philosophical Perspectives on Computer-Mediated Communication*. C. Ess (ed.). Albany NY, State University of New York Press: 115–45.

Hewson, B. (2004). Can men withdraw consent to infertility treatment? http://www.hardwicke.civil.co.uk/resources/articles/04030101.htm (accessed 27 August 2004).

Heyd, D. (1982). *Supererogation: Its Status in Ethical Theory*. New York, Cambridge University Press.

Himanen, P. (2001). *The Hacker Ethic and the Spirit of the Information Age*. London, Secker & Warburg.

Howcroft, D. and M. Wilson (2002). Re-conceptualising failure: social shaping meets IS research. *European Journal of Information Systems* 11: 236–50.

Hwang, F.-M. and K.-B. Yang (2004). Internet dating and female middle-school sexual abuse victims. *Journal of Taiwan Normal University* 49(1). http://www.ntnu.edu.tw/acad/epub/j49/j91–2.htm (accessed 27 August 2004).

Igbaria, M. and M. Chidambaram (1997). The impact of gender on career success of information systems professionals. *Information Technology and People* 10(1): 63–86.

Jackson, S. and J. Jones, eds (1998). *Contemporary Feminist Theories*. Edinburgh, Edinburgh University Press.

Jaggar, A. M. (1992). Feminist ethics. *Encyclopedia of Ethics*. L. Becker and C. Becker (eds). New York, Garland Press: 361–70.

Jerin, P. A. and B. Dolinsky (2001). You've got mail: you may not want it: an analysis of safety issues with online dating services. *Journal of Criminal Justice and Popular Culture* 9(1): 15–21.

Jimroglu, K. M. (2001). A camera with a view: JenniCAM, visual representation and cyborg subjectivity. *Virtual Gender: Technology, Consumption and Identity*. E. Green and A. Adam (eds). London and New York, Routledge: 286–301.

Johnson, D. (1994). *Computer Ethics*. Englewood, NJ, Prentice-Hall.

Johnson, D. (2001). *Computer Ethics (3rd edition)*. Upper Saddle River, NJ, Prentice Hall.

Jordan, B. (1978). *Birth in Four Cultures: A Crosscultural Investigation of Childbirth in Yucatan, Holland, Sweden and the United States*. Quebec and St Albans, Vermont, Eden Press.

Jordan, T. and P. A. Taylor (2004). *Hacktivism and Cyberwars: Rebels With a Cause?* London and New York, Routledge.

Kember, S. (2003). *Cyberfeminism and Artificial Life*. London and New York, Routledge.

Khazanchi, D. (1995). Unethical behavior in information systems: the gender factor. *Journal of Business Ethics* 15: 741–9.

Koehn, D. (1998). *Rethinking Feminist Ethics: Care, Trust and Empathy*. London and New York, Routledge.

Kohlberg, L. (1981). *The Philosophy of Moral Development*. San Francisco, Harper and Row.

Kramer, J. and C. Kramarae (1997). Gendered ethics on the Internet. *Communication Ethics in an Age of Diversity*. J. Makau and R. Arnett (eds). Urbana, IL and Chicago, IL, University of Illinois Press: 226–43.

Kramer, M. H. (1997). *John Locke and the Origins of Private Property: Philosophical Explanations of Individualism, Community and Equality*. Cambridge, UK, Cambridge University Press.

Kreie, J. and T. Cronan (1998). How men and women view ethics. *Communications of the ACM* **41**(9): 70–6.

Kuhn, A. (1985). *The Power of the Image*. London, Routledge & Kegan Paul.

Ladd, J. (1995). The quest for a code of professional ethics: an intellectual and moral confusion. *Computers, Ethics and Social Values*. D. Johnson and H. Nissenbaum (eds). Upper Saddle River, NJ, Prentice Hall: 580–5.

Lancaster, A.-M. (2003). Acknowledging the significance of gender, http://www. southernct.edu/organizations/rcss/resources/adap_tech/equity_access/lancaster/ intro.html (accessed 20 January 2003).

Lander, R. and A. Adam (1997). *Women in Computing*. Exeter, UK, Intellect.

Lane, F. (2000). *Obscene Profits: The Entrepreneurs of Pornography in the Cyber Age*. New York and London, Routledge.

Langford, D. (1999). *Business Computer Ethics*. Harlow, UK, Addison-Wesley.

Larrabee, M. J., Ed. (1993). *An Ethic of Care*. New York and London, Routledge.

Law, J. and J. Hassard (1999). *Actor Network Theory and After*. Oxford and Malden, MA, Blackwell.

Levy, N. (2002). Virtual child pornography: the eroticization of inequality. *Ethics and Information Technology* **4**(4): 319–23.

Levy, S. (1984). *Hackers. Heroes of the Computer Revolution*. Harmondsworth UK, Penguin.

Lewis, J. J. (2004). Property rights of women, Encyclopaedia of Women's History, http://womenshistory.about.com/library/ency/bluh_property.htm (accessed 30 August 2004).

Lloyd, G. (1984). *The Man of Reason: 'Male' and 'Female' in Western Philosophy*. Minneapolis, University of Minnesota Press.

Lovegrove, G. and B. Segal (1991). *Women into Computing; Selected Papers, 1988–1990*. London and Berlin, Springer-Verlag.

Ludlow, P. (1996). *High Noon on the Electronic Frontier: Conceptual Issues in Cyberspace*. Cambridge, MA and London, MIT Press.

Lyon, D. (1994). *The Electronic Eye: The Rise of Surveillance Society*. Minneapolis, MA, University of Minnesota Press.

Lyon, D. (2001). *Surveillance Society: Monitoring Everyday Life*. Buckingham, UK and Philadelphia, PA, Open University Press.

MacCannell, D. and J. F. MacCannell (1993). Violence, power and pleasure: a revisionist reading of Foucault from the victim perspective. *Up Against Foucault: Explorations of Some Tensions Between Foucault and Feminism*. C. Ramazanoglu (ed.). London and New York, Routledge: 203–38.

McDonald, G. and P. C. Pak (1996). It's all fair in love, war and business: cognitive philosophies in ethical decision making. *Journal of Business Ethics* **15**: 973–96.

MacKenzie, D. and J. Wajcman, eds (1999). *The Social Shaping of Technology.* Milton Keynes, UK, Open University Press.

MacKinnon, C. A. (1979). *The Sexual Harassment of Working Women.* New Haven, CT, Yale University Press.

MacKinnon, C. A. (1987). *Feminism Unmodified: Discourses on Life and Law.* Cambridge, MA and London, Harvard University Press.

Mason, E. S. and P. E. Mudrack (1996). Gender and ethical orientation: a test of gender and occupational socialization theories. *Journal of Business Ethics* **15**: 599–604.

Mason, R. (1986). Four ethical issues of the information age. *MIS Quarterly* **10**(1): 5–11.

May, L. and S. Hoffman, eds (1991). *Collective Responsibility: Five Decades of Debate in Theoretical and Applied Ethics.* Savage, MD, Rowman & Littlefield.

Meloy, J. R. (1998). The psychology of stalking. *The Psychology of Stalking: Clinical and Forensic Perspectives.* J. Meloy (ed.). New York, Academic Press: 1–23.

Meloy, J. R. and S. Gothard (1995). A demographic and clinical comparison of obsessional followers and offenders with mental disorders. *American Journal of Psychiatry* **166**: 258–63.

Meyers, D. T. (1994). *Subjection and Subjectivity: Psychoanalytic Feminism and Moral Philosophy.* New York and London, Routledge.

Mill, J. S. (1970). The subjection of women. *Essays on Sex Equality.* A. S. Rossi. (ed.). Chicago, IL, University of Chicago Press: 125–56.

Mill, J. S. (1998). Utilitarianism. *Ethics: The Big Questions.* J. P. Sterba (ed.). Malden, MA and Oxford, Blackwell: 119–33.

Miller, L. (1995). Women and children first: gender and the settling of the electronic frontier. *Resisting the Virtual Life: The Culture and Politics of Information.* J. Brooks and I. Boal (eds). San Francisco, City Lights: 49–57.

Mingo, J. (2000). Caught in the net: an online posse tracks down an Internet stalker, http://www.houston-press.com/extra/cyberstalk.html (accessed 24 March 2000).

Moor, J. (1985). What is computer ethics? *Metaphilosophy* **16**(4): 266–75.

Moor, J. (2001). Towards a theory of privacy for the Information Age. *Readings in Cyberethics.* R. A. Spinello and H. T. Tavani (eds). Sudbury, MA, Jones and Bartlett: 349–59.

Moravec, H. (1988). *Mind Children: The Future of Robot and Human Intelligence.* Cambridge, MA and London, Harvard University Press.

Moravec, H. (1998). *Robot: Mere Machine to Transcendent Mind.* Oxford, Oxford University Press.

Myers, C., T. Hall and D. Pitt, eds (1997). *The Responsible Software Engineer: Selected Readings in IT Professionalism.* London, Springer-Verlag.

Nagel, T. (1986). *A View From Nowhere.* Oxford, Oxford University Press.

Nissenbaum, H. (1995). Should I copy my neighbor's software? *Computer Ethics and Social Values.* D. G. Johnson and H. Nissenbaum (eds). Upper Saddle River, NJ, Prentice Hall: 200–13.

Oakley, A. (2000). *Experiments in Knowing: Gender and Method in the Social Sciences.* Cambridge, UK, Polity.

Oakley, A. (2002). *Gender on Planet Earth.* Cambridge, UK and Oxford, Polity.

Ofori-Amanfo, J. (1999). Gender differences in computer ethics decision making. MSc dissertation, Department of Computation, UMIST, Manchester, UK.

Okin, S. M. (1998). Gender, the public and the private. *Feminism & Politics.* A. Phillips (ed.). Oxford and New York, Oxford University Press: 116–41.

Olsen, F. (1984). Statutory rape: a feminist critique of rights analysis. *Texas Law Review* 63: 387–432.

Orwell, G. (1949). *Nineteen Eighty-Four: A Novel.* New York, Harcourt, Brace and Co.

Packard, A. (2000). Does proposed federal cyberstalking legislation meet constitutional requirements? *Communication Law and Policy* 5: 505–38.

Panorama (2001). Transcript of The Wonderland Club, Broadcast on BBC, 11 February 2001, http:www.bbc.co.uk/panorama (accessed 12 February 2001).

Panteli, A. and J. Stack (1998). Women and computing: the ethical responsibility of the IT industry. ETHICOMP98, Rotterdam.

Panteli, A., J. Stack, and H. Ramsay (1999). Gender and professional ethics in the IT industry. *Journal of Business Ethics* 22(1): 51–61.

Parent, W. A. (1983). A new definition of privacy for the law. *Law and Philosophy* 2: 305–38.

Pateman, C. (1988). *The Sexual Contract.* Cambridge, UK and Oxford, Polity.

Pateman, C. (1989). *The Disorder of Women.* Cambridge, UK and Oxford, Polity.

Phillips, A. (1991). *Engendering Democracy.* Cambridge, UK and Oxford, Polity.

Puka, B. (1993). The liberation of caring: a different voice for Gilligan's different voice. *An Ethic of Care: Feminist and Interdisciplinary Perspectives.* M. J. Larrabee. (ed.). New York and London, Routledge: 215–39.

Rainsford, D. and T. Woods (1999). *Critical Ethics: Text, Theory and Responsibility.* Basingstoke, Macmillan.

Raymond, E. (2001). *The Cathedral and the Bazaar: Musings on Linux and Open Source by an Accidental Revolutionary.* Sebastopol, CA, O'Reilly.

Reiss, M. C. and K. Mitra (1998). The effects of individual difference factors on the acceptability of ethical and unethical workplace behaviors. *Journal of Business Ethics* 17: 1581–93.

Reno, J. (1999). Cyberstalking: a new challenge for law enforcement and industry. A Report from the Attorney General to the Vice President. http://www.usdoj.gov/ag/cyberstalkingreport.html (accessed 30 November 1999).

Rheingold, H. (1993). *The Virtual Community: Homesteading on the Virtual Frontier.* Reading, MA, Addison-Wesley.

Richardson, H. (2003). CRM in call centers: the logic of practice. *IS Perspectives and Challenges in the Context of Globalisation.* R. Montealegue, M. Korpela and A. Poulymenakou (eds). Boston, MA, Kluwer.

Riley, D. (1996). Sex, fear and condescension on campus: cybercensorship at Carnegie Mellon. *wired_women: Gender and New Realities in Cyberspace.* L. Cherny and E. Wise. Seattle, WA, Seal Press: 158–68.

Robins, K. and F. Webster (1999). *Times of the Technoculture: From the Information Society to the Virtual Life.* London and New York, Routledge.

Robinson, B. A. (1994). Social context and conflicting interests in participant understanding of information systems failure. Information Systems Methodologies conference, BCS Information Systems Methodologies Specialist Group.

Robinson, F. (1999). *Globalizing Care; Ethics, Feminist Theory, and International Relations.* Boulder, CO, Westview Press.

Roiphe, K. (1993). *The Morning After: Sex, Fear and Feminism.* London, Hamish Hamilton.

Room, S. (2004). Meeting the challenges of the Victoria Climbie & Soham cases, http://www.dpalaw.info (accessed 24 August 2004).

Rose, H. (1994). *Love, Power and Knowledge: Towards a Feminist Transformation of the Sciences.* Cambridge, UK, Polity.

Rowbotham, S. (1973). *Hidden from History; 300 years of Women's Oppression and the Fight Against it.* London, Pluto.

Ruddick, S. (1989). *Maternal Thinking: Toward a Politics of Peace.* Boston, MA, Beacon.

Rumsey, J. P. (1997). Re-visions of agency in Kant's moral theory. *Feminist Interpretations of Immanuel Kant.* R. M. Schott (ed.). University Park, PA, Pennsylvania State University Press: 125–144.

Ryan, A. (1989). Distrusting Economics. *New York Review of Books*: 25–7.

Salecel, R. and S. Zizek (1996). *Gender and Voice as Love Objects.* Durham, NC, Duke University Press.

Schroeder, R. (1994). Cyberculture, cyborg post-modernism and the sociology of virtual reality technologies: surfing the soul in the information age. *Futures* **26**(5): 519–28.

Segan, S. (2000a). Female of the species; hacker women are few but strong, http://more.abcnews.go.com/sections/tech/dailynews/hackerwomen000602. html (accessed 20 January 2003).

Segan, S. (2000b). Facing a man's world: female hackers battle sexism to get ahead, http://more.abcnews.go.com/sections/tech/dailynews/hackerwomen000609 (accessed 20 January 2003).

Shade, L. R. (2002). *Gender and Community in the Social Construction of the Internet.* New York, Peter Lang.

Shapiro, S. (1998). Places and spaces: the historical interaction of technology, home and privacy. *The Information Society* **14**: 275–84.

Sherwin, S. (1992). *No Longer Patient: Feminist Ethics and Health Care.* Philadelphia, Temple University Press.

Slotkin, R. (1998). *Gunfighter Nation: The Myth of the Frontier in Twentieth-Century America.* Norman, OK, University of Oklahoma Press.

Smart, C. (1989). *Feminism and the Power of Law.* London and New York, Routledge.

Smith, M. R. and L. Marx, ed. (1998). *Does Technology Drive History?: The Dilemma of Tecnological Determinsm.* Cambig, MA and London, MIT Press.

Smith, P., ed. (1993). *Feminist Jurisprudence.* New York and Oxford, Oxford University Press.

Sollfrank, C. (1999). Women hackers – a report from the mission to locate subversive women on the net, http://www.obn.org/hackers/text (accessed 20 January 2003).

Sollfrank, C. (2000). Unauthorized access: have code, will destroy! Artbyte the magazine of digital arts & culture. http://www.artbyte.com/mag/Jul_aug_00/ femalehackers_content.shtml (accessed 20 January 2003).

Sollfrank, C. (2002). Not every hacker is a woman, *Technics of Cyberfeminism*, C. Reiche and A. Sick (eds). http:www.obn.org/reading_room/writings/html/ notevery.html (accessed 30 August 2004).

Spender, D. (1980). *Man Made Language.* London, Routledge and Kegan Paul.

Spier, R. (2001). *Science and Technology Ethics*. London and New York, Routledge.

Spinello, R. A. and H. T. Tavani, eds (2001). *Readings in Computer Ethics*. Sudbury, MA, Jones and Bartlett.

Spitzberg, B. H. and G. Hoobler (2002). Cyberstalking and the technologies of interpersonal terrorism. *New Media & Society* 4(1): 71–92.

StalkingBehavior (2000). Stalking behaviors, definitions and links, http://onour.com/stalking (accessed 28 March 2000).

Sterba, J. P. (1998). Introduction. *Ethics: The Big Questions*. J.P. Sterba Malden, MA and Oxford, Blackwell: 1–18.

Sterling, B. (1992). *The Hacker Crackdown: Law and Disorder on the Electronic Frontier*. London, Viking.

Stone, L. (1977). *The Family, Sex and Marriage in England, 1500–1800*. New York, Harper and Row.

Strossen, N. (1995). *Defending Pornography: Free Speech, Sex and the Fight for Human Rights*. New York, Scribner.

Tannen, D. (1992). *You Just Don't Understand: Women and Men in Conversation*. London, Virago.

Tavani, H. (1998). Information technology, social values and ethical responsibility: a select bibliography. *IEEE Technology & Society* 17(2): 26–40.

Tavani, H. and F. Grodzinsky (2001). Is cyberstalking a special type of computer crime? ETHICOMP 2001, Gdansk.

Taylor, P. (1999). *Hackers: Crime in the Digital Sublime*. London and New York, Routledge.

Thomas, A. M. and C. Kitzinger (1997). *Sexual Harassment: Contemporary Feminist Perspectives*. Buckingham, UK, Open University Press.

Tong, R. (1993). *Feminine and Feminist Ethics*. Belmont, CA, Wadsworth.

Tong, R. (1999). Feminist ethics, in The Stanford Encyclopedia of Philosophy (Fall 1999 Edition), E. Zalta (ed.), http://plato.stanford.edu/archives/fall1999/entries/feminism-ethics/ (accessed 24 November 1999).

Tronto, J. (1993). *Moral Boundaries: A Political Argument for an Ethic of Care*. New York and London, Routledge.

Turkle, S. (1984). *The Second Self: Computers and the Human Spirit*. New York, Simon & Schuster.

Turner, E. (1998). The case for responsibility of the computing industry to promote equal presentation of women and men in advertising campaigns. ETHICOMP98, Rotterdam.

Turner, E. (1999). Gender and ethnicity of computing, perceptions of the future generation. ETHICOMP99, Rome.

Twining, W. L. and D. Miers (1991). *How to Do Things With Rules: A Primer of Interpretation*. London, Butterworths.

Ulshofer, G. B. (2000). A Whiteheadian business ethics and the western hemisphere. *Journal of Business Ethics* 23(1): 67–71.

Urmson, J. O. (1958). Saints and Heroes. *Essays in Moral Philosophy*. A. I. Melden. (ed.). Seattle, WA, University of Washington Press: 202.

USAToday (1999). Gore asks Reno to study cyberstalking. 26 February. http://www.usatoday.com/life/cyber/tech/cte509.html (accessed 30 November 1999).

Vehviläinen, M. (1994). Reading computing professionals' codes of ethics – a standpoint of Finnish office workers. *Feminist Voices on Gender, Technology and*

Ethics. E. Gunnarsson, and L. Trojer (eds). Lulea, Sweden, Center for Women's Studies, Lulea University of Technology: 145–61.

Wajcman, J. (1998). *Managing Like a Man: Women and Men in Corporate Management*. Cambridge, UK, Polity.

Wajcman, J. (2004). *TechnoFeminism*. Cambridge, UK and Malden, MA, Polity.

Walker, M. U. (1998). *Moral Understandings: A Feminist Study in Ethics*. New York and London, Routledge.

Warren, S. and L. Brandeis (1890). The right to privacy. *Harvard Law Review* **4**: 193.

Warwick, K. (1997). *March of the Machines: Why the New Race of Robots will Rule the World*. London, Century.

Weber, M. (1930). *The Protestant Ethic and the Spirit of Capitalism*. London, Routledge.

Webster, J. (1996). *Shaping Women's Work: Gender, Employment and Information Technology*. London, Longmans.

Weizenbaum, J. (1976). *Computer Power and Human Reason: From Judgement to Calculation*. San Francisco, W.H. Freeman.

Welsh, S. (2000). The multidimensional nature of sexual harassment: an empirical analysis of women's sexual harassment complaints. *Violence Against Women* **6**: 118–41.

White, M. (2001). Visual pleasure in textual places: Gazing in multi-user object-oriented worlds. *Virtual Gender: Technology, Consumption and Identity*. E. Green and A. Adam (eds). London and New York, Routledge: 124–49.

Willcocks, L. P. and S. Lester, eds (1999). *Beyond the IT Paradox*. Cichister, UK, Wiley.

Wilson, E. O. (1975). *Sociobiology: The New Synthesis*. Cambridge, MA, Harvard University Press.

Wilson, M. and A. Greenhill (2004). Gender and teleworking identities in the risk society: a research agenda. *New Technology, Work and Employment* **19**(3): 207–21.

Winner, L. (1997). Cyberlibertarian myths and the prospect for community. *ACM Computers and Society* **27**(3): 14–19.

Winner, L. (1999). Do artifacts have politics? *The Social Shaping of Technology*. D. MacKenzie and J. Wajcman (eds). Buckingham, UK, Open University Press: 28–40.

Woffinden, B. (1987). *Miscarriages of Justice*. London, Hodder & Stoughton.

Wollstencroft, M. (1988). *A Vindication of the Rights of Women*. Brody, M. (ed.). London, Penguin.

Womack, S. (2003). Men's brains 'are programmed to ignore dust' http://www.telegraph.co.uk/news/main.jhtml?xml = /news/2003/10/03/ndust03.xml&sSheet = /news/2003/10/03/ixhome.html (accessed 3 October 2003).

Wright, M. (1995). Can moral judgement and ethical behaviour be learned? A review of the literature. *Management Decision* **33**(10): 17–28.

Wright, C. (2000). Murder.com, The Boston Phoenix, 10–17 August 2000. http://www.bostonphoenix.com/archive/features/00/08/10/MURDER.html (accessed 24 November 2000).

Yahoo (2000). Service provider Demon settles Internet libel case. http://uk.news.yahoo.com/000330/91/a2nba.html (accessed 30 March 2000).

Zuboff, S. (1988). *In the Age of the Smart Machine: The Future of Work and Power*. New York, Basic Books.

Index